I0817345

No Place Like Home

The Auburn that for so many generations has been loved and cared for by so many is disappearing before the onslaught of bulldozers, wrecking balls, and the lamentable replacement of humanely proportioned business and residential areas . . .

The post-Civil War Cullars family store at College and Magnolia was replaced in 1906 by a brick and stone version that was home to the Bank of Auburn and other businesses and organizations and still stands, though much altered, on its old corner opposite Toomer's Drug Store.

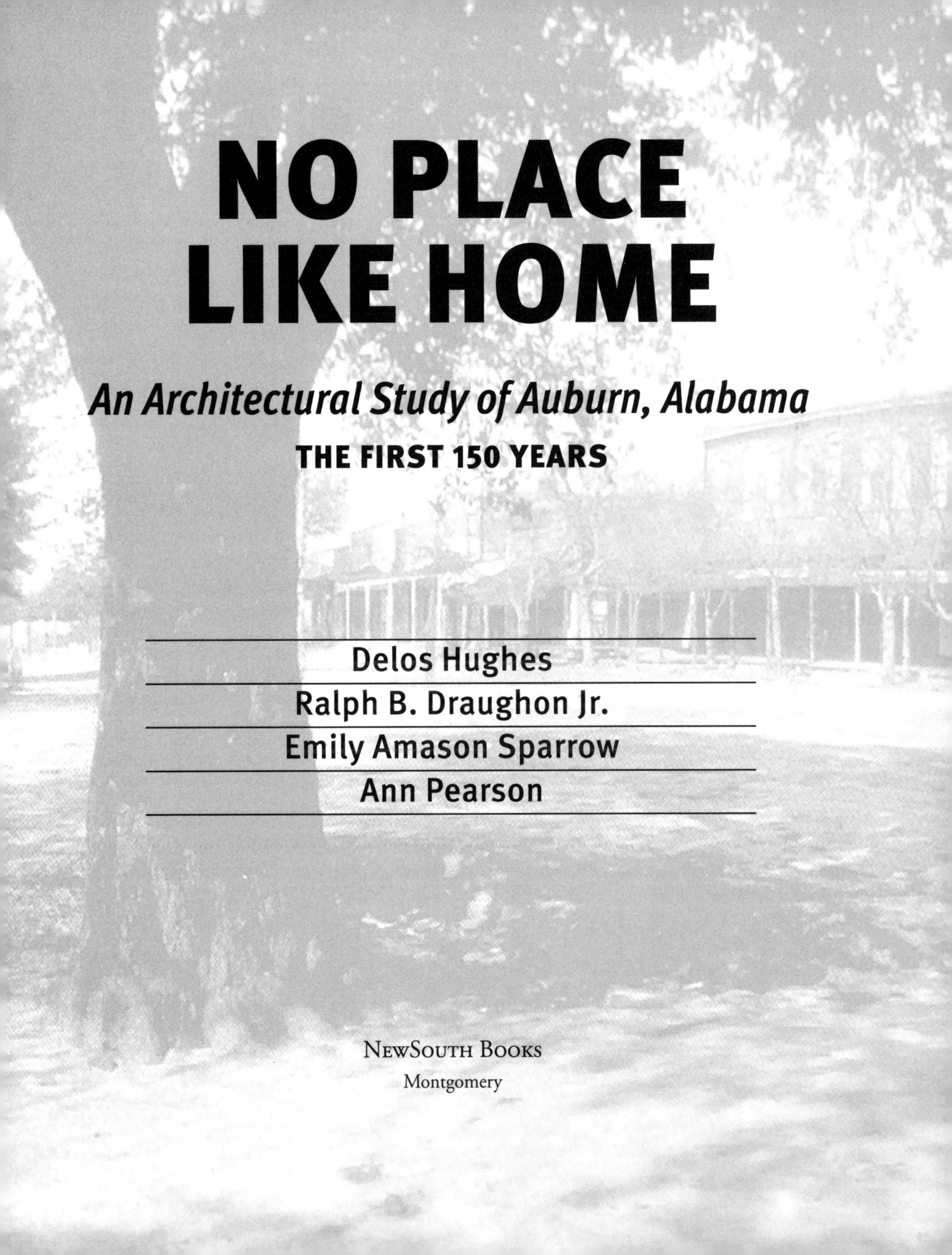

NO PLACE LIKE HOME

An Architectural Study of Auburn, Alabama

THE FIRST 150 YEARS

Delos Hughes

Ralph B. Draughon Jr.

Emily Amason Sparrow

Ann Pearson

NewSouth Books

Montgomery

NewSouth Books
105 S. Court Street
Montgomery, AL 36104

Publisher Cataloging-in-Publication Data
Hughes, Delos D.
No place like home: an architectural study of Auburn, Alabama, the first 150 years / Delos Hughes, Ralph B. Draughon Jr., Emily Sparrow, Ann Pearson.
p. cm.
Includes index.
1. Auburn (Ala.)—History—Pictorial works. 2. Auburn (Ala.)—Buildings, structures, etc.—Pictorial works.
3. Historic buildings—Alabama—Auburn—Pictorial works. 4. Auburn (Ala.)—Biography.
I. Draughon, Ralph B., Jr. II. Sparrow, Emily Amason. III. Pearson, Ann B. IV. Title.

Library of Congress Control Number: 2019952548

ISBN: 978-1-58838-400-3 (hardcover)
ISBN: 978-1-58838-419-5 (ebook)

Editing and proofreading by Beth Marino; design, composition, and indexing by Randall Williams; jacket design by Breuna Baine/Scott Markel; production, print coordination, and proofreading by Matthew Byrne; proofreading by Kelly Snyder and Isabella Barrera; publicity and promotion by Lisa Harrison; accounting by Lisa Emerson; publishing, sales, and marketing by Suzanne La Rosa.

Printed in the United States of America by Sheridan Books

The Black Belt, defined by its dark, rich soil, stretches across central Alabama. It was the heart of the cotton belt. It was and is a place of great beauty, of extreme wealth and grinding poverty, of pain and joy. Here we take our stand, listening to the past, looking to the future.

Contents

Preface

ABOUT OUR WORK

Gertrude Stein's famous characterization of another place, "There is no there there," might seem an unpromising characterization to introduce the pages that follow this one. If her description refers to a place's loss of identity, however, it might well be said of Auburn, Alabama, hometown of the authors of this book. The identity of this place once was that of "lovely village," but today it is not still a village and no longer so lovely as it was when the sobriquet was, much earlier, applied to it. In places Auburn is arguably "attractive," yet in others dishearteningly less than that. In *Lost Auburn* these authors recorded those parts of the lovely village that have been destroyed by time or by catastrophe or by a misguided impulse for "progress." Here we record some of what has not been destroyed, what we feel is worth preserving and celebrating, not just because it is old—for not everything pictured here is old—but because it has survived or deserves to survive for reasons that we will try to explain.

A traditional procedure for the evaluation of architecture has it that the qualities of a suitable building are: (1) that it serves the purpose for which it was built; (2) that it is structurally sound; and (3) that it pleases the senses. The Italian architect and critic Palladio gave us the mantra—*commodity, firmness, and delight.* In considering what is most important, interesting, and worthwhile to include in this volume of Auburn buildings, our judgments have been guided, more or less, by these criteria. We propose that age is a reliable indicator of *firmness.* Certainly, any ante-bellum structure in Auburn meets that standard, so we have gathered them all in these pages. Arguably, *firmness,* is the responsibility of architects and builders, so we emphasize them in our presentation of Auburn buildings. By and large responsibility lies with the architects for the quality of *delight.* The public, customers, or clients, obviously play a part in imparting beauty or awe or charm to a building. Still, it falls to the architect to translate these values and assemble them into structural terms. *Commodity* or usefulness, as we shall see as our investigation proceeds, is in some ways, a middle term. Though *firmness* is objective and *delight* subjective, *commodity* or *usefulness* has a foot in both camps. Analytically, this quality suggests continuum between structures that are understandable purely in utilitarian terms and structures which are "useful" in a figurative sense. We encompass all of these utilitarian possibilities in our pages.

An obvious danger in selecting the buildings and topics discussed here is that the connections between these criteria are overlooked. Although our purpose is seldom to judge, but mostly to record Auburn architecture, the most admirable buildings, a traditional critic would claim, must exhibit all three characteristics to a high degree. But those that do are the monuments of architecture. The buildings recorded here do not attain such exalted heights; nonetheless, Auburn buildings occasionally reached for excellence and we hope will continue to do so, and will occasionally, if modestly, succeed.

To account for why things are the way they are—in this case, why the built environment of Auburn is the way it is—one could do worse than to invoke an ancient notion of *cause*. The Greek philosopher Aristotle advised that there are four types of cause—*material cause, formal cause, efficient cause, final cause*—and that the combination of all four accounts for what anything is. We have found this a handy way to organize the material in this book. Concerning architecture, "*material cause*" is easily understood as referring to the wood or bricks or cement of which a building is composed. "*Formal cause*" points one to the patterns in which the materials of a building are assembled. The "*efficient cause*" is how the assembly takes place—by sawing or nailing or raising/lowering, in other words applying labor or changing the disposition of the materials in some way. And the "*final cause*" refers to what the intended end of using the materials, patterning them, working them, and the purpose for which all this is done.

Following Aristotle's analysis, we begin by exploring the design function by examining the architects and builders whose work lies behind the *formal cause* of Auburn's built environment. In the early years of Auburn building, as in most communities at the same stage of development, builders often were designers as well, so we have proceeded on to an account of the later development of Auburn to examine the contributions of building contractors, building to the designs of others, who may be said to govern the *efficient cause* of Auburn buildings.

It is obvious that the material of which any building is constructed is a consideration for both the architect and the contractor. Even in those rare instances in which a masonry building is built to the same plan as a wood-framed one, it will not be the case that, appearance aside, they are the same building. Subtle, but significant differences will be dictated by the materials

The purposes for which any Auburn building

was intended, which Aristotle designated the final cause, is the theme of our treatment of every building. We have gathered groups of some that share common purposes in order to show the range of architectural expression in our town, or sometimes to show the absence of architectural imagination in varying designs for similar purposes.

We have prepared the text and assembled the photographs in a way that we hope will be of interest to a wide variety of readers, be they purely Auburn *aficionados* for whom anything about Auburn is interesting, or more systematic students and scholars of the history and development of the variety of phenomena of which this account is a part—architecture, building construction, urban development, genealogy, town-gown relationships, to name only a small sample.

The rate at which the Auburn that for so many generations has been loved and cared for by so many is disappearing before the onslaught of bulldozers, wrecking balls, and the lamentable replacement of humanely proportioned business and residential areas with high-rise apartments and fast-food sprawl, also motivates the presentation in these pages. It will be obvious, and so ought to be acknowledged, that a hope to save what is left of the old Auburn and to guide what is to come in the Auburn yet to be, is the prejudice lying behind the work before you.

Acknowledgments

In all of what readers will find in this volume, we have the advantage of building upon the work of others who have gone before us, of those who have provided us with memories, records and other materials relevant to the buildings of Auburn, and many others who have supported this effort in a variety of ways, including the forbearance of our families, friends, and associates. We extend our thanks to all of them, and directly to:

Auburn University Special Collections, Joy Waller Aldarando, Madrid Bailey, Jennifer Baughn, Daniel Bennett, Dan Benson, Roger Birkhead, Marjean and Daniel Blessing, Dave Bottoms, Glenn Bottoms, Winifred Hill Boyd, Margaret Young Brown, Madge Williams Burton, Lucinda Samford Cannon, Walter Clement, Danny Sue Gibson Conner, Vandy Copeland, Mr. and Mrs. William Copeland, Bobby Crew, John and Sara Ann Curry, Christian and Rebecca Dagg, Christine Blackburn Danner, L. L., "Jr." and Pat Davis, William and Linda Dean, Bobby Dees, Jan Dempsey, Fran Pick Dillard, John Dodd, Jim and Cathy Donald, George and Pat Harper Echols, Kathy Enzor, Ed and Pat Johnson Evans, Totsie Farr, Bob Gamble, Beverly Chrietzberg Garcia, Walter Giddens, Mary Ann Godwin , Harvey Gosser, Anne Cullars Graves, Richard Guthery, Vandy Harper, Bert Harris, DeLisa M. Harris, Robert Harris, the Rev. and Mrs. James Helms, David Hill, Bert Hitchcock, Mary Hoffschwelle, Daniel W. Hollis, Guy W. Hubbs, Joe and Betsy Judkins, Linda Pauline, Wilkins Klein, Earl and Katherine Lancaster, Julie Wright Littlejohn, Nancy Nunnery Lowe, Jim Lowery, Robert and Janie Marino, Anne McChesney May, Barbara Wittel McIntyre, Anita Meadows, Helen Coppedge Middleton, Kaye Minchew, Linda Montgomery, Sidney James Nakhjavan, Dickson and Mary Pruett Norman, Joe Nunnery, Marty Oliff, Ginny Pearce, Charles Pick, Susan Jordan Pillgreen, Clyde and Deana Prather, Virginia Young Priest, Karen Rogers, Kenneth Rogers, John Saidla, Katherine Davis Savage, Larry and Anne Tamblyn Shaw, Jerry and Mary Elizabeth Gregory Shaw, Alex and Annette Screws Simmons, Thomas Sparrow, Tom Sparrow, Jim Spence, Edward Lee Spencer Jr., Spence Spencer, Steve and Starla Spencer, Delores Spinks, Jimmy Sprayberry, Carolyn and Billy Tamblyn and Family, Virginia Taylor, Beverley Burkhardt Thomas, Martha Thomas, Susie Thomas, Sharon Tolbert, Joel and Lynda Vowell Tremaine, Pat Wittel Tremaine, Ellen Kerr Vanoy, Edna Ward, Beverly Webster, Charles Wessinger, Linda Pauline Wilkins, Betty Grimes Williams, J. Michael Williams, Billy and Anne Womelsdorf, Emil and Margaret Wright, Cecil Meadows Yarbrough, Joe Yeager, Eugenia Malone Zallen, John Zellers.

No Place Like Home

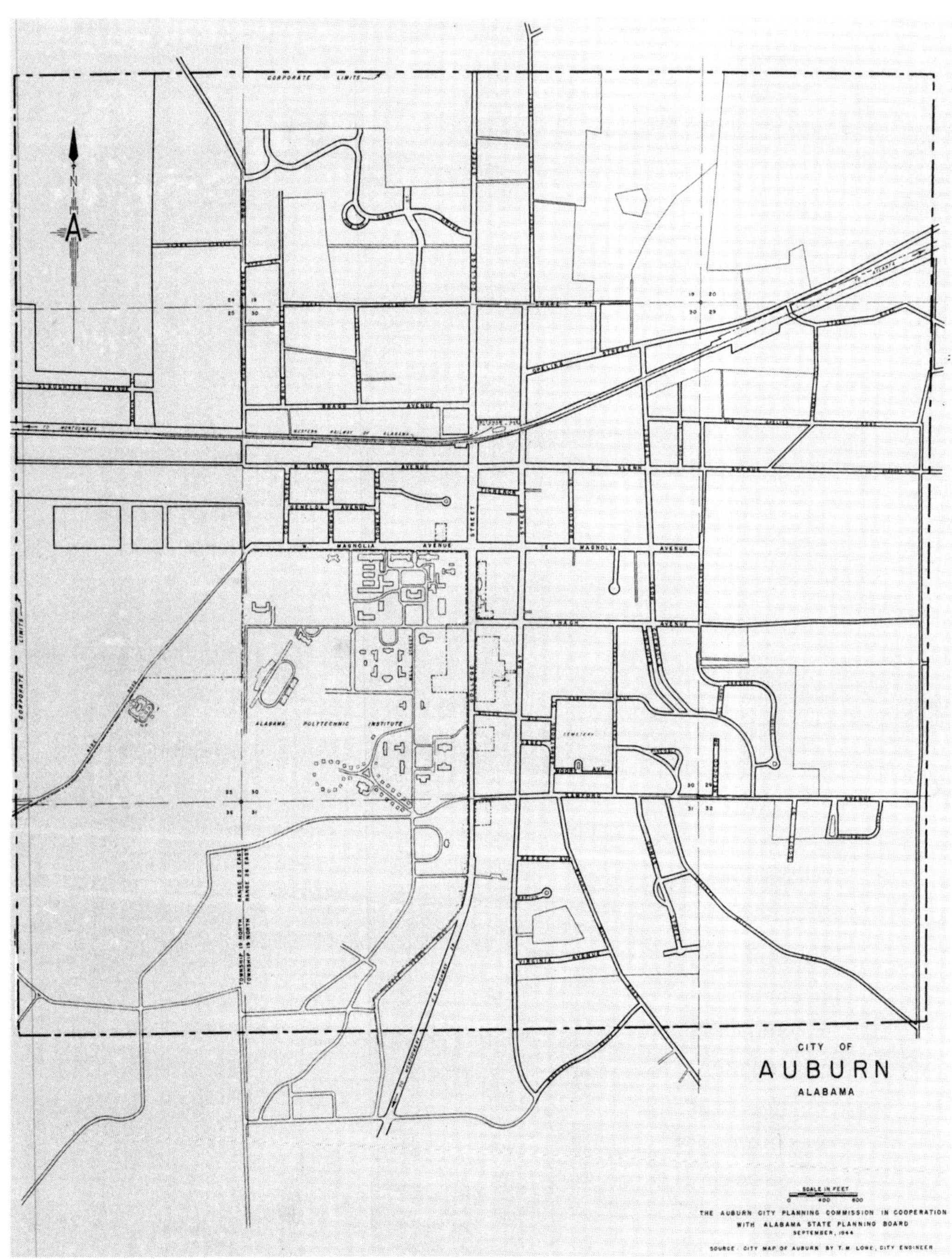

1944 city map of Auburn, Alabama.

1

Auburn, 1836–1900

Antebellum Auburn

Seeking a new promised land in the wilds of East Alabama, a band of thirty-six Methodists from Georgia parted the waters of the Chattahoochee by ferryboat and in late 1836 settled an outpost that they soon named Auburn, after an Oliver Goldsmith poem that celebrated "the loveliest village of the plain." In choosing this flowery sobriquet, the settlers exercised considerable poetic license—their settlement was not situated on a plain and certainly was not lovely. Auburn began as a rough-hewn hamlet of log cabins, log dogtrots, log outbuildings, two log churches, a log schoolhouse, and a log post office. Indeed, some have hinted that this abstemious community of professed teetotalers even contained a log tavern.

Top, cabin on the Nunn plantation; bottom, ruins of a Noble Hall outbuilding.

Although a professional architect did not appear on the scene until the late 1850s, the new village could boast of some fairly sophisticated structures, most, if not all, built with slave labor. Although their names never have been recorded, men and women held in bondage served as the foundation stone of the village of Auburn, which rose on the backs of their labor, even as many of the slaves themselves were quartered in primitive log quarters, similar to the living conditions of the men, women, and children held in bondage locally and across the American South.

The top photo adjacent shows a tenant cabin, probably postbellum, with plank board windows, used by African American laborers and situated on the grounds of the Nunn plantation on the Wire Road. At another site, a plantation outbuilding intended for slaves has fallen into ruin on the grounds of Auburn's antebellum Noble Hall, where many once labored.

Antebellum Auburn afforded lawbreakers only primitive accommodations. No image exists of the antebellum village jail, locally referred to in nineteenth-century slang as "the Calaboose," but Professor Bennett Battle Ross left a written record of it in his memoir of his boyhood in the community. The ramshackle "Calaboose" remained in use into the Reconstruction era and stood quite unsteadily in the middle of Main Street, immediately to the south of today's Toomer's Corner. According to Ross's memoir, one prisoner confined there overnight set it on fire, somehow avoided being burned alive, and made his escape as the rickety prison went up in smoke. By torching the Calaboose, this malefactor dramatically removed from today's Toomer's Corner area one of the most remarkable landmarks ever to stand in downtown Auburn.

So-called "professional" builders did not arrive on the local scene until later, but the pioneers of the 1830s possessed building skills that they and their antecedents had learned as they moved westward, from settlement to settlement, on the advancing frontier. A few scholars claim that the model for the American log cabin was imported from faraway Sweden and that hardy frontiersman and their womenfolk adapted it as their wagons trekked south and west on the long trail to antebellum Alabama. But whatever the origin of the log cabin model, most pioneers were familiar with it for this reason: they had been born in it.

Auburn's prime mover, and the Moses of this new search for the promised land, was "Judge" John Jackson Harper, who apparently considered his judicial title in Harris County, Georgia, to be a lifetime honorarium, even in Alabama. His motive for choosing the Auburn site to settle with his band of Methodists remains puzzling, since he held forty-three slaves in the 1840 census, and his slave holdings had almost doubled to seventy-two by the time of his death in 1847. With the vast rich soil of the Alabama Black Belt spread out before him, why did he choose to stop short and settle in the relatively unpromising agricultural vicinity of the loveliest village?

In 1836, businessmen in Montgomery planned a railroad from that city to West Point, Georgia, and in the same year, whether by accident or design, Judge Harper settled a village that lay precisely on that route. The Panic of 1837 temporarily derailed the project, but in 1847 the railroad line reached Auburn, and Judge Harper contracted for his slaves to clear the way and lay the tracks. He died before he could begin the project, but he must be given credit for bringing the vast economic engine of a railroad to the community he founded.

Mary Eleonora Reese, whom Professor George Petrie described as an early and exceptionally perceptive local historian, provides another economic motive for Harper's founding of a new settlement. According to Ms. Reese, Harper "soon set to work" and "built many houses in and around the town" during his lifetime. Thus, it can be said that Harper not only founded Auburn but also profitably developed it by building houses and selling real estate.

All of Harper's buildings were constructed before his death in 1847, and time has swept them all away. Nevertheless, Ms. Reese, an eyewitness, described three of the buildings Harper constructed, and a photograph of one of the three remains. These three structures document, if not Harper's sophistication as a builder, at least his ability to construct larger and more multifaceted buildings as time went on.

According to Ms. Reese, Harper built for himself first a log cabin, second, a frame I-house "plantation plain" structure for his son Thomas, and third, a large residence of two stories and some pretension that Harper constructed for himself. The first two of these structures were so common in early nineteenth-century Georgia and Alabama that Harper and his workers hardly needed a pattern book to put them up.

Ms. Reese writes that Harper built for himself the first residence in the village: "a double log house connected by a wide hall with shed rooms in the rear and a half story above." More commonly, "a double log house connected by a wide hall" would be described as a dogtrot cabin, and a log cabin that fits that description still survives on the Calloway Plantation in Washington, Georgia, the community in which Judge Harper was born. Indeed, anyone who rambled down the trail through Georgia to Alabama

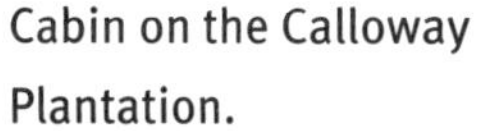
Cabin on the Calloway Plantation.

Auburn's first frame house, west side of College Street.

in the early nineteenth century would be familiar with many examples of the model for the first Auburn house, and Judge Harper and his slaves could have easily could imitated them.

Incidentally, Ms. Reese locates this first house in Auburn, which later became rental property, "in a field behind Mr. Julius Wright's home," an unidentified location. A later historian, Mollie Hollifield (Jones), said Harper's cabin was situated off East Samford Avenue somewhere between Dumas Drive and Moore's Mill Road. Nevertheless, the exact location of this first house in Auburn still puzzles historians.

Although only Ms. Reese's brief description of the first house in Auburn remains, a photograph of a second house that Harper's work force indisputably built has survived. The first frame house in the village, it was situated in the middle of downtown on the west side of today's College Street. Judge Harper intended the simple plantation house, popularly known as "plantation plain," to be home to his handsome second son, Thomas, and Tom's new bride, an attractive young woman with a long name: Elizabeth Swepson Taylor Harper. After tuberculosis took the life of his older brother, Thomas came to occupy a special place in his father's affections. Furthermore, Judge Harper particularly delighted in Lizzie, Thomas's bride, who persuaded the Judge to name the village he had created "Auburn," so Judge Harper put his numerous slaves to work to build Lizzie a suitable residence when she came to town.

Judge Harper upgraded his various places of residence throughout his years in Auburn, and his last residence was large, two-storied, and at the time something of a local showplace. It stood just south of Pine Hill Cemetery (for which Harper donated the land and in which he is buried) on today's Armstrong Street. William Flewellen Samford lived at Harper's house next to the cemetery in the Civil War era, after Samford's former residence, Sunny Slope Plantation, had been converted into a Confederate recruiting camp.

Samford had a penchant for dubbing each of his residences with a literary flourish, and he chose to call this house "Cedre Villa." The house itself, according to Samford's granddaughter, burned to the ground, of causes not connected to the war, in 1863. Its remaining straggly cedar trees date at least from the Civil War era.

So little information survives about Judge Harper's last residence that any generalization about its architecture remains problematic. Nevertheless, he had the labor force, including skilled carpenters, to undertake a more sophisticated domicile, perhaps using the pattern books and style manuals circulating in the period.

The Harpers also constructed commercial structures. Next door and to the south of the first frame house built for Tom Harper and his bride (on today's College Street), the Harper work force built a store that Tom Harper operated. Some claim it to have been the first store in the village. It certainly can be dated before 1843, when Tom Harper died. The structure remained in situ until the twentieth century, when two Auburn landmarks, the Tiger Theater and Bayne's Drugstore, replaced it.

In building Tom Harper's store, the workmen introduced locally a new technique. During its lengthy existence, people called it "the pebble store" or "the pebble building" because it was constructed of a kind of stucco studded with pebbles. After the Dickerson Thomas Halliday family settled in Auburn shortly before the Civil War, an inventory of their downtown properties included several commercial buildings of pebble construction that also may have been built by Judge Harper or his son.

Tom Harper collaborated with his father in the building trade. At Tom's early death in 1843, only about six years after the founding of Auburn, the inventory of his estate (according to county historian Peavy Wright) included about seven local houses that then were offered for sale.

Judge Harper had an enslaved labor force to undertake challenging tasks in local construction. At his death, an inventory and appraisal of his seventy-two slaves included Let, a blacksmith, at $1,000, the most valuable in the estate. The appraisal listed Jack, a carpenter, at $900. Let, another carpenter, who had the same unusual name as the blacksmith, also was appraised at $900, again indicating a value far above his fellows. The two carpenters, Let and Jack, must surely deserve substantial credit for Harper's extensive involvement and success in local building.

But the most valuable disclosure in the appraisal of the Judge's estate comes in a list of the numerous slaves that had been put out to hire in the village after Harper's death. Most had been hired by reputable figures in the village, many of them relatives and associates of the deceased. A typical entry, for example, reads: "Littleton Wynn for the hire of the Boy Solomon 140.00." But the most expensive rental listed for a slave appears as follows: "Bob Jack to himself at $200." This exceptional entry means that a valuable slave, who obviously could earn money in the community, was (incredibly enough to modern eyes) paying a high price to his masters to rent himself!

But who is Bob Jack? As previously mentioned, a Jack, but not a Bob Jack, is listed as a carpenter worth $900, the second highest value for a slave in the estate. (The only other Jack mentioned in the appraisal, Little Jack, was assigned a value of $700 with no particular skill listed.) By the process of elimination, Jack the valuable carpenter and Bob Jack appear to be one and the same.

What an incongruity for a slave to rent his own labor! It would not only be exceedingly unusual, it also would be completely illegal in Auburn, in Alabama, and in the lower South in the 1850s. Furthermore, there can be little doubt that this decision to allow Bob Jack self-employment would have been extremely controversial in the charged atmosphere of the late 1840s, when the Methodist Church had divided on sectional lines and a furious debate over slavery in the territories once again was sweeping the nation. As a result, Bob Jack's talent and industry probably proved to be his undoing, and his independent employment ended soon thereafter. While no record of community disapproval has yet been found, there can be little doubt that some townspeople would regard this slave's particular arrangement to be an illegal and unwise loosening of the chains and restraints of bondage.

Littleton Wynn, Harper's son-in-law and the executor of the Judge's estate, soon put Bob Jack up for sale. A pious Methodist ever concerned about Christian marriage, Wynn also assigned Bob Jack's wife, Mit, to join him on the auction block so that the married couple could be "sold down the river" together. Their fate thereafter, whether together or apart, remains unknown, but at least posterity can record the name and the bitter experience of one of the most noteworthy of the many enslaved craftsmen and builders of antebellum Auburn. But, how sad to say, how heartbreaking to admit, we know next to nothing about him, or his handiwork, or the ultimate fate of this talented worker and his wife.

Ms. Reese describes the work that slaves did in the 1850s building the Auburn Presbyterian Church—the oldest surviving public building in Auburn and now the Auburn University Chapel—for her father, Edwin Reese, a plantation owner and prominent Presbyterian. She wrote that her father ". . . burned the brick and the lime, sawed out the lumber, and his own [slave] carpenters did the work under the supervision of a white first class workman." Lime for the building came from the Chewacla lime works, the chief source of Edwin Reese's fortune. Furthermore, according to Meredith Harvey's early study of slavery in Auburn, Edwin Reese had a slave carpenter who could read, and Reese bequeathed to him, as a token of respect, the Reese family Bible.

First Presbyterian Church and detail of roof framing.

According to Robert Gamble, a respected Alabama architectural historian, the restoration of the structure that is now the University Chapel, after a century and a half of varied use, has been particular felicitous. At the time of the restoration, the interior late nineteenth-century ceiling consisted of flat, beaded, rotting, wood planking. The architect who directed the restoration, Nicholas Davis, removed the beaded ceiling and left the sturdy, hand-sawed, mortised and pegged beams exposed. Thus, the visitor to the chapel today can appreciate the steadfast labor and immense talent of the enslaved carpenters who in 1850 raised high the roofbeams and positioned the chapel's substantial structural details.

The brick Presbyterian church of 1850, in its original modified Greek Revival configuration, followed a common rural architectural pattern, with two doors that, at least according to legend, were intended to be separate entrances for men and women. In a published history of her family, Ms. Reese suggests that the Auburn church closely resembled a brick church that her kinsmen built in the vicinity of West Point, Georgia, but whether this other church still stands has not been determined.

Ms. Reese's first cousin, Dr. James O. McDowell, a young medical doctor, emigrated from North Carolina to Auburn, where, she reported, he, too, acted as developer and perhaps amateur contractor and "built many houses in the town." Unfortunately, she provided no details about which houses her cousin erected, and the doctor has gone down in local history and legend not as a developer, but as the principal in a much repeated (and possibly much embroidered) love story. It seems that when he first saw sixteen-year-old Maria Wynn portray Pharaoh's daughter in a local Methodist Sunday School pageant, he became so infatuated that he proposed to marry her at once! But Pharaoh's daughter in the pageant turned out to be offstage not only a granddaughter of Judge Harper, the pharaoh of the loveliest village, but also a daughter to Littleton Wynn, the judge's grand vizier. These worthies vehemently objected to a hasty courtship, but after a year they capitulated, and the seventeen-year-old bride and her twenty-three-year-old groom were joined in matrimony in 1845. The doctor then built for his bride a large house just off Opelika Road. Later, the couple migrated to Argyle, Texas, where (after bearing the doctor four children) Maria died in 1860. Shortly thereafter the doctor married Maria's younger sister Lavonia.

Dr. McDowell's importance in local building is difficult to determine. After he and Maria migrated to Texas, the William Crawford Dowdell family acquired the house McDowell built for his bride. Many additional architectural flourishes added by owners through the years made its original architectural configuration difficult to determine, and ultimately the house was one of many antebellum structures demolished in a neighborhood severely damaged by Auburn's fierce tornado of 1953. So the antebellum house Dr. McDowell built for himself and Maria in Texas, if it survives, is the only remaining structure that can be credited to him as a builder, and it would be a useful comparison for a study of architectural developments in antebellum Auburn.

Ms. Reese's history includes this intriguing observation:

> Mr. Howe, Mr. [George W.] Shelton and Mr. Sam Williams, contracters [sic] who built many houses, among them the house occupied by Dr. McAdory, the one known as the old "White place" and many others of the old houses, the Methodist church [of 1850] before it was remodeled which still stands as a monument to them.

Happily for local history, photographs survive of the three structures in Ms. Reese's account: the Methodist church of 1850, the Murphy summer residence in Auburn, later occupied by Dr. McAdory, and the White-Harris house. Two of the three have been demolished and the third rescued but moved out of town.

The census through the years identified George W. Shelton as a carpenter and Sam Williams as a carpenter and joiner, but Ms. Reese describes them more accurately as contractors, significant in the chronicles of Auburn.

Sam Williams, about twenty years older than his partner, migrated from his South Carolina birthplace to Alabama, where he made an auspicious marriage to a daughter of Dr. Pleasant Phillips, a prominent physician and planter in Russell County. In 1850, at the time of their first recorded collaboration in erecting the Auburn Methodist Church, the younger partner, twenty-four-year-old George Shelton, a native Virginian, was a bachelor. Sam Williams apparently served as matchmaker. A year later, on June 5, 1851, Shelton married Dr. Phillips's younger daughter, Mary Sharp Phillips, and the two contractors thus sealed their partnership by marrying sisters. The Sheltons were blessed with a daughter, Lucy, in 1852, but Mary Sharp Phillips Shelton died about the time of the birth of her second child, George P. Shelton, in 1855.

The 1850 Methodist Church.

In her treatment of the buildings constructed

A typical Alabama antebellum Methodist church, this one off Highway 14 in Autauga County.

by Shelton and Williams, Ms. Reese considers the Methodist church of 1850 a particular "monument" to the contractors, and in her history of Auburn's early Methodist congregation, Letitia Ross provides a description of the structure, which she attended from her early childhood for about thirty years. The church stood on a high raised basement that was never fully finished for use; to reach the chapel, according to Miss Lettie, a worshipper had to climb some nineteen steps. Only a grainy snapshot of the structure survives, but several Methodist churches built in antebellum Alabama to the same design happily exist, and they illustrate its architectural appeal. A lovely church of the same style, just off Highway 14 in middle Alabama, serves as an example.

Shelton and Williams are also associated in Ms. Reese's account with some antebellum Greek Revival buildings of great consequence in Auburn. Because of its healthy water supply from natural springs, Auburn served as a refuge, by railroad, from the life-threatening cholera epidemics that struck Montgomery in the nineteenth century; furthermore, the mosquitoes of Auburn cooperated by not spreading yellow fever to refugees. Mrs. William Lowndes Yancey and her children fled from Montgomery in the summer of 1853 (and probably stayed at Pebble Hill). Among other exiles from the state capital were members of the well-to-do Murphy family, whose handsome mansion in Montgomery still stands as an antebellum landmark. John H. Murphy, cotton merchant and railroad entrepreneur, hired Shelton and Williams to build a pre-Civil War summer residence, which stood on a hill on the north side of West Magnolia Avenue. A series of photographs of the house date from the postbellum era, when Professor and Mrs. Isaac McAdory and her daughter, the future Freddie Lipscomb, occupied the house. A later photograph illustrates the house before it burned around 1931.

In his *Alabama Catalog*, Robert Gamble has written that "plain untapered piers complemented by equally plain bold trim were peculiar characteristics of the Greek Revival in the Auburn area." These "peculiar characteristics" certainly were evident in the three structures that Shelton and Williams built and for which we have photographic evidence. Perhaps their "peculiar characteristics" can be attributed to an idiosyncrasy in Shelton and Williams's interpretation of the style.

Ms. Reese also credits Shelton and Williams with the construction of the James A. White house, which once stood on Warrior Court but now has been moved to the country and handsomely restored by the family of John T. and Eleanor Harris who, in the late 1930s, were married in the parlor of the old mansion. A comparison of photographs of the Murphy-McAdory house and the White-Harris house, both constructed by Shelton and Williams, reveal a striking resemblance. The White-Harris house, however, contains a fine winding staircase, while there is no record of a comparable staircase in the Murphy-McAdory house.

Top, the Murphy-McAdory House; bottom, the White-Harris House.

Another local historian, Varian Feare (the pen name of Mrs. Walter Burkhardt), also has written a description of antebellum Auburn buildings. Her account, which dates from 1935, has an occasional error, but it benefits from her husband's contribution in directing the Historic American Buildings Survey in Auburn and throughout Alabama at the time of her writing—she had access to the extensive notes he took on Auburn's antebellum buildings. Mrs. Burkhardt's work notes further contributions of George Shelton, the contractor. She credits him, for example, as contractor for the Perry-Cauthen house, now demolished, which dated from after 1859, when, according to newspaper reports, the original Perry mansion (valued at $25,000) burned to the ground. Auburn tradition has it that the original Perry mansion was built

Staircases in the White-Harris House, top, and the Drake-Samford House.

in the early years of the Auburn community, well before George Shelton appeared on the local scene.

The Historic American Buildings Survey describes the Perry-Cauthen house as a raised cottage that is, like the Halliday-Cary-Pick house, on a raised basement. Mrs. Burkhardt connects the Perry-Cauthen house and the Halliday-Cary-Pick house by crediting George Shelton as the contractor for the noted spiral staircase in the Halliday-Cary-Pick house (see p. 167). Further studies may establish the reputation of George Shelton as a major figure in the construction of the buildings of antebellum Auburn. Three handsome antebellum homes in Auburn were constructed around the same time: the now-moved White-Harris house, the now-demolished Drake-Samford house, and the Halliday-Cary-Pick house, which survives in place. All three of these houses featured notably striking staircases. According to Ms. Reese, Shelton and Williams served as contractors for the White-Harris house; Mrs. Burkhardt credits Shelton as contractor for the Halliday-Cary-Pick staircase, but it remains undetermined who actually constructed its staircase and the staircases in the Drake-Samford and White-Harris houses. So far no information has been found showing whether the same or different carpenters constructed these three remarkable staircases that were such important architectural features of antebellum Auburn.

Even though the history of Auburn's domestic buildings contributed to its reputation as a lovely village, without the construction of its college they might hardly be remembered today. Langdon Hall was not the first but is now the oldest surviving public building still on its original site. The ancestor of the present Langdon Hall, the frame chapel of the Auburn Masonic Female College, was first constructed at a different site, the northeast corner of today's Gay Street and Magnolia Avenue (where the Bank of Auburn now stands). The cornerstone of this structure was laid on October 1,

1853, but the auditorium was not ready for occupancy until 1856, and its construction cost probably exceeded the initial estimate of $2,500.

Like the Methodist church across the street, the chapel stood on a high basement, in which Professor John Darby had his office. A distinguished scientist, as a young man Darby had pioneered and published a noteworthy study on botany in the Southern states but perhaps because of his eccentricity had not found major academic appointments. In his later years, besides teaching at both the male and female colleges at Auburn, he devoted himself to the manufacture and sale of a purple-tinted antiseptic, Darby's Prophylactic Fluid, which later proved useful in treating injuries in the Civil War.

According to the *Montgomery Advertiser*, the chapel at the female college could accommodate eight hundred people, and it became a popular forum for political events in antebellum east Alabama. At one time student guides to today's Langdon Hall embarrassed themselves and Auburn University by claiming that Abraham Lincoln once spoke there, but the chapel did serve as a center for debates between states' rights Democrats like William L. Yancey and Whig and American Party advocates like Robert Toombs of Georgia and William P. "Parson" Brownlow of Tennessee. When the female college closed during the Civil War, the chapel stood abandoned for many years, whereupon it was moved across town to the campus of the former East Alabama Male College.

Stephen Decatur Button.

By 1857, the first professional architect in Auburn, Stephen Decatur Button, had appeared on the local scene. Born in Connecticut, Button first went south in the 1840s. Starting in Apalachicola, he moved upstream to Columbus, Georgia, where he designed a church. Very successful in drumming up business, he designed other buildings that still survive in Montgomery and Savannah. Most importantly, he won a competition to design the Alabama state capitol in Montgomery, which was erected in 1847 but burned two years later.

When the trustees of Auburn's fledgling East Alabama Male College approached Button in the mid-1850s to design an academic building, he presented them with an elaborate proposal of Gothic design, which the trustees rejected.

Button then proposed a tall, Italianate-style structure that

Top, Button's rejected Auburn College proposal; center, the extant 1857 East Alabama Male College cornerstone; bottom, the design built in 1858–9.

would be cheaper to build. Wary of cost, the trustees initially authorized only the expenditure of $25,000 for the building, with its million bricks. In the end it cost more than $60,000 to build, though its cost has been reported erroneously as far larger than that.

On August 12, 1857, the cornerstone of the new building was laid (and it still can be seen at the base of today's Samford Hall). The Methodist Bishop of Georgia, George E. Pierce, presided over the day-long event. He stood in for the Methodist Bishop of Alabama, who cold-shouldered the ceremony since he preferred rival Greensboro as a site for a Methodist college in the state. Two renowned political orators spoke on the occasion: the fiery Southern rights advocate, William Lowndes Yancey (a Presbyterian with local ties), whose oratory, it was said, struck like the lightning from heaven, and the mellifluous and more politically moderate Henry W. Hilliard (an ordained Methodist minister). Hilliard's devotees proclaimed that they would travel the length of the state just to hear him reverentially enunciate the word "Alabama"! Furthermore, according to Ms. Reese, "the finest feast ever served in Auburn" was spread out and served, and "the marshal of the day, Hon. Frank Dillard, mounted upon a spirited white horse, [and] kept excellent order."

Construction of the building proceeded but was suspended during the winter of 1858–1859. According to the minutes of the board of trustees, it was resumed in the spring of 1859, "under the supervision of Wm. G. W. Shelton," and plans were "happily approaching completion in full time for the expected opening of the College in October next."

These minutes identify another significant local structure (after the

Button's Evergreen Cemetery Gatehouse, Gettysburg, Pennsylvania.

Methodist church of 1850, the Murphy house, and the White-Harris house, the Perry-Cauthen house, and the staircase at the Halliday-Cary-Pick house) for which Shelton is suggested as supervisor of construction, and it can be conjectured that he served as contractor on many other local buildings. His partner, Sam Williams, who emigrated first to Louisiana and then to Texas in the Civil War era, may have left the village of Auburn by 1859.

As for the architect, by the late 1850s Button had settled in Philadelphia, where he practiced with distinction until his death in 1897. He actually lived across the Delaware River in Camden, New Jersey, at one time next door to Walt Whitman. Button's five-story buildings in Philadelphia used metal-frame (skeleton) construction that anticipated by thirty years the method later used in tall office buildings, and in the mid-twentieth century, architectural historians credited Button with influencing the advances in building construction of Louis Sullivan, the master of tall-building design (and the mentor of Frank Lloyd Wright). Besides the Philadelphia office buildings, Button's best known surviving works are a significant number of highly regarded resort structures on the New Jersey shore and a major Civil War battlefield landmark, the gatehouse to the Evergreen Cemetery at Gettysburg, Pennsylvania. The towering gateposts of Button's Gettysburg entryway could be distant cousins of the two towers of his East Alabama Male College academic building, and, like the gatehouse, Old Main at Auburn also had landmark status in the Civil War as the Texas Hospital, subsidized by that state for its soldiers wounded in the conflict.

Notable Buildings in Postbellum Auburn, 1860–1900

The professional architect found little patronage in the village of Auburn in the decades after the Civil War. As alumnus C. C. Grayson recalled in his memoir, *Remember Auburn in '64?*:

> Auburn was almost a deserted village at this time, the early sixties. I can't remember a single store that was open for business, though there must have been some. There were vacant buildings and grass-grown

The Beasley-Bidez House.

streets where goats by the hundred took possession, and adding to the desolation, a terrible storm [the tornado of December 1864] wiped out many homes, ours among them.

Professor B. B. Ross also remembered the devastation, especially the goats roaming the streets, and he particularly noted that only one house was built in the community in the ten years after the Confederate surrender in April 1865. That one house was significant enough that though it now has been demolished, it has a part to play in this narrative.

It was built, probably to his own design, by the Rev. Isaac Taylor Tichenor, a distinguished Baptist clergyman, who had been appointed by the state to take over the old East Alabama Male College in Auburn, purge from it any lingering Methodist influence, and convert it into a state institution—the Agricultural and Mechanical College of Alabama. The Beasley and then the Bede Bidez family subsequently lived there, and Beasley's pasture became an Auburn landmark, the site of a primitive golf course that local sportsmen, led by Dr. George Petrie, hacked out. Today the former pasture is the site of an extensive collection of municipal buildings on Ross Street, between Glenn and Magnolia Avenues.

Though very little construction was done in Auburn after the Civil War, the Baptists did construct, perhaps with the aid of an unidentified architect, one notable building in the era of Reconstruction, the third such structure, and the most elaborate, that the congregation had built so far in the village. This third Baptist church no longer stands, but it may have left behind an adopted offspring.

Though segregated and usually confined to a gallery, slaves and their enslavers often worshipped together in antebellum Auburn, but after 1865 there was a movement for freedmen to seek separate houses of worship. Consequently, with some financial and material aid from their former enslavers, African American Baptists in the Reconstruction Era built for themselves a sanctuary that still stands: an enduring symbol of these emancipated citizens' devotion to their faith and a local landmark of far more than local significance. It stands at a location still known as Baptist

Hill, even though Unitarians now occupy the building.

This church presents an intriguing architectural puzzle. The structure gives the appearance of having begun on an ambitious scale but never completed in that vein, suggesting perhaps that the volunteers who built it were trying to follow a design that was more expensive than they could afford. Is it possible that the white Baptists offered the black Baptists the same architectural plan that they used to build their own church? A comparison of images of Auburn's third Baptist church and the church that the freedmen built does offer suggestive comparisons. Furthermore, since both white and black congregations enthusiastically supported the division of the antebellum congregation, the shared use of the same architectural design seems possible. Since the Baptist Hill church is such a valuable local landmark, the suggestion that the two churches might have shared a common plan offers a new and intriguing hypothesis that could be studied and debated by architectural historians, preservationists, and interested local citizens to good effect in understanding the history of Auburn building.

Ebenezer Baptist Church, top, and Auburn's third Baptist church, above.

Chroniclers and local historians sometimes mistakenly refer to William Daniel Wood as an architect rather than a civil engineer. But he did not, like an architect, design new buildings; instead, he painstakingly recorded the design of an existing building, measuring how it was put together so that in the future it could be taken apart. Specifically, he calculated and recorded the dimensions and framework of the long-abandoned auditorium of the defunct Auburn Masonic Female College so that the structure could be dismantled and moved in sections to the campus of the Agricultural and Mechanical College of Alabama, where it would be re-erected.

After Wood's father died, his maternal relatives, the Wadsworth family, took him in. They had a large lumber company near Prattville, Alabama,

William Wood; below, Langdon Hall.

where Wood, in a sense, served as apprentice. He showed promise, learned the business, and went on to attend Auburn, where he majored in civil engineering. For his senior project in engineering drawing, he undertook the challenging task of recording the dimensions and structural configuration of the long-abandoned Auburn Masonic Female College chapel. There is no extant record of the day-to-day difficulties he confronted in that task, but he surely must have encountered plenty of dust, creaking floorboards, and general dilapidation. Climbing up and measuring the tower would have required strenuous effort and might even have presented some physical danger.

Wood's formidable undertaking met with resounding success. His project received much praise and a special commendation at the college commencement of 1883. As a prize, he also was rewarded with a Bible, which one of his descendants still retains. After graduation, the young man, with the support of his Wadsworth relatives, went on to establish a successful lumber company in Birmingham, where he was long active in business and civic affairs.

With Wood's careful work as a guide, the college was able to take the female chapel apart and then transport portions of it, section by section, about a block and a half down a wide, dusty street to its new site, next door to the Stephen Decatur Button-designed building, Old Main. B. B. Ross recorded his memories of the move. While he did not specify that the sections of the chapel were rolled down the street on logs, that is a logical assumption and an image that has long appeared in local lore.

Auburn's exhibit of student engineering drawings at the New Orleans World's Fair of 1884—the World's Cotton Exposition—included Wood's prize-winning drawings of the chapel. After the Exposition closed, the significant collection of drawings was housed in Old Main, where all were lost in the fire of 1887.

No image of the chapel on its original site survives, but a photograph of the chapel, soon after its move to today's Auburn campus, does exist, and it illustrates the chapel in its original Italianate style. In the future, the structure was to undergo a transformation from an Italianate to a classical style. The person in charge of that extensive remodeling was J. A. Cullars, not a professional architect, but a remarkably talented local builder. A jack-of-all-trades, Cullars was, seemingly, a master of them all. He wore many hats, including that of amateur architect, but he really belongs in a separate section, that of master builder, and not in this general discussion of the professional architect.

Top, Alexander Bruce; above, Thomas Henry Morgan.

A fire on June 24, 1887, altered the architectural design of the college at Auburn. Stephen Button's Old Main caught fire, probably from rats overturning test tubes in the chemistry lab, and the antebellum structure burned down, leaving only a charred, soot-stained shell behind. Since many in the Alabama legislature doted on the state university and regarded Auburn as an unnecessary and regrettable stepchild, rumors spread that the college in the loveliest village would have to close, but the state senator from Auburn's district, William James Samford, mustered friends and spearheaded an effort that, rather surprisingly, resulted in a $100,000 state appropriation for the college to rebuild. As a result, the Agricultural and Mechanical College had the resources to hire the largest and most influential architectural firm in the Southeast, Bruce and Morgan of Atlanta.

The firm of Alexander Bruce (1835–1927) and Thomas Henry Morgan (1857–1940) designed so many prominent buildings in the late nineteenth century that the volume of their work is hard to comprehend today. Their clients were spread throughout the Southeast, and their buildings extended from the Cherokee County Courthouse in North Carolina to the Cotton Exchange in Mobile, noted for its statue of the goddess of commerce perched upon its parapet. The firm's clientele centered in Georgia, where many of the state's numerous counties feature a courthouse designed by the firm. It is not entirely an exaggeration to say that in the late nineteenth and early twentieth century Bruce and Morgan designed downtown Atlanta.

One of the firm's early advertisements declared: "We make a specialty of planning Court-Houses, Colleges, Churches, Opera Houses, Libraries, and all public buildings." In addition to Samford and Hargis halls at Auburn, a probably incomplete list of the college buildings designed by the firm of Bruce and Morgan includes the main administrative buildings at Clemson, Georgia Tech, and Agnes Scott, as well as significant buildings at Winthrop College, Georgia College at Milledgeville, and Oglethorpe University. Describing the firm's administrative buildings, the *Georgia Encyclopedia* observes that they ". . . were usually symmetrical in plan with great bell towers, terra-cotta decorations, and an array of Romanesque arches."

In his walking tour guide to Auburn University, architecture professor R. G. Millman described Samford Hall: "It is a prototypical land-grant college building featuring multiple gables, brick richly ornamented with stone, terra-cotta decoration, and a tall clock tower. Georgia Tech's administration building by the same firm is another example."

Besides its decorative elements, Samford tower supposedly had practical features: a bell that summoned students to chapel and announced the changing of classes as well as a clock that was meant to support undergraduate punctuality. Alas! The bell soon fell into disuse, and each of the four faces of the clock told different versions of the time, thus providing incontrovertible alibis for the habitually tardy.

In 1929, the board of trustees named Samford Hall to recognize William James Samford and the many members of his family who had loyally supported the college in many capacities through the years.

Samford Hall.

Sad to say, a college architect imported from the University of Florida and completely insensitive to historic preservation undertook a drastic alteration of Samford Hall in 1969. He gutted the double staircases, lowered the ceilings, and converted many of the offices to dark cubbyholes. Quite a few older graduates of Auburn actually wept when they entered the altered structure; many others were outraged. Since that time, the college administration has made efforts to mitigate the damage done by this mutilation of a historic Bruce and Morgan landmark.

2

Town and Gown in Auburn Architecture

THE PROFESSORS

It seems almost inevitable that an agricultural and mechanical school would early recognize that courses in architecture might be, if not a necessary development, at least a highly desirable one and certainly a comfortable complement to its "mechanical" side. At the same time, the formal study of architecture neatly fit the artistic impulse on Auburn's campus and did not threaten the scientific impulse, allowing itself to claim to be one of the many disciplines composing a "polytechnic" institution.

Nathaniel C. Curtis

On June 3, 1907, President C. C. Thach came to a decision of far-reaching consequence for the study of architecture in the South. He recommended to the board of trustees that the Alabama Polytechnic Institute establish a new faculty position, a chair of architecture and drawing, which would be the first such full-time faculty position in the Southern states. In New Orleans, in 1907, local architects taught classes from time to time on temporary appointment to the art department at Tulane University, but no full-time position had been established there. Consequently, when the A.P.I. board of trustees agreed to Thach's recommendation, they made a decision of regional significance.

The alumnus William Warren, already represented on the campus by the greatly admired Smith Hall, was an obvious first choice for the position, but Warren had no desire for a college professorship. As the old saying goes, he was "a doer rather than a thinker," a go-getter who wanted to design lots and lots of buildings and watch them spring up about him. But Warren had a candidate for the position at Auburn, and it was probably on his recommendation that Nathaniel Cortland Curtis got the job.

Warren and Curtis first became acquainted at Columbia University. Although Warren was further along in his studies at the architectural school, they both looked to a favorite professor, William Robert Ware, for guidance. Professor Ware not only taught courses on the practice of architecture, he also developed an innovative method to teach future architects. Furthermore, he perceptively recognized that young Mr. Curtis might have a bent for teaching.

When the twenty-three-year-old Curtis received his degree from Columbia in 1904 he accepted a minor appointment as instructor of drawing and geometry at the University of North Carolina at Chapel Hill, from which he held an undergraduate degree. Nevertheless, despite his rather insignificant instructorship, he had local credentials of consequence. As an undergraduate, he belonged to the mystic Order of Gimghoul, a secret student society dating from 1884 that, for a time in the twentieth century, had as much social status at Chapel Hill as Skull and Bones had at Yale. In 1924, when he was practicing architecture in New Orleans, Curtis was invited to design what, from the viewpoint of his fellow members in that secret order, would become his most noteworthy structure—the celebrated and fantastical stone landmark, Gimghoul Castle, which still sits at the edge of the hill on which the college town is situated and commands a striking view over the North Carolina Piedmont.

In 1907, young Mr. Curtis was looking for a better paying and more prestigious assignment. He was pleased to receive the appointment at Auburn, and the village was pleased to receive him. For one thing, he was an eligible bachelor—nice-looking with good manners. He attended the local Episcopal church, and dating back to colonial America, various ancestors of the same name (Nathaniel Curtis) had been active in civic affairs. An amateur musician, Curtis played the violin in the elite local group that formed the small college orchestra. Furthermore, he joined the would-be local "highbrows" in the Lupton Conversation Club and even gave a paper there. Curtis's reputation as an author grew mostly from his later experiences

NATHANIAL COURTLANDT CURTIS
B. S.
Professor of Architecture and Drawing.
Ph. B., University of North Carolina, '00; Special Assistant, U. S., G. S., and N. C. G. S., '00–'01; Morgan Scholar, Columbia University, 1901–'4, B. S. in Architecture ibid, 1904; student free-hand drawing National Academy Design, 1904; Draughtsman Carrel & Hastings, Architects, 1901–'02., etc; Instructor in Drawing and Descriptive Geometry, University of N. C., 1904–'07; Practicing Architect; Professor of Architecture, Alabama Polytechnic Institute, 1907; Honorary Member N. C., Architecture Association; Engineering Society A. P. I., Architectural Society Columbia University, A. T. O.

From the *Glomerata.*

in New Orleans, but it began in Auburn with the publication of his first book in 1909, *Elements of Graphics*.

As to his academic assignment, he turned out to be a successful teacher, and he popularized the study of architecture at Auburn. Indeed, as a tribute to his success as chair (and recruiter), the college created the Department of Architecture in 1912. He had been an Alpha Tau Omega at Carolina and got along well with college boys. He also got along well with ATO alumni in the community, including prominent local leaders like Shel Toomer, Professor B. B. Ross, and, in Opelika, various members of the Samford family.

Another possible explanation for Nathaniel Curtis's unquestionable success at Auburn: he dated Nellie Thach, the daughter of the president of the college. Dating the boss's daughter can involve perils as well as possibilities, but in Curtis's case, it probably proved helpful. (And, incidentally, he married her!) Curtis's appointment at Auburn was not without special benefit to the university. In 1908, President Thach reported, somewhat smugly, to the board of trustees that Professor N. C. Curtis "kindly volunteered his services to draw the plans and specifications for the library building" and that "plans, elevations, etc., for the agricultural building were designed and drawn by Professor N. C. Curtis, free of charge . . ."

Still, an important question remains. Curtis arrived at Auburn at the beginning of Mike Donahue's revered era of coaching college football on the plains. How did Nathaniel Curtis score on the inevitable and always relevant issue of supporting college football at Auburn? The answer: very high! Incredibly enough, in 1911, the first graduate to receive a degree in architecture from A.P.I. was John Eayres Davis—the captain of Auburn's varsity football team of 1910; a star fullback noted in particular for a spectacular play in the winning game in 1911 against Georgia Tech; a varsity letterman for four years in basketball and track, as well as football; a record holder in the South for the pole vault; an academic honor student for four

years; and, incidentally, the future third partner in the immensely influential architectural firm of Warren, Knight & Davis!

From the early days of Curtis's role as the first chair of architecture in the American South, Auburn trained students to carry its influence out beyond their small world to mold the wider built environment. The leaders of instruction in the school also brought the world's architectural expertise into Auburn's built environment. The North Carolina native, Nathaniel Curtis, brought degrees from the University of North Carolina and Columbia University, an architecture program devoted to Beaux-Arts training. His impact on the Auburn building scene consisted of three campus buildings. To accommodate the expanding engineering programs at the college, Curtis produced designs for additions to the original Broun Hall, greatly expanding it along West Magnolia Avenue. Two of his "freely offered" designs are acknowledged as Beaux-Arts masterpieces—the agricultural building, Comer Hall, and the Carnegie Library.

Top, Broun Hall, original footprint, and above, as expanded. Below, Comer Hall.

In collaboration with the celebrated Auburn graduate William Warren, Curtis was responsible for the design of a home for the Alpha Tau Omega fraternity on the corner of North Gay Street and Glenn Avenue. In 1916, four years after he left Auburn, Curtis also designed the Lambda Chi Alpha fraternity lodge on West Magnolia, which stands today but is virtually unrecognizable by virtue of the uninspired commercial

Top left, Curtis's Carnegie Library; above, an earlier Curtis design sketch for the library. Left, the A. L. Thomas house. Below, the ATO fraternity house.

developments that have swallowed it up (see page 207).

Curtis's son, N. C. Curtis Jr., who became a celebrated architect in his own right, was born in the president's house in Auburn in 1917. These family connections tied Curtis to the college and the community even after he had established a significant reputation at Tulane and in New Orleans generally. In 1920, Curtis designed the house of his friends on North College Street, Mr. and Mrs. A. L. Thomas. The design did not follow the usual taste in Auburn at the time of its construction, and today it occupies a unique position on Auburn's North College Street Historic District. The house is among the few masonry buildings constructed by the Cullars family (see p. 75).

The Judd house.

The soft, nearly pink color of the plain plastered walls suggests a Spanish influence in the design and is complemented by the shallow balconies that accent the upper floor full-length door/windows and by the semi-circular arch at the front door. By the time that Curtis produced this design, he had carefully studied New Orleans design, which included significant Spanish influences.

The possibility that still another building design by N. C. Curtis once rose on South College Street has recently been discovered. Turpin Bannister, dean of the School of Architecture and Art in the late 1940s, wrote to his graduate professor, Joseph Hudnut, then dean of Harvard University's School of Design, and once also head of the Department of Architecture in the School of Engineering at Auburn, recounting his conversation with Dean Judd (School of Education). As Bannister tells the story, Judd claimed his house had been designed by N. C. Curtis for Joseph Hudnut, who had succeeded Curtis in Auburn's chair of architecture. The house had been altered on a number of occasions, Judd reported, and remaining photographs picture quite a large building, often described as "Dutch colonial." Assuming later alterations and perhaps expansions, further research may allow that a Curtis-Hudnut provenance is possible.

Joseph Hudnut

Joseph Hudnut.

During his distinguished career as an architectural educator, Joseph Hudnut had a profound impact on the profession, but at his first post as academic administrator at Auburn, he had only the less challenging task of establishing the academic Department of Architecture, newly created in 1912.

Nathaniel Curtis Sr. had taken on Auburn's village ways like a well-fitting glove; for his successor, Joseph Hudnut, the fit was not so comfortable. Born in Michigan, he had an undergraduate degree from Harvard and an architectural degree from the University of Michigan. Neither he nor his wife were Southerners. They joined the local Lupton Conversation Club but do not seem to have been active in other activities in the village. He did not say so, but Hudnut may have regarded his stay at the Auburn of a century ago as an assignment in the sticks. But that did not preclude his taking a strong interest in his students and a genuine concern about their education.

By his own account, he had determined to inculcate in his Auburn students and in the first building he designed for the campus—the first president's home in 1915—an appreciation for the elements of classical architecture. The house, now named Cater Hall, and now the central element of a collection of women's dormitories, exhibits exactly the Old South style that Hudnut originally promoted. He claimed that his inspiration for the design was the early nineteenth-century Federal style version of the standard five-part Georgian Palladian mansion, "Homewood House," now the location of the Homewood campus of Johns-Hopkins University in Baltimore.

Top, Cater Hall. Center, Homewood. Bottom, Hamill Sunday School Building.

Hudnut's other important local client was the Auburn Methodist Church, for whom he designed the Hamill Memorial Sunday School Building. Ideas that later defined Hudnut as one of the founders of American architectural modernism could be sensed in this second Auburn building. Its architectural design has been much admired, but to some eyes its yellowish brick clashed with the red brick of the nearby Victorian church, which still stands; the Hamill Building has been demolished and replaced.

In 1916, Hudnut resigned to seek a Master of Science degree at Columbia. By 1923, he was teaching architecture and serving as director of the McIntyre School of Fine Art at the University of Virginia. He became dean of Columbia in 1933, and in 1936 was chosen as dean of the newly created Harvard School of Design, which brought together architecture, landscape architecture, and design. And in the late 1930s he brought modernist architect Walter Gropius, founder of Bauhaus, and Marcel

Breuer to Harvard, thereby changing the focus of American architectural education from historicism to new ways of addressing design.

Frederic Biggin; below, his Women's Building on the campus of Oklahoma A&M College.

Frederic C. Biggin

Frederic Child Biggin arrived in Auburn in 1916 as head of the "curriculum in architecture in the Civil Engineering Department," as had N. C. Curtis and Joseph Hudnut before him. Before coming to Auburn, he spent some years in private practice, then accepted an academic position at Oklahoma A&M College in Stillwater (now Oklahoma State University), where he became dean of the School of Architecture.

Frederic Biggin's years in Auburn were largely devoted to development of the college's program of architectural education, so that when his efforts produced the organization of the School of Architecture, he was appointed dean (1927). Dean Biggin's contributions to the school and the college were impressively recognized two years later when, as reported in a publication of the Theta Chi fraternity, of which Biggin had been a member:

> In grateful appreciation of his many years of fruitful labor in building up a small, unimportant department of architecture at the Alabama Polytechnic Institute into the School of Architecture and Applied Arts, that is second to none in the South, the architectural students, faculty, and a few alumni, presented Dean Frederic Child Biggin . . . with an extensive trip abroad as a Christmas gift.

With the benefit of a grant of six months leave from the college, the trip was, indeed, extensive, taking Professor Biggin to the Adriatic, through Greece and Italy, down to the Southern Mediterranean sites in Egypt, and on to Western European countries before his return to Auburn.

Frederic Biggin built a reputation as a skillful and resourceful administrator, but some earlier accomplishments as scholar and designer lay behind his administrative talents. In 1897 he produced, with his co-author, J. S. Siebert, a study titled *Modern Stone-cutting and Masonry*. The book is still in print, which argues for labeling it something of a classic.

Although Biggin produced designs for several campus projects at Oklahoma A&M College (armory, gymnasium, science hall) no records remain to show whether they were ever built. The only building on the Oklahoma A&M campus with a recorded Biggin connection is the Women's Building, still in use, for which he is listed as supervising architect.

In Auburn, Dean Biggin directed the further redesign of Langdon Hall in 1921 but thereafter was apparently seldom distracted from efforts to build the School of Architecture and to serve in related administrative capacities for the college. He also produced the design for his own home, still standing at what was once the north edge of Auburn. His family occupied what continues to be the only Auburn house designed in authentic Dutch Colonial Revival style.

Below, Biggins House. Bottom, A.P.I. faculty during his tenure. From left, Frank W. Applebee; Biggin; Sidney W. Little; W. N. Womelsdorf; E. W. Burkhardt; L. B. Ambler, E. H. Gray; Roy H. Staples; F. W. Lincoln; A. E. James; and Frank M. Orr.

Frederic Child Biggin served as dean of the School of Architecture at Alabama Polytechnic Institute for twenty-seven years until his death in 1943. In their tribute to him, the board of trustees included this remembrance: "[H]is life and character are exemplified in the words of Kipling, which for years he kept in his office for all of his students to see."

> And only the Master shall praise us. And only the Master shall blame. And no one will work for the money. No one will work for the fame. But each for the joy of the working, And each, in his separate star, Will draw the thing as he sees it. For the God of things as they are!

An abbreviated version of these lines from Rudyard Kipling's poem "When Earth's Last Picture is Painted" is inscribed on Biggin's tombstone

Top, Biggin Hall. Above, Turpin Bannister.

in Auburn's Pine Hill Cemetery.

The first campus building created expressly for the School of Architecture, an L-shaped international-style structure designed by the Montgomery firm of Pearson, Tittle & Narrows, and completed in 1951, was named Biggin Hall to mark Frederic Child Biggin's pioneering work in creating the Auburn University School of Architecture. The building is now home to the Department of Art.

Turpin Bannister

By the time Bannister succeeded Biggin (1944), the Beaux-Arts tradition was firmly established at A.P.I. Change, however, was afoot. The School of Architecture and Arts at Auburn was in turmoil as older, traditional Beaux-Arts values clashed with newer approaches associated with the Bauhaus, Walter Gropius, and former Auburn faculty member, Joseph Hudnut, who was leading the movement at Columbia and finally at Harvard.

Little known and hardly remembered in Auburn, Turpin Bannister was a pioneer and giant in the field of American architectural history. He was a founding member of the National Trust for Historic Preservation and a principal founder and first president of the Society of Architectural Historians (SAH) in the United States. As the first editor of the SAH journal, he launched a major instrument for the development of architectural history as a discipline in college and university schools of architecture and departments of art history. Holding degrees from Denison College (BS) in his home state of Ohio, Columbia University (BArch), and Harvard University (PhD), he accepted the invitation of the Alabama Polytechnic Institute to become its dean of the School of Architecture and Arts in 1944. After four years in Auburn, he moved to the University of Illinois to serve as head of its Department of Architecture and later to the College of Architecture and Fine Arts of the University of Florida to serve as dean.

Aside from his strong interest in music and architectural history, Turpin Bannister was best known for his interest in and talents for architectural education administration—an account of which was presented in his major work, *The Architect at Mid-Century*. In his few years at A.P.I., it fell to Bannister to smooth a transition from the Beaux-Arts tradition to a more Bauhaus orientation, which was then beginning to transform the discipline in most major American schools of architecture.

Although he was a trained architectural designer and taught design courses before coming to Auburn, unlike most of his predecessors, he did not design a house for himself in Auburn. The Bannisters recorded as living at 123 Burton Street for all of their four years in Auburn. They had, however, purchased property on which an existing house stood shortly before leaving Auburn. Their son, Thomas Turpin Bannister, recalls living in that house only briefly and that no changes were made to it while the family occupied it.

He recalls, too, that his father did design houses for the family in both Illinois and Florida. The biographical sketch of him that appeared in the *Journal of the Society of Architectural Historians* included the claim that in Auburn "he designed and built his 'perfect home,'" the quotation marks giving the impression that Banister himself was the source of the information. This perhaps resulted from a misunderstanding of a comment he made about another house of his design in Urbana, Illinois, or Troy, New York.

Following the precedent set by N. C. Curtis and followed much later by Walter Burkhardt of faculty members providing designs for campus buildings, Dean Bannister apparently served as associate architect for a men's dormitory, Magnolia Hall, erected in 1948. A set of plans left by him at the University of Florida names Bannister, along with principal architect Norman Holman of Ozark, Alabama, as designers of the building. Magnolia Hall acquired some notoriety for containing dorm

Drawing from the plans for Magnolia Hall.

rooms so small that state attorneys made it an example in defending the state in a civil suit brought by Alabama prison inmates. The prisoners claimed that the size of their jail cells constituted cruel and unusual punishment. The state responded that the prison cells were larger than the student rooms in Auburn University's Magnolia Hall and therefore the prisoners had no reasonable objection to the size of their own accommodations. Students celebrated the state's case with T-shirts showing a convict with ball and chain and the slogan, "Mag. Not just a dorm, a way of life." Magnolia Hall was demolished in 1987.

Frank M. Orr

Frank Orr. Below, the Orr family home on North College Street.

Turpin Bannister departed Auburn in 1948; to succeed him in the deanship, the college chose Frank Marion Orr, a faculty member in the department since 1928, whose specialty was architectural construction. Orr served there until 1956, holding the fort, it might be said, for a traditional approach to architectural education that was being threatened on every side by a newer set of values both in theory and practice.

The site of the Orrs' house was one of the earliest improved lots in what was called the Edwards-Irvine subdivision, a strip of building lots between North College and Sanders streets, adjacent to what became known as Cary Woods, the large tract that the Cary family developed. Aside from his administrative duties on the campus, Frank Orr conducted a vigorous private architectural practice. In a single block of Auburn, along North College Street, one finds a representative collection of his designs. First among these is his own home at 501, a 1937 two-story Colonial Revival house. The first story is finished in smooth plaster, while the overhanging upper story, or "jetty," with decorative drops, is clad in weatherboard, which, like most of his houses, is without vertical corner boards.

For the lot abutting his own, Orr designed a house for Charles

W. Edwards, the long serving registrar of A.P.I., his first wife, Orlean, and their four children.

The Edwards House, on an attractive elevation above street level at 521 North College Street, dating from 1937, exhibits more Southern regional style than does the "garrison" style of its neighbor, which is ordinarily thought of as a more Northern version of the Colonial Revival. The main block of the two-story Edwards home, with a wing to the north side, is a three-bay design, but with the front door in a side bay rather than centered. Four slender, square columns with minimal bases and capitals support the veranda roof that shelters the street facade. Arches above the first-floor openings sport brickwork decorations, while raised bottom panels and floor-length shutters provide some regularity to the openings along the first-story front.

Two more Orr designs on North College, the Edwards House, top, and the Smith-Askew-Godwin House, bottom. Below, one on Samford Avenue, the Coppedge House.

The collection of Orr designs continues to 535 North College where, well hidden from the street, is the Urban-Shaeffer house. Scattered through the town are a number of other Orr-designed houses, most of which have been handsome additions to their neighborhoods.

On Sanders Street (543), the house built for E. B. Smith, later, with substantial 1950 additions, the home of the Askew family (and presently owned by the Godwin family) is practically a lesson in mitered weather-board corners. Although the roof's collection of gables and dormers seems unusual for Orr designs, it complements appropriately the towering trees of the wooded lot around it.

Orr designed a house on Samford Avenue where an open space west of the Three Little Pigs became the site for the Coppedge House. Later additions of elaborate decorative cast-iron work to the front of this house have obscured the original clean lines of the design. The rear elevation reveals a larger building than the front elevation suggests. Fortunately, family members have preserved the complete set of

building specifications that the builder, Isaac Newton, followed. The architect paid careful attention to interior fittings in the house. The living room fireplace was designed without a mantel on the instructions of Mrs. Coppedge, who found mantels to be generally collection places for unattractive bric-a-brac. The master bedroom was supplied with two clothing closets, one for Mr., one for Mrs.; built-in shelving was also part of the design.

As property to the south of town along College Street opened to development, large building sites were acquired for homes. On one of these, Professor Henry Good and his wife, Myrtle, began to plant what became a large collection of camellias and engaged Frank Orr to design a house to sit among them, facing the street from the edge of a large lawn. Other neighborhoods feature Orr designs such as the larger Greene house.

Top, Good, and above, Greene houses. Below, Sidney Little. Bottom row, sketch for Church of Christ, the built church.

Sidney Little

Sidney Little joined the Auburn architectural faculty in 1937, after a short stay at Clemson. A 1919 Cornell University graduate in architecture, Little did additional study at the American School of the Beaux-Arts in Fontainebleau, France. Later he earned an M. Arch. degree from Tulane. Little's teaching responsibilities in nine years at A.P.I. centered on architectural design, so it is unsurprising that he contributed designs for two eye-catching buildings in the town—his own house on Drake Avenue that now is home to the local Montessori school, and the Church of Christ on

Glenn Avenue, lamentably a victim long ago to spreading commercial development.

It is obvious from the images of these buildings—the church drawing by Little himself—that he had abandoned the Beaux-Arts tradition and opted for a modernist approach, which was gaining popularity at many American schools of architecture, including Auburn's. Both the Auburn designs of his own house (top) and that of the Cureton House (bottom) were published in national architectural journals.

Little acquired two lots on Hudson Terrace, around the corner from his home on Drake Avenue. On one of them is a small flat-roofed house of modern design, and of a modern material—concrete. The design is Little's. Next door is a similar house, probably also designed by Sidney Little but for which no documentary evidence has yet been found. The roof of this house has been altered; the chimney stack on the front of the house is the same as that on its Little-designed neighbor.

The house Sidney Little designed for the Brackeen family on East Samford Avenue was quite unlike the three neighboring Little houses on the Drake-Hudson Terrace corner. Auburn architectural taste may not have been quite ready for the modernism that Little's other houses displayed, for he produced this small house of great charm and a more traditional appearance for the Brackeens. The used brick exterior and off-center entrance suited the small lot bordering on the creek at the bottom of the Samford hill.

As Curtis, Hudnut, and Bannister had, Sidney Little also would build a reputation as a successful educational administrator. Between his years at Auburn and his death in 1972, Sidney Wahl

From top, Little and Cureton houses, two concrete houses on Hudson Terrace, and the traditionalist Brackeen house.

Little served as dean of the School of Architecture at both the University of Oregon and the University of Arizona. According to an obituary, after 1952 Dean Little's professional practice had been limited to consultation in design and urban planning.

Walter Burkhardt

For some, Auburn was merely a way-station on a professional path to national prominence. N. C. Curtis himself, though he designed three major Auburn campus buildings and married the president's daughter, spent scarcely five years in Auburn before accepting the offer to build an architectural program for Tulane University in New Orleans, where he became a major contributor to the development of Southern regionalism as an architectural theme.

Not every architectural school faculty member, however, decamped for opportunities elsewhere. Chief lion among this pride was Walter Burkhardt, who not only shaped the careers of his students but also shaped much of the built landscape both on the campus and in the town beyond it and in surrounding parts of the state as well. All that while he gave to his adopted state an invaluable lesson in appreciation and preservation of its architectural heritage through his direction of the Historical American Buildings Survey program for Alabama, to which his wife, writing as Varian Feare, also contributed by continuing her husband's extensive series of articles in the *Birmingham News* (later collected in a volume called *Alabama Ante-Bellum Architecture*). Burkhardt traveled hundreds of miles over the state, with Auburn photographer W. N. Manning, among many others, to identify and record historic Alabama architectural treasures. Two of those

Walter Burkhardt. Below, his Auburn-Opelika airport terminal.

treasures were restored under the direction of Walter Burkhardt—Noble Hall and the Halliday-Cary-Pick House (see p. 145).

Following some early years in Florida, Burkhardt's career in Auburn, where much of what he designed still exists, shows his versatility as a planner and architect in command of a variety of building types and styles. Beginning in 1929, his work included, among many other projects, site plans for the Gardner, Pineview, and Meadowbrook subdivisions and for the Auburn-Opelika Airport. He created building designs for the airport terminal, Auburn's First Presbyterian Church and education building, Frederick's Funeral Home, St. Michael's Catholic Church, many building alterations in Auburn and surrounding towns, as well as an addition to the Lee County Courthouse in Opelika.

Top, Frederick's Funeral Home. Bottom, the Graves Center Amphitheater.

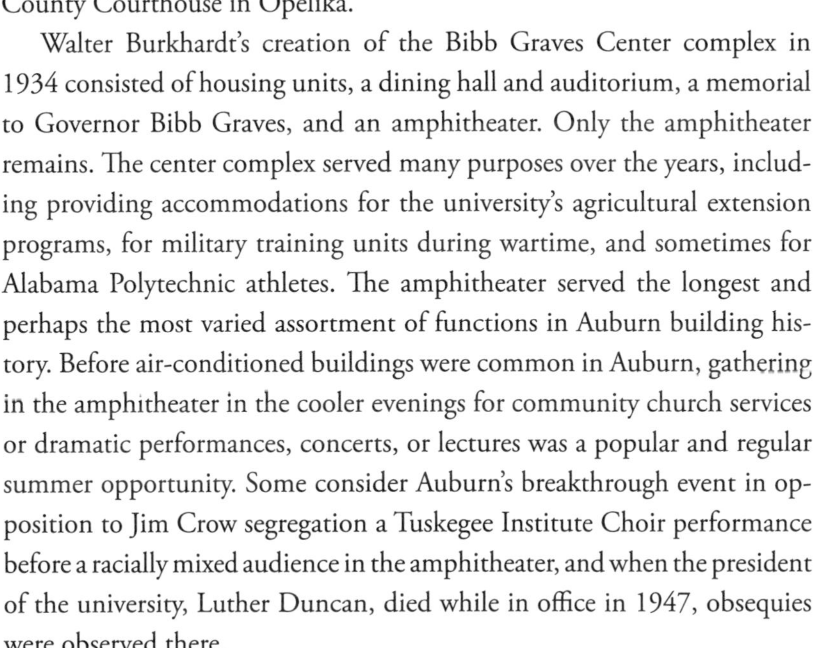

Walter Burkhardt's creation of the Bibb Graves Center complex in 1934 consisted of housing units, a dining hall and auditorium, a memorial to Governor Bibb Graves, and an amphitheater. Only the amphitheater remains. The center complex served many purposes over the years, including providing accommodations for the university's agricultural extension programs, for military training units during wartime, and sometimes for Alabama Polytechnic athletes. The amphitheater served the longest and perhaps the most varied assortment of functions in Auburn building history. Before air-conditioned buildings were common in Auburn, gathering in the amphitheater in the cooler evenings for community church services or dramatic performances, concerts, or lectures was a popular and regular summer opportunity. Some consider Auburn's breakthrough event in opposition to Jim Crow segregation a Tuskegee Institute Choir performance before a racially mixed audience in the amphitheater, and when the president of the university, Luther Duncan, died while in office in 1947, obsequies were observed there.

The entwined history of two Auburn churches, St. Michael's Catholic and the First Presbyterian, is so often told it has almost become Auburn legend. Burkhardt's very contemporary design for the Catholic church, according to one local account, was first presented to the Presbyterians when they decided to replace their Akron Plan church, unique in Auburn, on the corner of Thach and South Gay. Those entrusted to approve a design had a more traditional view of what a church should look like, rejected the design, and charged Professor Burkhardt to try again. Traditional they wanted and traditional he gave them, though at least one feature of the building was both traditional and unique in Auburn—the column capitals. Burkhardt's Presbyterian church capitals are neither Tuscan, Doric, Ionic, Corinthian, nor Composite, but most closely resemble Egyptian columns, which use a palm leaf decoration at the top.

When Professor Burkhardt was enlisted to design a new Catholic sanctuary—also, sadly, replacing a handsome, classical church building—it is often alleged that he presented the modernist design that the Presbyterians had turned up their noses at. It suited Catholic tastes just fine, the story continues; they built it and worshipped in it until they outgrew it.

This popular story of the connected histories of the Catholic and Presbyterian churches, however, is not accurate. Professor Burkhardt, a Presbyterian himself, did offer the Presbyterians a design that was rejected, reportedly because it lacked a steeple. Ms. Lucille Burton, a major financial contributor to the project, is believed to have vetoed the design and requested Burkhardt produce another—less modernistic, more traditional. He complied, and the Presbyterians built

Top, St. Michael's Catholic Church; above, First Presbyterian Church; right, two earlier First Presbyterian sketches.

his revised design. No explanation survives for the two versions of the original designs used to illustrate early fundraising pamphlets. This revision of the Catholic-Presbyterian story concludes by noting that St. Michael's Church was not a castoff design from the Presbyterian project but had been specifically designed according to the wishes of the Catholic congregation. Recently the Auburn Catholic community left their Burkhardt church for a larger facility far out on North College Street, selling the building on East Magnolia to their former Methodist neighbors, who have added it to their substantial campus.

Above, Auburn United Methodist Church; below, Gosser House; bottom, front and rear views of Burkhardt House.

At the same time the Presbyterian congregation was building its new Burkhardt designed sanctuary, the Methodists were extending their campus to fill more of the quarter of the block defined by Magnolia and Thach to the north and south and South Gay and Ross to the west and east. This expansion would place a new United Methodist Church sanctuary next to the old one, which would be re-designated the Founders' Chapel. Construction of the new Methodist church, a common speculation had it, was delayed until the Presbyterians had finished their new church so that the Methodists could claim pride of height, with the tip of its soaring belfry exceeding the heavenward reach of the new Presbyterian spire. The Presbyterians broke ground for their building in December 1952 and completed it in January 1954; groundbreaking for the new Methodist church occurred in August 1954, and the building was completed in September 1955.

Among the many Auburn residences that

Above, four more Burkhardt houses; top right, the Burkhardts at home; bottom right, the Girl Scout Hut on Drake Avenue.

Burkhardt designed, six in the Pinedale neighborhood alone, the most generally known are the rustic Gosser house on Cedarcrest Circle, now demolished, and the house on the corner of Pinedale and Payne Street that he created for his own family.

In brick, with a cottage-like appearance, the 1941 building, constructed by Opelika builder R. W. McMillan, has several features that showcase Professor Burkhardt's talent in combining innovation and tradition. The interior of the house features a step-down living room, a feature hardly known in town at the time, while on the exterior the architect placed two side-by-side roof dormers with different but harmonious treatments. He also combined dormer roof types on the Brown House just a block away on Pinedale and used the stepped chimney stack that appeared on the Gosser House as well.

Architectural importance is a function neither of size nor of public acclaim. One of the smallest and least noticed of Professor Burkhardt's buildings deserves a special place in this account of his work. The Girl Scout Hut, lately given a glaring red paint job in place of its original color (remembered as a dark forest green) has served the Auburn community of Brownies and Girl Scouts for some seventy years on Drake Avenue, once the edge of town.

Edwin and Earl Lancaster

Separating the architectural lives of two Lancasters, father Edwin and son Earl, is not easy, nor is there a reason to do so. Both were first introduced to architecture as a profession in the classrooms of Alabama Polytechnic Institute. The father returned to his alma mater first in an administrative role and then as a designer. The son was a designer foremost, both as his father's partner and as principal in his own firm. From beginning to end, theirs is a story revealing of the world and of the lives of architects in Auburn.

After graduating summa cum laude with a degree in architecture from A.P.I., Edwin Lancaster began an architectural practice in Birmingham in 1920. Although physically handicapped from boyhood by the loss of one leg, he became a star high jumper at Auburn. In his architectural studies, he seems to have excelled as well, becoming the president of the student architectural society in his senior year and graduating with high honors.

Top, Edwin Lancaster; bottom, Earl Lancaster.

By the early 1940s, wartime personnel requirements had decimated both student enrollments and faculty availability. With exemption from military duty and a sterling record in his student days, Edwin Lancaster was a valuable prospect to help the college keep the architectural program running during the war years and prepare it for an expected surge of prospective students and returning faculty when hostilities were over. Lancaster was named acting dean while Orr was away and remained on the faculty until 1947 when the University again called on him to represent its interests by assuming the chair of the Alabama State Building Commission in Montgomery. He later returned to private practice in Auburn.

Known particularly as a skilled draftsman, even before he graduated he had served in the Montgomery drafting room of the eminent architect,

Top, "Fort Nash" in Decatur, Alabama; bottom, (Conn) Anderson House.

Frank Lockwood (see p. 141). After some years of practice in various locations both within and outside of Alabama, including at his own firm in Birmingham, Lancaster returned to Auburn as a faculty member in what had become the School of Architecture and Allied Arts in 1942. He was appointed acting dean of the school from 1944 to 1945. Afterwards he resumed private practice with an office in Montgomery while maintaining his home in Auburn.

Lancaster's reputation as a talented designer was built in part on the spectacular art deco house he designed in 1939 in Decatur, Alabama—Fort Nash, as it is known, was a wedding gift from the Coca-Cola bottling Nash family to their daughter.

Of two Auburn houses designed by Lancaster, one, the Col. Conn Anderson house, is still standing. Colonel Anderson was commandant of cadets for the college's ROTC program. With training as a civil engineer, Anderson remained in Auburn after completing his military service and became an active assistant to the Cary family in planning their major real estate development in an area of northwest Auburn bounded by North College Street and West Drake Avenue. This large and sprawling area, by no means flat, required careful planning to accommodate the terrain by winding the streets through the previously undeveloped forest that covered it—just the sort of challenge that civil engineers would be trained to meet. One of the lots available in what became the Cary Woods subdivision was chosen by Col. Anderson for his own house, and Edwin Lancaster was the architect he chose to design it.

Additions to the left obscure some of the features of the main block, but otherwise the original design remains intact, maintained by today's owners, Carol and Jeff Jakeman. From the street, observers can appreciate that the architect handled the slope of the site quite deftly so that the horizontal quality of the design does not seem threatened. Details of what is basically a classical design are not fussy or overdone, and the symmetry that traditional style requires is only compromised by the quite noticeable chimney stack piercing the roof to the right.

A second house designed by Edwin Lancaster—for Duck Samford, an Auburn insurance representative—has unfortunately been demolished to allow further (and arguably regrettable) commercial development along what once was considered the "back road" between Auburn and Opelika. Duck Samford was the generous donor of Duck Samford Park, which included the Auburn High School football stadium, along the eastern edge of University Drive between East Glenn and the edge of Indian Pines (formerly Saugahatchee) Golf Club.

Top, Baptist Student Center; center, TKE fraternity house; bottom, C. J. Rehling Laboratory building.

Edwin's son Earl graduated from A.P.I. in 1950, and father and son formed a partnership in 1960. A partnership between two architects, one of whom is self-described as a modernist and the other as a traditionalist apparently raises few problems when they develop separate projects. But what will be the result when both are working on the same project? Earl Lancaster himself explained one such situation, the design of the Baptist Student Center on the west side of North College Street (135) in downtown Auburn. In response to the clients' request for an up-to-date design for the street facade, Earl designed the front of the building, while his father designed the rear. Except for the signage, the design from the College Street side is virtually an international-style composition.

The approach was somewhat different for another joint Lancaster project, the design of the Tau Kappa Epsilon fraternity house at 554 West Thach Avenue. The facade of this building, facing the street across a deep front lawn, was given the formal symmetry of classical design and the flat roof associated with modernism. In addition, the centered main entrance is covered by a portico with pediment, again revealing a classical inheritance, yet it is absolutely without ornamentation. The door surround, however, is composed of transom and sidelights, the ordinary accompaniments of a traditional entrance. Perhaps it is the scale of the building that contributes to the successful merging of these alternate design approaches.

A third Auburn building designed by the Lancaster father-son team is the Alabama State Toxicology Laboratory (1051 Wire Road), formerly designated the C. J. Rehling Laboratories to recognize Alabama's pioneering state toxicologist.

An interesting sidelight in comparing the experiences of father and son—the whole design career of the elder Lancaster was conducted "on the board," an expression that refers to plans, elevations, and other graphic presentations drawn by hand and generally reproduced by a blueprinting process. Edwin Lancaster died in 1981; the first AutoCAD program was introduced the following year. Earl Lancaster once called the company for instructions about drawing a slanting line (so easily done by hand) and was told a modification of the program would soon be available that included this technique.

Keith Reeve; below, his family home on Woodfield Drive.

J. Keith Reeve

Architect Keith Reeve came from Illinois, with an architectural degree from the University of Illinois, to join the Auburn faculty twice—from 1928 to 1937 and again from 1946 to 1954. Apart from college class responsibilities, Reeve began an Auburn career in the partnership of Rush & Reeve and later served as chief draftsman in the studio of prominent Columbus architect T. Firth Lockwood. Reeve left much of his early design work back in Illinois but then renewed this part of his career in both Opelika and Auburn. One notable Opelika building was the semi-circular Sunday school addition to the Methodist church campus there, a classic Akron Plan auditorium.

Just as his colleagues ordinarily did, Reeve designed a house for himself, his wife Minerva, and their two daughters. The Reeves' house was on Mrs. Cauthen's wooded development along what she named Woodfield Drive, extending from Wright's Mill Road to South College Street. The boxy structure had little decorative detail but was perhaps a pioneering effort among Auburn domestic buildings of the 1940s for the divided picture window that, with the front door next to it, makes a tripartite combination that occupies most of the first-floor facade of the main block. Neighbors recall that on

EARL LANCASTER REMEMBERS AUBURN ARCHITECTURAL LIFE

My father, Edwin Lancaster, was originally from York, Sumter County, Alabama, and came to Auburn in 1916 to study architecture—was graduated in 1920. He was married to Minnie Lucile Morgan from Senoia, Georgia. My father and I had an architectural partnership from 1960 to the time of my father's death in 1981; I continued to practice until retirement in 1996.

The Lancaster family moved from Birmingham to Auburn in 1942 when I, age fourteen, was in the tenth grade. My father, Edwin, came to fill in for Dean Frank Orr, who was leaving for military service. When the dean offered him the position at Auburn, there was an exchange of letters to settle on the terms of his employment. When the question of salary came up, my father suggested a salary of $3,800, and the dean said, "Mr. Lancaster, that won't work because that is more than I currently make." Obviously, an agreement was reached and my father was on the faculty.

One house I can think of that my father designed in Auburn was the Conn Anderson House on Cary Drive; another was the Duck Samford House on the back road to Opelika. Mr. Samford said this was really two houses—one level for his wife and one for him. There was a story about the house costing Mr. Samford some ridiculous sum of something like seventy-five dollars—that was because when his brother started an insurance company [Liberty National] he talked his brother into buying some stock. The value of the stock soared, and when Mr. Samford sold the stock to pay for his new house, it didn't cost him but seventy-five dollars above the value of the stock he sold.

My parents owned the lot where our house currently sits, and after the war they built a two-story garage apartment on the property, which they lived in for thirty-six years. After the war, building supplies were scarce, so at the time the garage was the best building choice.

In 1947 Auburn asked my father to take a position with the state building commission to help Auburn by giving them an inside man in Montgomery. My dad commuted the sixty miles to Montgomery on a two-lane highway and served as the director of the Alabama State Building Commission.

In the 1950s my father went to Paris to run an office for a company building an air force base in Wiesbaden, Germany. My mother accompanied him, and he tried to get me to go, but I declined. At one time he had ninety French architects working under him.

After Germany my father worked for Sherlock, Smith & Adams in Montgomery. He quit that in 1960, and he and I formed a partnership. Daddy had the Alabama State Toxicology Laboratory under construction and the promise of the Tau Kappa Epsilon fraternity house and the Baptist Student Union. On the student union building my father and I divided the project. I was a student of modern architecture, so I designed the front of the building and father was a man of classical architecture, so he designed the back part of the building.

Although my father had no formal education beyond his degree from Auburn, he had excellent job experience—this is what counts for a good architect.

My father lost his left leg when he was eight years old, but that never stopped him. He walked with a crutch that was made out of hickory, and I buried him with that crutch in his casket. He was on the AU track team—a high jumper! My daughter, Lauren Lancaster, wrote an article for AU athletics, and in it David Housel is quoted as saying my father was the best athlete to ever play for Auburn. My father and Frank Vandergrift's father were in the A.P.I. class of 1920. In later years they loved getting together and recounting the night they climbed the Auburn water tower. As the story goes, Frank's father carried a bucket of paint and a stepladder up the hundred-foot tower ladder and assisted my father in stepping over the outside rail of the tower. My father climbed the stepladder and painted a ten-foot-high "20" on the side of the tower.

About the faculty, when my father was serving as dean and when I was a student, I remember Orr, Burkhardt, Reeve. I would say the faculty was weak. Keith Reeve (whose daughter, Patty, I once dated) was caught between what he was trained in and what he was being asked to do. Pretty much the students were helping each other, learning together as we went along. Dean Bannister was a very smart man, but he went off somewhere else. My father said he had to work hard to stay ahead of his students. I think he didn't have time for much private design work. He was absorbed in learning and working, not designing.

On the faculty in 1948–50, there was an excellent architect named Gabriel Guevrekian on a temporary appointment who was a modernist, but Orr wouldn't hire him permanently because he said the man didn't have a "structural conception."

The only job I had in high school was working at the *Lee County Bulletin* stuffing papers. I was fascinated by the printing process and the part I and the other young men played. When I was about to graduate from high school my father asked me what I wanted to study in college, and I said I didn't know. He said I might want to work in his office during the summer. I did, and I knew being an architect would be something I would enjoy. That summer I worked for my father, the college architect, for thirty-five cents an hour. I started Auburn in 1945 and was graduated in 1950.

One of my classmates was Art Pomponia from New York. He came to Auburn because his sister had married an Auburn music professor.

Paul Rudolph was older than I. I was president of the student AIA, and through Dean Orr I had to work out all the details for a student field trip to the Frank Lloyd Wright campus in Sarasota, Florida. We saw Rudolph on the trip but never saw the Frank Lloyd Wright sites. Someone proudly mentioned to Rudolph that he was an Auburn graduate, and he said, "I am a Harvard man," and that he was ashamed to admit he went to Auburn.

I saw some of Paul Rudolph's designs from when he was a student at Auburn, and they were awful. His work as an Auburn student certainly could not be described as extraordinary. Professor Brown, who taught structural design, had to do some major adjustments on [Paul Rudolph's design for the Applebee house] because it was sagging—the cantilevered plan was faulty.

— RECORDED BY EMILY SPARROW

warm evenings Minerva Reeve could be seen through the window at the baby grand piano and could be heard banging out the "Beer Barrel Polka."

The Reeve house was not nearly so admired as most of his colleagues' houses, but he built a solid reputation with those he designed for others. Perhaps the best among these was a house for Wilbur Hutsell, the legendary A.P.I. coach who supervised the track and field program for forty-two years. The site was a small lot on the corner of South Gay Street and Samford Avenue that Reeve had acquired out of the holdings of the Cullars family in the neighborhood where their construction business had begun.

Top, Hutsell House; bottom, Grimes House.

The Hutsell house is almost a model for the classic American Colonial Revival house. Though on a small lot, for proportion, detail, simplicity, and siting, it could hardly be bettered. The design echoes the standard model in its symmetry and simplicity, a plainness that calls attention, intentionally, to the one elaborate element—the front door surround. The heavy broken pediment focuses the composition more adequately than, one assumes, any other treatment could have. While the facade features one other decorative element—the corner brickwork suggesting quoins—it does not distract at all from the central doorway but, with a plain entablature above the second-floor windows, completes a frame for the facade.

When Keith Reeve created this design for Wilbur and Corinne Hutsell, Mrs. J. C. (Lottie) Grimes, a neighbor to Keith Reeve when earlier their families both lived on Bragg Avenue, so admired the design that she persuaded him to design a similar house for the undeveloped lot the Grimeses had acquired across South Gay Street from the Hutsell house. While both designs fall easily into the Colonial Revival category and share many similarities, disregarding the exterior color, neither could be mistaken for the other. An elaborate entrance marks both, but the Grimes version consists of a portico with a full pediment at the roof and sidelights framing the front door. The height of the portico roof required shrinking the size of the center upstairs

Toomer's Drug Store, then and now.

window, so although necessary symmetry of the style is not compromised, some of the plan of the house is revealed, for beyond the smaller window must lie a bathroom or perhaps a closet.

One design produced by Keith Reeve is remembered by most members of the Auburn family but not necessarily admired by them. In a misguided attempt to update the exterior of the Toomer's Drug Store building, Reeve redesigned both its Magnolia Avenue and College Street facades. The attempt produced the modern look asked for, sleek and bland, but Auburn lost an irreplaceable part of its appearance as a lovely village.

William and Helen Womelsdorf

William Norvell Womelsdorf was born in Birmingham in 1913. He attended the Citadel in Charleston and graduated from the Alabama Polytechnic Institute in 1937 with a degree in architecture. During his undergraduate years at A.P.I., he was employed during the summers as a draftsman for several Birmingham architectural firms: D. O. Whildin; Miller, Martin & Lewis; and E. B. Van Keuren. Upon graduation, he accepted a teaching position at Auburn, worked locally as draftsman for Walter Burkhardt, and as draftsman and designer with Frank Orr. Womelsdorf served as an associate professor at A.P.I. from 1939 to 1951, with the exception of the war years, when he was a first lieutenant in the U.S. Army Air Corps.

In his private architectural practice, which Womelsdorf conducted from the Peacock Building in Opelika, he contributed to the built environment of the Auburn and Opelika communities both through the work of his students and with the commercial and residential buildings he designed. Among his commercial designs is the Wright drugstore (now Cheeburger Cheeburger) on the southeast corner of College Street and Tichenor Avenue. The building was a relative latecomer to the Auburn drugstore scene, serving both as a conventional drugstore entered from College Street and as a bus terminal entered on Tichenor. At one time a high canopy was attached to its north side to shelter arriving buses and their passengers.

For his friends the Hitchcock brothers—Jake, Jimmy, and Billy—Womelsdorf produced a double commercial structure to accommodate the A&P grocery store and Markle's Drug Store on the south side, toward the eastern end of the first block of Magnolia Avenue as the business district was extending toward the Methodist Church into what had once been a premier residential area. The second floor of the two-story building was fitted for student living spaces. The Doctors' Building, a Felton Little project on the west side of the first block of North Gay Street, was also a Womelsdorf design. In the spectacular explosion of the Kopper Kettle in 1978, the Doctors' Building was a collateral victim.

William Womelsdorf, top, and two of his Auburn projects, the *Lee County Bulletin* building and the Jordan-Womelsburg-Anders House.

For the *Lee County Bulletin*, Womelsdorf designed a new plant on Tichenor Avenue that included not only office space but also large printing facilities that accommodated the *Bulletin* as well as the college newspaper, the *Plainsman.* Felton Little was the owner and longtime landlord of the Bulletin Building, the first in what is today a long row of business structures of approximately the same height along the north side of Tichenor. Worth noticing on the Bulletin Building are several decorative elements worked into the brick facade—the corners presumably meant to suggest quoins, the splayed arches over door and window with an unusual keystone feature, and the outlined panel at the top into which an identifying sign might be placed (but so far as is known never held a *Lee County Bulletin* sign).

William Womelsdorf's design skills were in regular demand for commercial projects, yet he also designed attractive residential projects, including the house at 529 Sanders Street, originally produced for Ralph and Evelyn Jordan. When Ralph Jordan accepted a coaching position at the University of Georgia, Womelsdorf bought the house for his own family. The home is currently owned by the Anders family.

While still living in Auburn, Mr. Womelsdorf was active in community affairs, including the Sigma Alpha Epsilon social fraternity, the Rotary Club, and the Episcopal Laymen's League; he also served as consulting architect for the Opelika Parks and Recreation Board.

During his undergraduate years, William Womelsdorf married fellow architectural student Helen Stowers. They celebrated their marriage with a grand tour of Europe, returning from France in the summer of 1937. To graduate early, Mrs. Womelsdorf changed her major to interior design but came back at the beginning of WWII and began work on an architectural degree at A.P.I. She was an instructor of interior design and architecture in the School of Architecture from 1942 to 1954. Her first contract with Auburn in 1942 was for $1,800 for a complete twelve months! One of the Womelsdorf's sons, Billy Jr., recalls his mother's claim that some of the men in the architecture department thought a woman's place was at home and not in a professional position. She said, always with a laugh, that the only reason she was employed was due to a shortage of male instructors during and after the war years. That can hardly have been the whole story, for by all accounts she was a much-respected instructor.

Build This Farm Home for the Ages

This house is so beautiful yet so basic that it fits all families from newlyweds to grandparents.

By HELEN S. WOMELSDORF

This Plan Gives You —

1. A U-shaped kitchen in the center of the house.
2. A dining area and an everyday living area connected with the kitchen.
3. A utility room near the kitchen.
4. An attached workshop-garage and breezeway.
5. Easy-to-clean floors in working area.
6. One, two, or three bedrooms.
7. One or two bathrooms.
8. Adequate storage space.
9. Good traffic pattern.
10. Cross ventilation in every room.

Helen Womelsdorf, top, and one of her popular designs in *Progressive Farmer* magazine.

After William and Helen Womelsdorf divorced in the early 1950s, Mr. Womelsdorf moved to Chicago for graduate studies at the Illinois Institute of Technology, where one of the leading architects of the day, Mies van der Rohe, had designed the campus and the program of architectural study. Womelsdorf went on to work with several government agencies as a consulting architect and later as an architectural advisor in Colombia, Chile, and Surinam.

Choosing to remain in Auburn, Helen Womelsdorf went on to design many of the private homes that are still regarded as major contributions to the town's built environment, a number of them in the Cary Woods development in the 1950s. On Cary Drive, she designed the homes of Herman and Edwina Alexander, the Jake

Hitchcocks, Dorsey and Jean Sims, and Jack and Lib Dunlop.

Charles Rush of Home Building and Supply, Inc., was the contractor for most of these attractive houses. Billy Womelsdorf Jr. recalls that his mother always liked working on a project where Rush was the contractor because he was a fine artisan and a trained architect. Rush's stepson, Vandy Harper, provides an interesting side note about the Alexander house. It was considered a big deal when the house was built because construction costs for the project were seventeen dollars per square foot while all other residential construction in town was going for fourteen dollars per square foot. The cost of this project was the talk of the town among those in the construction business.

Helen Womelsdorf reached an audience wider than her Auburn students and clients with a series of house plans in a variety of styles published by the *Progressive Farmer* magazine. Its editor once wrote Auburn President Ralph Draughon that one of Mrs. Womelsdorf's house designs was the periodical's most requested plan.

THE STUDENTS

Ralph Dudley

Legend has it that Ralph Dudley, a student at the Alabama Polytechnic Institute, designed the railroad station that replaced the burned building across the street from Mrs. Terrell's boarding house, where he was living. The Terrell family's account is the only proof to support this claim, which has been confidently repeated and elaborated as historical fact, as in this account by the proprietors of a restaurant recently opened in the new building:

> The train station was hit by lightning in 1904 and incinerated. Auburn alumnus Ralph Dudley had dreams to restore the train station once again. At 21 years old, he designed a Victorian railroad station and renewed transportation to the station.

Ralph Dudley and the Auburn train station attributed to him.

Above, Langdon Annex; right, Dudley's bookplate; below, the Dudley family.

Fortunately for Mr. Dudley's reputation, nothing has been found that contradicts this local legend, and there are reasons enough to believe it to be true. His training at the college with preparation in architectural arts was certainly sufficient for the job, and with further training in engineering disciplines it is even likely that another Auburn design may have been his—the handsome building now named Langdon Annex that has served a variety of purposes since its original construction as the Electrical Building, which housed Auburn's first electrical generating system powerful enough to serve both the college and the town.

Frank Dudley, Ralph's father, was also an A&M College of Alabama graduate (1882, civil engineering) and operator of a prosperous Columbus, Georgia, building supply and construction company—the Dudley Lumber Company, said to be the second largest building supply concern in Georgia. Frank Dudley not only advertised himself in Columbus as an architect but also had demonstrated that ability in Auburn by designing the house for Professor and Mrs. Mell that was so much a part of the "beyond classroom" social and intellectual life of the town. Auburn University Special Collections holds a set of drawings by Frank Dudley, presumably designs for a building that would replace the destroyed Old Main.

After his Auburn graduation, Ralph Dudley headed for New York, certainly with the material support of resources from the family business, and entered Columbia University's architecture program.

By the time he had completed a tour as Capt. Dudley in the U.S. Army, his attention was fixed on the engineering side of his interests and training. He was attached to several New York electrical engineering companies—ending with his own Edison Electrical Corporation—to exploit the innovations in electrical engineering he had developed, especially those allowing a fuller development of the benefits of skyscraper construction. In life, Ralph Dudley was often recognized for his entrepreneurial skill, financial success, neighborliness, and generous contributions to the arts in New York; Columbus, Georgia; and Auburn.

Dudley Hall.

Ralph Dudley remembered his alma mater with a substantial estate benefit that in part funded the construction of a new home for architectural education—replacing Biggin Hall—named Dudley Hall in recognition of his gift.

William T. Warren

In addition to William T. Warren's considerable talent as an architect, he also had significant ability as an entrepreneur. The large architectural firm he founded, Warren, Knight & Davis, put its stamp on an extraordinary number of local, county, and state buildings in Alabama. Locally, Warren's firm transformed the campus of Alabama Polytechnic Institute from 1920 to 1940.

Warren was born in Montgomery, Alabama, in 1877 and attended public schools and the Stark Military Academy, from which he received his high school diploma. His father, a wholesale grocer, had gone to work at an early age and perhaps impressed on his son the importance of hard work and a job well done. Whatever the case, young Warren entered the Agricultural and Mechanical College of Alabama, class of 1897, and proved to be a bundle of energy. He majored in electrical engineering, a popular calling to pursue at the time. Besides being an active member of his social fraternity, Alpha Tau Omega, he sang with the college glee club and served on the hop committee, which arranged the college dances. He cut a dashing figure brandishing a racket in a yearbook photograph of the tennis club, and he also managed the college baseball team. With his military school background, he served as captain of his cadet company, and, perhaps most interesting to posterity, he acted as staff artist and helped put together the college's first yearbook, the *Glomerata*. One of his satirical sketches depicted

William T. Warren.

two figures: a spit-and-polish cadet officer with a sword reviewing his company in 1897 and a bearded and slightly bedraggled farmer with a hoe viewing his potato patch in 1927.

After graduation, Warren liked to recall that he turned down a relative's promise of employment in a funeral home and instead set off for New York, where he enrolled from 1898 to 1902 in the Columbia University School of Architecture. From an undergraduate degree in electrical engineering to advanced study in architecture may seem quite a leap, but at the time incorporating electrical service into architectural design was considered to be a priority. Whatever the case, at Columbia, Warren found his true calling, put electrical engineering behind him, and devoted himself entirely to the study of architecture.

Columbia professor William Robert Ware, a noted architectural educator, recognized Warren's talent and took him under his wing. A few years later Professor Ware also recognized the talent and encouraged the aspirations of another young Columbia student, Nathaniel Curtis, class of 1904, who later would have a significant impact on Auburn and would collaborate with Warren on a local project.

After graduation from Columbia in 1902, Warren secured an apprenticeship at the prestigious New York firm of McKim, Mead & White, where he remained until 1906. In the meantime, he kept an eye open for opportunities in Alabama. In 1905, for example, he submitted a design in a competition to add wings to Alabama's state capitol. He did not succeed, but he did, rather cleverly, win local publicity. His sketches for the capitol appeared in his hometown newspaper, the *Montgomery Advertiser*, on July 16, along with his commentary. He wrote:

> Architectural proportion is as critical on the inside as out. The skilled designer of the old [capitol] building understood that larger rooms must have more height than small ones, and made the rooms for the Senate and the House of Representatives two stories high accordingly. Not only is the extra height necessary for the dignity and beauty of the rooms, but it is essential for thorough ventilation in a Southern climate.

As he wished, Warren in 1907 returned to Alabama to practice in

Birmingham. At the same time, he acquired a partner, William Welton, also a McKim, Mead & White employee, with whom Warren practiced for three years. Although the partnership succeeded both financially and esthetically, the affable Mr. Warren later recalled, "Welton was a very unattractive man, and we soon separated."

In 1907, Warren won the competition to design a dining hall and dormitory, Otis Smith Hall, at his alma mater, the Alabama Polytechnic Institute. The president of the college, C. C. Thach, had supported Warren's entry in the competition and indeed favored the study of architecture as an academic discipline at Auburn. When just a professor, Thach had posed with Warren in the tennis club photo in the first *Glomerata* of 1897 and knew him on a first-name basis as "Will." Students also knew Thach on a first-name basis, at least behind his back. They nicknamed him "Cholly" for his Southern accent, but when he became college president, they referred to him, more respectfully, as "King Cholly." When Warren won the competition for the dining hall, President Thach wrote another Auburn man in New York City, Champe Andrews (a much-publicized volunteer in the Spanish-American War): "You will be pleased to know that out of five or six competitors for the new Dining Hall, Will Warren was the successful competitor yesterday in Montgomery."

During the construction of Smith Hall, Warren and President Thach

Smith Hall.

corresponded. When the local contractor, J. A. Cullars, balked at some details of the design and wanted to narrow the mortar joints of the brick and to color the mortar red, Warren complained in a letter (see p. 75) to Thach. The president turned Warren's complaint over to the building committee, which Warren also personally addressed, and they sided with the architect in this controversy.

Concerned with every detail, Warren also contacted Thach about the brick itself. He wrote: "Please tell Mr. Cullars to save his dark hard burned red brick and black headers for the outside work, and keep the lighter colored brick for the inside work of the walls." As the work progressed, Thach took pleasure in the building and asked for a rendering of the structure to hang in the faculty room. William Warren was delighted with the building as well; it was his design alone. He kept a signed copy of his rendering of Smith Hall among his personal souvenirs until the end of his life. Posterity has rendered a positive verdict on Smith Hall. It remains a significant structure on the Auburn University campus today.

William Warren could watch over construction details like a hawk, but he had no influence on the decisions made by the Building and Grounds Department of the college. Warren designed the main entrance to Smith Hall to be in a carefully surveyed straight line from the main entrance of Samford Hall, across the street. But rather than building a sidewalk that leads from one entrance to another, the Building and Grounds Department built a sidewalk that leads from nowhere to nowhere. Illogically placed, it avoids any consideration of entrances to either building and ignores any connection to a street crossing. The sidewalk starts in the middle of Samford Hall and does go straight to the street—but not to a pedestrian crossover on that thoroughfare. The sidewalk from nowhere to nowhere remains a time-honored eccentricity on the front campus of Auburn University.

Warren, Knight & Davis Remodel Auburn's Campus

In 1921, John E. Davis, Auburn's first graduate with a degree in architecture (as well as an honor graduate and a football hero), joined William Warren and Eugene Knight to create the partnership of Warren, Knight & Davis, the most prestigious architectural firm in Alabama for many years. The new partnership also successfully acquired clientele in Florida and

Tennessee, and some of the firm's loyal adherents argued that it was, in its time, the leading architectural firm in the South.

After his graduation from Auburn, John Davis served an architectural apprenticeship for a year in Philadelphia with Horace Trumbaur, best known for designing the original campus of Duke University. He then served an apprenticeship for five years with Lewis Kamper, who successfully transplanted the McKim, Mead & White style to urban Detroit. After his years in Detroit, Davis wanted to return to practice in Alabama, and in 1921 both Knight and Warren urged him to do so. Knight wrote a letter of formal invitation to Davis to join the partnership.

Eugene Knight, a rather modest and quiet individual, at least in comparison to his gregarious partners, had no connection with Auburn or indeed with any formal education. He was self-taught but extremely meticulous and had served a long apprenticeship with a number of architects. He was particularly noted for his talent, precision, and attention to detail in drafting and his supervision of others in that task. In a large, bustling firm, he quietly did his job and always earned the approval and affection of the founding partner, William Warren.

The new partner, John Davis, was energetic, affable, and (unlike Knight) outgoing. Quite bright, Davis had talent around the office, but his primary task was to secure work in the field. He soon proved to be successful at that assignment. After he joined the partnership, the firm's work with colleges expanded everywhere but particularly at A.P.I. From 1921 through the 1940s almost every building at Auburn rose to the designs of Warren, Knight & Davis. Both Warren and Davis promoted the firm with their alma mater, but Davis probably deserves even more credit than William Warren for all the business at A.P.I. that came the firm's way.

An early example of John Davis's extraordinary access to the inner circle that ruled the Alabama Polytechnic Institute—he was in Governor Thomas Kilby's office in the state capitol in Montgomery on December 1, 1922, for an executive committee meeting of the A.P.I. Board of Trustees. Dr. Spright Dowell, president of the college, and Charles DeBardeleben, president of Auburn's alumni association, also attended. According to the trustees' minutes, Davis "submitted the plans for two dormitories, one for the boys and one for the girls, to be built out of Alumni funds." In a follow-up comment, President Dowell reported that after consulting with several alumni committees he had chosen the firm of Warren, Knight & Davis as architects to prepare plans for the two buildings. The executive committee of the board of trustees then approved the choice of architects and the building plans.

Davis again proved his unique access to A.P.I. matters by attending a second meeting in Montgomery a few days later on December 6. On this occasion, the executive committee of the board of trustees dealt with an effort by a group that wanted to cancel the plans for the dormitories and move A.P.I. to Montgomery! The committee responded by deciding to build only one dormitory in Auburn but to open bids on it. Secondly, the committee agreed not to award a final contract to the contractor proposed by Warren, Knight & Davis until the Montgomery group could make a presentation to the entire board of trustees.

The entire board of trustees met in Montgomery on December 21 to hear the Montgomery group present their argument to move A.P.I. to the state capital. John Davis not only attended the meeting, he also took the floor. He argued that the contractor for the dormitory at Auburn had presented a reliable bid. After he spoke, the trustees rejected the plan to move A.P.I. to Montgomery and awarded the contract to build the dormitory to the contractor Davis had recommended. John Davis was present throughout these high-priority deliberations, and he also influenced their outcome.

In the first year after Davis joined as partner, Warren, Knight & Davis began an extraordinary expansion, for which Warren and Knight gave Davis credit. The new partner's influence extended far beyond the campus at Auburn. Among many new opportunities for the firm, he probably deserves credit for the 1923 contract to design the elaborate stone mansion atop a Birmingham mountain for Charles DeBardeleben, president of the Auburn Alumni Association and Birmingham coal and iron baron.

The dormitory that Davis promoted, known as Alumni Hall, still stands on College Street on the main campus, but it has been converted from a dormitory and now bears the name of Travis Ingram Hall. A second building that John Davis promoted, Erskine Ramsay Hall, for which the Scottish-born tycoon donated $100,000, also remains in place on West Magnolia Avenue.

WARREN, KNIGHT & DAVIS BUILDINGS ON THE AUBURN CAMPUS

1-Duncan Hall, 1928; 2-Alumni Hall, 1923; 3-Ross Laboratory, 1929; 4-Ramsay Hall, 1924; 5-Textile Engineering, 1932; 6-Drake Infirmary, 1938; 7-Animal Husbandry (Upchurch Hall), 1929; 8-Women's Quadrangle, 1938.

(Continued on next page)

1-President's House, 1938; 2-Tichenor Hall, 1939; 3-Georgian Practice Hall (Glanton Hall), 1939; 4-Cary Hall, 1939; 5-Nursery School, 1939; 6-Field House (Petrie Hall), 1939; 7-Stadium West Stands, 1939; 8-Stadium East Stands, 1949.

Paul Rudolph

Paul Rudolph.

Of hundreds of Auburn University graduates in architecture, Paul Rudolph achieved the greatest national reputation. Though his acclaim stemmed mostly from his work in Florida among the so-called Sarasota school of architects and in New Haven where he became dean of the Yale School of Architecture, his connection to Alabama began in his youth and one more was in negotiation until his unexpected death in 1997.

In his earlier years, Rudolph's ties were to Kentucky and, peripherally, to the pastoral pursuits of his father, a Methodist minister, whose profession offered Rudolph his first exposures to his two passions—architecture, through drawings for an addition to a church, and music, through church services. At A.P.I., Rudolph was notable on campus for accomplishments in music and architectural design, out of which originated his first building on the grounds. At the request of a faculty acquaintance, Thomas P. Atkinson, professor of modern languages, Rudolph developed as his senior project a house for Atkinson on a small lot in a developing area on the eastern side of Auburn at the corner of Samford Avenue and Scott Street. The design differed from the prevailing architectural values in Auburn at the time, which tended toward traditional and regional expression. Rudolph's Atkinson house, while not avant-garde in any sense, tended clearly toward what most of the neighbors would recognize as somehow "modernist."

The Atkinson house is a small, one-story brick structure, marked particularly by its low-pitched roof and windows that wrap around the corners of the building. Borrowing from Frank Lloyd Wright in a modest way, Rudolph specified the locally quite unconventional central heating system, now referred to as radiant heating, in which heated water is circulated through the concrete floor pad. The design for the house includes a large living room through the center of the plan, with a fireplace set against an inner wall. The left side of the living room is a bedroom wing extending toward

Atkinson House, top, and its overmantel, bottom.

the street, while past the fireplace wall is the kitchen and dining area. (At the far right side of the building, what originally was a carport has since been enclosed to provide additional living space.)

One decorative element was built into what might be said to be a modern equivalent of a fireplace overmantel. Rudolph incised a scene of fishermen into a manufactured wall covering called Homasote, said by its manufacturer to have "scores of uses, from decorative wall coverings to fire-retardant roof insulation." One student of Rudolph's work claims that the panel was the first homoerotic art produced in the whole town, though how this was determined is hard to imagine.

The history of Paul Rudolph's creation of the Atkinson house design is well known, but one glitch in the chain of events has sometimes confused the attribution. The Atkinson design was produced just prior to Rudolph's graduation, and construction did not begin until afterwards. Protocols required that a building permit could only be issued if a registered architect had prepared the plans. The builder, J. J. Hodges, a busy local contractor, would hardly risk his professional status by ignoring the requirement. By this time, Rudolph was employed by the Birmingham firm of E. B. Van Keuren. Because Rudolph was not yet a licensed architect, the obvious solution to the problem was to make Van Keuren's firm the architect of record. The firm was so recorded; the permit was obtained; the Atkinson house rose. It still stands at 628 East Samford Avenue.

When Paul Rudolph entered Harvard's School of Design in 1942, he was taught by the international architectural design star Walter Gropius. As further training and opportunities arose for him, in Auburn he cemented his growing reputation as a thorough modernist with his second local project, the spectacularly cantilevered house on Chewacla Drive designed for Martha and Frank Applebee.

In the combined School of Architecture and Arts, Frank Applebee was a professor of art, whose specialties were drawing, watercolor, modeling, and applied art. The episodes that surrounded the acquisition, display, and finally archiving at Auburn of the collection of modern paintings once a part of the Advancing American Art brouhaha were largely due to Professor Applebee's initial and energetic efforts. By the time Rudolph's design was solicited, both he and Applebee were enthusiastically, even notoriously in some eyes, in the modernist camp, and Rudolph was developing his attraction to the internationalist style.

The oblong flat-roofed box that is the Applebee house was firmly anchored into the sloping site at one end by the contractor, Harold Swindell of Opelika. From the street view, one bedroom lies to the right, while the more public areas of living room, dining space, and kitchen are centered, and a two-bedroom wing leaves earth behind and juts into the air at the left, providing some protection to a parking area below.

According to the present owners, Anne and Larry Shaw, the Applebees could not afford to complete the house to the exact specifications that Rudolph had proposed. With the original plans in hand, the Shaws are now renovating the building to those specifications and will at some future time open to the public as a house museum.

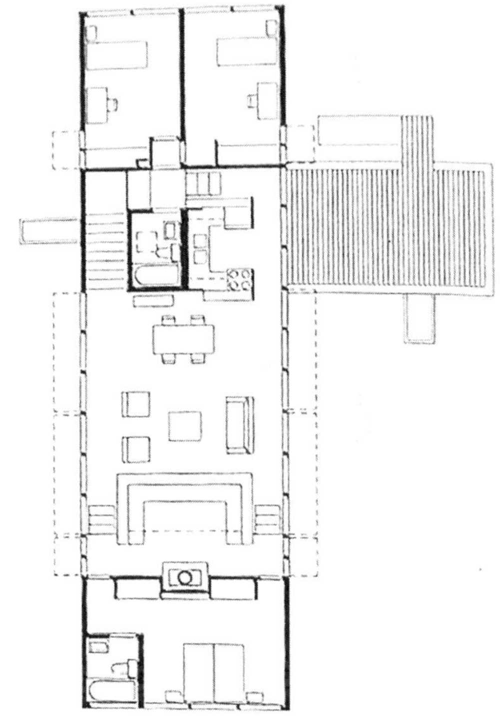

Applebee House, top, and a sheet from its plan.

The third Rudolph building in Auburn was planned for the university's Kappa Sigma fraternity, of which Rudolph had been a member as an A.P.I. undergraduate. Its unusual plan placed the dormitory accommodations in a long, centered run of rooms with entertainment, meeting, cooking, and eating spaces at the ends. Through 2015, the building stood vacant and

Top, Kappa Sigma House; bottom, Tuskegee University Chapel.

threatened with demolition after having been seriously damaged by fire. It was finally demolished in 2016.

Paul Rudolph had made his early reputation in Florida as a designer of residences, but when larger projects came his way, he enhanced his reputation with designs of larger buildings, most notably the Yale Art and Architecture Building when he was dean there. Through some acquaintances he had developed over the years, in the mid-1960s he was persuaded to create one design close to Auburn, the spectacular chapel on the campus of Tuskegee University, which continues to draw admiring visitors and architectural students.

Perhaps due to the success of those buildings or simply because he was a son of Auburn, he was invited to design the proposed Jule Collins Smith Museum of Fine Arts. Negotiations involving Thomas Tillman, Auburn's Director of University Planning, had not proceeded far when Paul Rudolph died in 1997. Ultimately the museum was built to designs of the Birmingham firm Gresham, Smith and Partners.

3

Builders

CONTRACTORS AND WORKMEN

The oldest public building in Auburn still on its original site is the Presbyterian church, built by the local planter Edwin Reese in the 1850s. When the college acquired the building, they put it to various uses over the years until its rebirth as the Auburn University Chapel, a restoration made possible by the generosity of the E. L. Spencer family. In the early nineteenth century, attempting to differentiate between architect and contractor hardly made sense. It was typical, and in this case probable, that little in the way of architectural plans or elevations or specifications guided the construction process. Since the builder was also the owner, there was no contract and thus no contractor in a modern sense. In all likelihood, Reese was both architect and contractor in that he decided what the building would look like, and he assembled and assigned tasks to the workers who made and laid the bricks, felled and sawed the trees, and milled and assembled the wooden roof structure, doors and windows, and interior woodwork. Most of Reese's talented builders were enslaved laborers, directed on the site by an experienced white supervisor, according to Mary Reese's "Early History of Auburn." Otherwise, so far as we know, no whites or free men of color were among them. According to the 1850 census, Edwin Reese owned thirty-one slaves—fifteen females and sixteen males—in the northern section of Macon County. Of these, seven were men between the ages of fourteen and thirty. None of the enslaved men was older than thirty, so these seven were the likely builders of the Presbyterian church.

A similar story unfolded on the outskirts of Auburn, when Addison Frazer brought the builder Henry Foster from Kentucky to direct the building of a plantation house by his slaves. No record is available of the enslaved population of the Frazer plantation before 1860, when the census shows that Frazer owned twenty slaves between the ages of thirty and sixty, not identified by sex, and twenty-two female slaves, aged ten years and younger. Foster and enslaved laborers built the house, known now as the Frazer-Brown House and as Noble Hall, of rubble (that is, unworked, rough) stone, collected from Frazer's two thousand acres and assembled into walls nearly two feet thick and covered with stucco.

The building has considerable architectural sophistication—tetra-style porticoes front and rear, a vernacular treatment of the Doric columns at the front, piers at the rear, and Greek Revival embellishments inside and out. The builders must have been skillful to have completed the hanging stair with a reverse flight that rises from the main floor of the center hall and the cantilevered front and rear balconies.

Little is known about builder Henry Foster. He is not easily recognized in Kentucky or Alabama censuses. Possibly Foster returned to Kentucky after his service in Alabama. According to the Louisville city directory, in 1865 both "Henry C. Foster, bricklayer," and "Henry T. Foster, brickmason," lived in Louisville on adjoining streets, one of them possibly the creator of Noble Hall.

The old Presbyterian church and Noble Hall—created without architects and built with enslaved labor—are probably representative of how all of the few surviving antebellum buildings in and around Auburn were created. Most surviving records from the early postbellum period do not show that the enterprise of building was carried on in any more systematic or modern way than before. But in the immediate postbellum period, at least one Auburn building sheds some light on the transition from an older tradition to a newer one. Many Auburn histories include the information that the builders of the Ebenezer Baptist Church on East Thach Avenue were former slaves, many of them church attenders. When the church was built in 1870, the congregation would likely have included former slaves who were experienced builders. The design was simple, straightforward, with just the features that mark it unmistakably as a church. It has stood just as built, still serving a religious community (though not the original one), on its original site for almost a century and a half.

No systematic study has recorded the extent to which in the post-Civil War years members of African American churches built their own sanctuaries. In Auburn, the AME Zion Church on Martin Luther King Drive is another example. In the face of an expanding membership, the congregation, which had been meeting in a small church building on Cox Street, decided in 1946 to build a much larger sanctuary. Under the direction of its pastor, Rev. Butler Williams, church members gathered, produced, and assembled resources for a church notable for its design and decoration and for the rock-faced concrete block produced and laid by the hands of the members to build it.

In Auburn, as in much of the South, building in the years after the Civil War first relied on newly freed black workmen for labor. As the composition of the workforce gradually shifted, building skills became more evenly distributed between white and black workers, but some of the old patterns remained. One source of information about these patterns is the United States Census.

The first people that the census identified as building contractors in Auburn were J. A. Cullars in 1900 and Milton T. Culver in 1910. Of Cullars, much is added below, but there is little record of Culver's life in Auburn. M. T. Culver of the Atlanta firm Culver, Eiseman, & Co., advertising itself as "machinists and contractors," moved his family to Auburn in 1894 so that his children—three boys and one girl—could attend the college, from which all graduated. No record yet discovered describes anything he built in Auburn.

"Building contractor" is a flexible term, and it was a late addition to the available vocabulary to describe the people responsible for developing our built environment. In Ms. Reese's history of Auburn, for example, Shelton and Williams are identified as "contractors" (actually, "contracters" in her text), while the 1850 census classifies them as carpenters. At one time a familiar description was "undertaker," denoting one who "undertakes" the responsibility for producing a building, usually by way of a formal contract. "Mechanic" was also occasionally used to describe someone skilled in a building trade. In earlier times, when most building was wooden, "master carpenter" often designated a person who directed the building process. For masonry buildings, the parallel term was "master mason." The term "contractor" was used for any project that involved a contract, be it transporting mail or leasing convicts, not just constructing buildings, so "building contractor" is the most useful term for a person who holds a contract to put up a building and who is responsible for managing the whole process required to accomplish that.

Census reports for Auburn, Alabama, from 1870 to 1940 (excluding 1890 because those reports are missing), identify only nine persons as building contractors: Joseph A. Cullars in 1900; Milton T. Culver in 1910; J. A. Cullars and Hull Cullars in 1920; and in 1930 and 1940, in addition to the Cullars brothers, Joseph H. Ceasers, W. Chrietzberg, Willis M. Conklin, Isaac S. Newton, Jake Pitts, and Carroll G. Temple. But to tell the whole story of Auburn building, the associated workmen (and they were all men) must be included—the carpenters and masons and their "helpers," the plasterers, painters, stone workers, and later, plumbers and electricians.

It should not go unremarked that the whole period examined here was racially segregated in Auburn. All of the contractors listed in the census reports were described as white. Although not all of the 1870 report is legible, it appears that fifteen persons listed there worked in building trades. One was a plumber (white) and one a brick mason (black). Thirteen were carpenters, of whom five were black and eight white. In 1880, ten workers were listed as carpenters—six white, three black, and one described as "mulatto." Three brick masons were included in that year—one white, two black. In 1900, of the fifteen building workers, twelve were black and three, including the contractor, Cullars, were white. By 1910, however, the census reported a large increase in the numbers of workers in the building trades. "House carpenter" was the designation for seventeen Auburnites who appeared in the census that year; five were white, three were black, and nine were mulatto. For brick layers and brick masons the figures were: one white, one black, six mulatto. Two plasterers were listed in 1910, one black, the other mulatto. Among house painters, two were black, nine mulatto, and none white. In the years up to 1910, then, it appears that within the building trades, the racial composition was fairly evenly divided between white and non-white tradesmen—with the exception of painters. Although we have not yet learned where the boundaries of the census subdivision called "Auburn" lay in these years, it may be safe to assume that a substantial number of non-white residents lived within the Auburn limits.

The count of building tradesmen expanded in the 1920s, '30s, and '40s. The town was growing, the need for housing keeping pace, and the population in the building trades expanding to meet that need. The whole numbers of builders of all descriptions in Auburn were as follows: 1870=15; 1880=13; 1900=16; 1910=49; 1920=45; 1930=88; 1940=94.

Building the College

While the college began to hire building tradesmen as their own employees, they were largely the maintenance crew; though listed in census reports, they are not included in the figures given above. But of the older buildings still standing on the campus, records give us some information about the architects who designed them and the contractors who built them, if not much information about the crews who actually assembled them.

Langdon Hall began life as a chapel for the Auburn Masonic Female College and was moved to its present location on the campus in 1883; little information survives about the history of its construction. Although one account claims that the intact building was rolled on logs through the town to its campus site, another account recalls that the building was disassembled, the pieces carted off to the campus, then reassembled. While the building was still on its original site, a college cadet, W. D. Wood, received an academic prize for his drawings of the building. It is supposed that those drawings guided the reassembling of the auditorium on the college campus. However true that might be, no record suggests who reconstructed it.

Some years after it was in place on the campus of the Agricultural and Mechanical College of Alabama, as the school was then called, the old chapel building sorely needed attention. The board of trustees authorized removing the tower and redesigning the front of the building in 1889, but the work was not done for lack of funds. The college president advised the board in 1890 that "for the preservation of the building [the tower] should be removed and an approved front substituted." An unnamed architect's plans required covering the building with eight inches of brick instead of the four inches that the $2,500 original appropriation anticipated. Finally, in 1892, the trustees allowed the president to accept a bid of $5,556 from J. A. Cullars, the local contractor whose role in building Auburn will be a

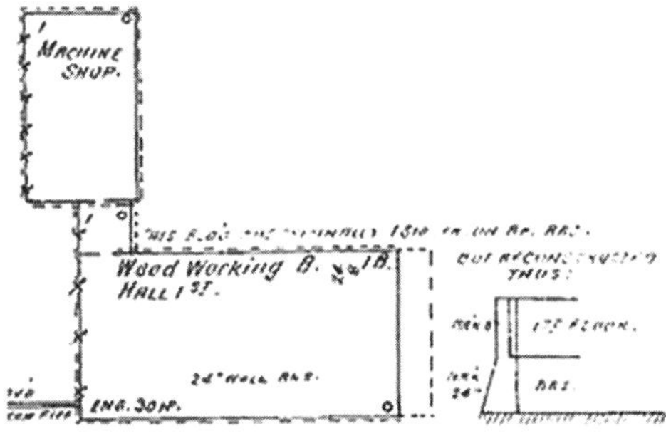

Top, Langdon Hall under reconstruction; center, construction details from the Sanborn Map; bottom, Langdon Hall reconfigured.

large part of this story hereafter. Cullars's renovation of the building produced a result that, with some later modifications, is the Langdon Hall that stands today.

Even before the 1892 improvements to Langdon Hall were made, the building assumed a role on the campus quite different from its original use as an assembly hall. When the principal college building, Old Main, burned in 1887, the college adapted Langdon (and other buildings) to shelter its operations while new college buildings were under construction. In the basement, contractor James Smith installed his shop. The Sanborn Fire Insurance Map for Auburn, Alabama, 1897, included the explanation, "This building was originally 1 story, frame, on brick basement / but reconstructed thus."

Records of the A&M College of Alabama suggest that it was well launched by the time disaster struck Old Main. After the fire in late June 1887, the institution missed hardly a beat in accommodating the cadets entering and returning in the fall of that year. Destruction of the main building occurred just at the time A&M was about to launch its new building project, a purpose-built chemistry building to satisfy the demand for space and special facilities needed for that increasingly popular curriculum. Recognizing the importance of chemistry to Alabama agriculture, the legislature had already appropriated funds for the building—skimpy though they were. For the college, it then became a joint project to rebuild the main building while concurrently putting up a new chemistry building.

The college trustees first instructed its building committee "to procure some competent architect." Ignoring the usual procedure to secure competitive bids for designing public buildings, the committee contracted the services of a very competent architect, the prominent Atlanta architectural firm, Bruce and Morgan, to design both the main building and the chemistry building. When their attention turned to securing a building contractor, however, the committee proved more careful with the public's money. As instructed, they advertised for contractors' bids and chose the low bidders.

With the architect's plans in hand, the low bidder for the chemistry building at $11,900—the partnership of Floyd and Stevens from Opelika—began work in early 1888 on a site just north of Langdon Hall where the building still stands, though threatened by two major fires over the years. Stylistically it is a standard Bruce and Morgan academic building, uneasily described as "Georgian-based" with a substantial complement of borrowing from non-Georgian styles. After the chemists departed, it proved useful enough to house a variety of other departments—architecture, pharmacy, and music—and now the administrative offices of the Graduate School. The university named it Hargis Hall after the distinguished surgeon Dr. Estes Hargis, a 1917 Auburn graduate, one-time assistant to Dr. Mayo at the Mayo Clinic, and later Birmingham physician and hospital founder.

Newly finished Hargis Hall.

Business developments in postbellum Opelika were like those in every part of the recovering South at the time. In particular, the development of the building contracting businesses in association with lumber mills and planing mills occurred in most Southern towns ambitious for economic and population growth. Messrs. Floyd, Stevens, and an associate named Andrews were at the center of such development in Opelika. W. D. Floyd opened his planing and sawmill in a large brick building in 1886, in association with C. E. Stevens. In fact, W. A. Andrews leased the mill from the company and would later become a principal partner in the business when it became Andrews & Stevens. Unfortunately, though he produced some signal accomplishments, such as Opelika's Lee County Courthouse, Andrews not only ran the mill but may have run the partnership arrangement into the ground. After fire had destroyed the mill and some of its machinery in 1898, the association with Stevens foundered, and a court-ordered division of the property ensued. When the business was sold "at public outcry in front of the courthouse door," Andrews himself purchased the "lot, buildings, machinery, etc." for $11,000. He continued the business as W. A. Andrews Lumber Company, offering building materials and "architectural service" in Opelika and Columbus, Georgia, newspapers.

Shortly after fire destroyed Old Main, President William LeRoy Broun reported to the trustees of the A&M College that $25,000 (about $600,000 in 2016 dollars) was available for "rebuilding the main college structure."

Four contractors submitted bids, including Floyd and Stevens, whose $44,745 offer was underbid by the successful bidder at $43,500. The result was reported in the trustees' minutes of October 27, 1887.

> The sealed bids for the erection of the main college building were opened and submitted; and after a consideration of the same it was resolved that James Smith of Sparta, Hancock County, Georgia, being the lowest bidder to build the main college building of the Agricultural and Mechanical College of Alabama according to the plans and specifications of Messrs. Bruce and Morgan, architects; that the contract for the erection of said building be awarded to him with the understanding and agreement that the said James Smith, Contractor, can use in the erection of the building all suitable brick on the grounds of the college except a sufficiency thereof to complete the laboratory building now in process of erection.

Top, Samford Hall under construction; bottom, as completed in 1893.

The college made an additional contract with Smith, reported in the trustees' minutes thus: "The second contract for the interior of the building was made with the same contractor for $25,000 with the provision that proper deductions were to be made for all parts of the specifications omitted by the building committee."

Even though James Smith had no reputation in Alabama, he was an experienced Georgia builder, often on projects designed by Alexander Bruce, an association that no doubt brought him to Auburn, Alabama. Among other projects, in Georgia Smith had built the Hancock County courthouse designed by Parkins and Bruce in 1882, the Walton County courthouse by Bruce and Morgan in 1883, and the Newton County courthouse by Bruce and Morgan in 1884.

With generous funding from the Alabama legislature and private benefactors, the college began an active building program toward the end of the aughts, including three major buildings still on the campus today—Smith

Hall (1908), Comer Hall (1909), and the Carnegie Library (1909), now Mary Martin Hall. The college was pleased to adopt the designs of faculty members and alumni for a number of its early buildings—Comer Hall and the Carnegie Library, designed by faculty member N. C. Curtis; the president's home, designed by faculty member Joseph Hudnut; and Smith Hall, designed by alumnus William Warren. Rarely, however, did the college rely on local builders to put them up. Domestic building was increasingly in demand in this period, thus Auburn and Opelika builders had plenty of modest-scale projects to occupy them. The college may also have been uncomfortable encouraging local builders to compete against each other to win their contracts. Although in these early years at least one Opelika firm, Floyd & Stevens (later Andrews & Stevens), was a likely bidder, among these early twentieth century campus buildings only Smith Hall had an Auburn contractor, the reliable J. A. Cullars, who was probably the only Auburn builder with the experience and resources to take on large projects.

As the new century opened, college administrators realized that the town could no longer offer enough housing accommodations for the growing student body. The decision to build a combined dormitory and dining hall facility across College Street from the main campus attracted attention across the state, especially when the design submitted by alumnus William Warren of Birmingham was chosen. Bids to erect the building were solicited, and J. A. Cullars won the contract over eight other bidders.

Correspondence between the architect and President Thach preserved in the Auburn University archives reveal that Cullars had clear opinions about the appearance of the building and was not shy about advancing them. He suggested to Thach that Warren's specification for wide white mortar joints would not harmonize with buildings already on the campus and proposed to lay the brick with narrow red joints. To the contractor's presumptuous suggestion, Warren replied:

> We made the joints thick and with white mortar for the express purpose of having a beautiful wall that would harmonize with the style of building [i.e., colonial revival]. Red mortar is never used by first-class architects in this kind of work and we want to register our most emphatic protest

Example of the brickwork on Smith Hall.

against such a blight being put upon the whole design.

When the building was completed in 1908 it attracted national attention with a spread in the November 10, 1909, issue of the *American Architect and Building News*, which included its plan, photograph, and a description by Warren:

> This recently completed building occupies a site on the wooded campus of the Alabama Polytechnic Institute and has a large banquet hall 40' x 105' on the first floor and twenty bedrooms on the second floor. The banquet hall contains a brick and faience fountain with an antique terra-cotta basin.
>
> There is a basement below the kitchen wing, and also a mezzanine story in this kitchen wing containing additional space for service.
>
> *The exterior is of selected dark red common brick, laid Flemish bond in white mortar joints.* [emphasis added] The arch keystones are marble and the other trimmings pine painted white. The interior is finished in hard pine.
>
> This building contains 227,000 cu. ft. and cost complete, $28,000 or 11c. per cu. ft.

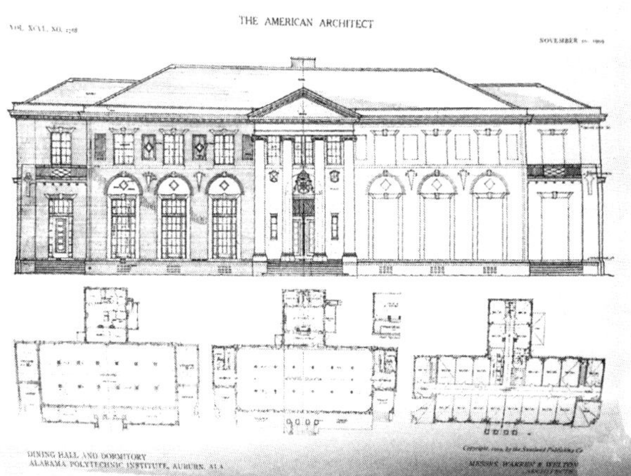

Top, Smith Hall as depicted in 1909 professional journal; bottom, elevation and plans.

For three of the college's early projects, winning bids (that is, *lowest* bids) were submitted by the same Birmingham company, variously referred to as Birmingham Building & Improvement Co. and Birmingham Building & Construction Co. Little has thus far been discovered about this firm. In Birmingham it is remembered mostly as a builder of houses. A historian of Birmingham's black middle class finds that Birmingham Building &

Improvement Co. not only built in the sections of Birmingham available to black families but also advertised in publications with largely black readership and even on occasion provided mortgage financing to its black clients. One of its advertisements read:

> ***If you own a lot,*** we will build you a house on plans to suit upon terms equal to paying rent. If you do not own a lot we will furnish one and build on plans to suit on terms about equal to paying rent, after a small payment is made. No one can afford to pay rent to others where such opportunities are offered.

None of what is known about Birmingham Building & Improvement Co. suggests a company equipped for the large and sophisticated construction projects credited to it for two of the most prestigious and stylish buildings now standing on the Auburn campus (and a third, the Broun Hall expansion, regrettably demolished). The first under construction was a new home for the agricultural program. This move was to emphasize the college's place as an agricultural institution under the land grant program specified by the Morrill Act and to make clear the direction of the agricultural program toward research rather than farming. Even before construction began the building was named Comer Hall in recognition of the governor who had secured a major appropriation ($75,000) from the legislature to build it.

The number of photographs of Comer Hall under construction is unusual for construction projects of that time. The images provide a good record of the building process of the period. The name of only one contributor to this process is known—S. L. MacIntosh of Opelika, later the builder of the 1917 Presbyterian church in Auburn and of a house for legendary J. A. "'Fessor" Parrish, principal of the Lee County High School. While J. J. Sudduth of Opelika was a large supplier of bricks in the area, and though bricks manufactured in Columbus were conveniently available, news reports show that the bricks for Comer Hall were

Comer Hall under construction in 1909. See photo of completed building at page 26.

produced in the Birmingham brickyard of Sibley-Minge Press Brick Co. and must have come into Auburn by train.

To relieve overcrowding of the Samford Hall library space, the college used a grant from the Carnegie Foundation to defray a large part of the cost of building the new Carnegie Library. N. C. Curtis, chairman of the college's department of architecture, designed both the new agricultural building and the new library. Apparently, negotiations to select the contractor for these buildings did not follow ordinary practices. The trustees' minutes for 1909 record that its building committee was in Birmingham pursuing a builder. John C. Brooks is named as president of the Birmingham Building & Improvement Co., and because his is the only name listed, he must be named the contractor for these two buildings. Brooks held BA and MA degrees in mathematics from Princeton, where he also instructed in mathematics. There is no known explanation for his move to Birmingham nor of his transition from mathematician to building contractor—his life as reported to a Princeton alumni group. After a short career in Birmingham, he moved to California in hopes of improving his poor health. He died there in his late forties.

Below, Cater Hall; bottom, Ross Chemical Laboratory.

OTHER EARLY BUILDERS

Despite the ordinarily detailed records of college building projects in Auburn, none has yet surfaced to identify the builder of the 1915 president's residence (now Cater Hall) designed by Joseph Hudnut (see p. 28) nor the architect or the builder of the Electrical Building (1896–97, now Langdon Hall Annex) that is particularly notable for its roof, the only mansard type on the campus.

Frost Construction Company was a large Tampa, Florida, builder mainly of commercial and institutional structures. Just as the American economy entered its bleakest period, Frost contracted to build two buildings for the Alabama Polytechnic Institute, the first of which was the imposing Ross Chemical Laboratory, seen here while under construction.

While the chemistry building was still unfinished, Frost began the Animal Husbandry and Dairy Building, completed in 1930, reportedly at a cost of $190,000, including equipment. It is now known as Upchurch Hall, home to the Animal Sciences Department. Both of these buildings were designed by Warren, Knight & Davis (see p. 61) in the neoclassical style of many of their Auburn University buildings. The bas-relief cow head over the front door of the Animal Husbandry and Dairy Building announced its original use.

Top, Animal Husbandry and Dairy Building (Upchurch Hall); bas relief decoration over its front door; bottom, the new president's home, completed in 1939.

With a distinctively different appearance but still within the classical revival style is the present president's home, another Warren, Knight & Davis design. The residence was part of a large, federally funded multi-project grant to the Alabama Polytechnic Institute in the later 1930s. The Brice Building Company of Birmingham was the contractor for the president's home, first occupied in 1939. The company had been founded only in 1931, with a view, the date suggests, of participating in the New Deal's efforts to stimulate the American economy through construction projects. The reach of the company expanded greatly in post-World War II years, with commercial and academic projects in Tennessee, Mississippi, and Louisiana.

THE CULLARS LEGACY

The story of early building in Auburn is incomplete without extended attention to the Cullars family, particularly to J. A. (Joseph Alpha) Cullars. His skills as a carpenter/woodworker, an apparent talent for organization and management, and a genial manner were the foundations of success. As a bachelor, it is also possible that freedom from the responsibilities of raising a family enabled the considerable scope of J. A. Cullars's interests and accomplishments. He earned a prominent place in the community, which he served as a Lee County commissioner and an active member of

J. A. Cullars. Below, Auburn Public School and the Cullars' family store.

the Methodist church. The Cullars Brothers Construction Co., as it was sometimes known, built a large number of the graceful Victorian houses that once helped make Auburn the "loveliest village of the plain." A few of them remain, though the village has become a rather ordinary medium-sized city today.

A scattering of news reports, some public records, some local memory, and the fortunate preservation of papers relating to the lives and business of the Cullars brothers by their descendants are the basis of this account. The building career of J. A. "Tobe" Cullars began at least as early as 1884, a date suggested from remarks he included in a letter to his nephew and namesake, Alpha, stationed in Brest, France, with the American Expeditionary Forces at the end of World War I. "There is no [contracting] work being done here—duller than it has been in thirty five years . . . I have done more work in the field [i.e., on the farm] this year than I have done in thirty-five years." Under the aegis of its patriarch, M. L. Cullars, the family farmed a large spread in Lee County south of the Auburn village (much of it now included within the Auburn city limits). M. L.'s three builder sons—Hull, J. A., and William A.—continued working on the farm even as their contracting business expanded. By the late 1880s, the brothers were at work helping James Smith build Samford Hall.

The Cullars legacy is remembered today largely by the houses that J. A. Cullars built. But his status as a builder was established early by his institutional work. He must have earned on Samford Hall a solid reputation as a workman that led to his contract to remodel Langdon Hall and to make some "repairs, improvements and changes" to the residence building of the Agricultural Experiment Station, as recorded in the A&M College Board of Trustees minutes for 1892. When James P. C. Southall arrived in Auburn in 1901 to join the A.P.I. faculty, some eight or nine years after Cullars's renovations and improvements, his family lived in this house. "The instant I saw it," he wrote in his memoir, *The Abbots of Old Bellevue*, "I was agreeably surprised. It was a modern, spacious frame building in the midst of a big yard with a flower-garden . . . pleasantly situated on a high hill . . . halfway surrounded by two porches and had six large rooms all on one floor."

An early climax to Cullars's building career at the college, however, came in 1908 with the low—and winning—bid to construct Smith Hall (see p. 75).

In addition to the institutional projects that he undertook for the college, he did another for the town in 1899, the Auburn Female Institute, which became the Auburn Public School.

The Cullars family built the store they operated in downtown Auburn on the corner of College (formerly Main) and Magnolia. In response to the growth of the village, in 1906 they replaced the old frame Cullars store building with a newer brick and stone one that was home to the Bank of Auburn and other businesses and organizations and that still stands on its old corner opposite Toomer's Drug Store, though lately so altered as to be nearly unrecognizable to patrons of its earlier businesses.

Even though J. A. Cullars is now remembered mainly as an Auburn builder, he did work elsewhere in the area, having built in Camp Hill the public school (1906) and the Methodist (M.E.) church. The former is noteworthy because it was designed by the prominent Montgomery architects Frank and T. Firth Lockwood.

A little farther afield, in Alexander City, J. A. Cullars built in 1907 the first workers' houses for the Alexander City Cotton Mill, precursor to the Avondale Mills. For projects such as these, Cullars was more supervisor than artisan. In the adjacent photograph, he can be seen—fourth from right, holding plans—with a large workforce constructing an unidentified building, perhaps the Camp Hill school.

Top, Cullars' Store became Bank of Auburn; center, Camp Hill United Methodist Church; bottom, Cullars and his crew on the job site of possibly the Camp Hill public school.

The Cullars family construction enterprise was anchored by three buildings that stood on the edge of the town and of the family's farm. Two houses, still in place, on and near the corner of South College Street and Samford Avenue were family residences, standing roughly on one corner of the properties that Cullars accumulated along Samford Avenue and South Gay Street. The two houses were certainly showpieces for the accomplished skill and taste of J. A. Cullars. They display, inside and out, a skillfully crafted array of the ornamental effects of popular architecture in the late Victorian period. Design versatility is displayed in these buildings as well. Although they were placed within sight of each other and were built on apparently the same grade when viewed from street level, the orientation of one is distinctly horizontal, the other distinctly vertical. To a prospective client, the message was that Cullars could build any way one might wish!

Top and above, 369 and 421 S. College Street; below, Cullars farm house, and, bottom, after its move to Chimney Acres.

The Cullars house at 369 South College Street was built for brother Hull Cullars. Family legend is that J. A. Cullars built the house at 421 South College for himself at the time of his intended marriage. The union did not take place, the prospective bride is not known, and Cullars remained a lifelong bachelor. He did not live in the house he had built but rather in the household of his sister. The house was rented occasionally and later became the home of his nephew.

A third family house, for the third Cullars brother, William Arlington Cullars, was built farther out on College Street on the Cullars farm property. A few photographs of this building in situ are known but of the whole building only one blurry shot exists. An image of the house after being moved, renovated, and substantially altered, however, shows its general configuration when it was a Cullars family home.

The third in-town anchor building was the Cullars' workshop, which stood empty for many years after the business closed and finally was demolished

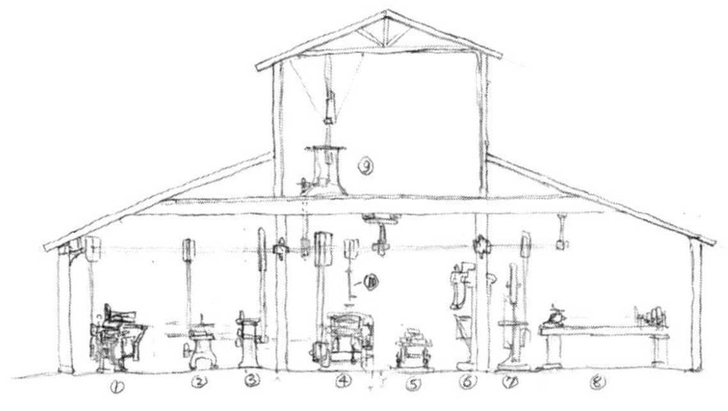

at the behest of the City of Auburn, which deemed it a hazard to public safety. In that shop were the highly complex woodworking machines with which the Cullars produced the elaborate decorations that the most picturesque Victorian styles required.

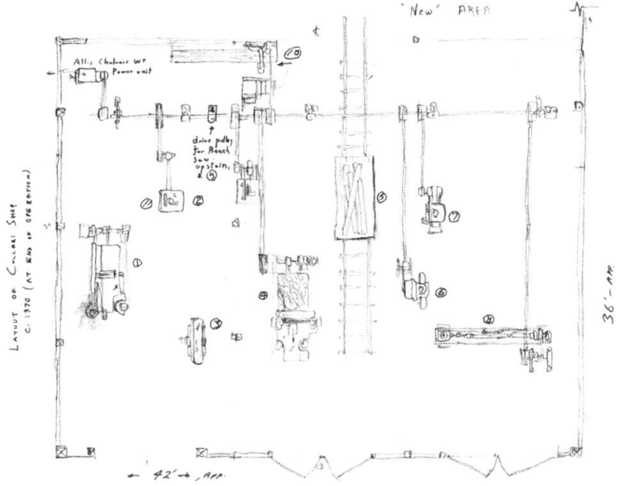

Although the workshop, shown here in 1890 soon after it was built, was often referred to as the Cullars barn, it had never been a farm building. A shop cart ran on double steel rail to carry supplies to the woodworking machines arrayed to either side of the rail. The machines were powered by belts driven from an overhead shaft originally powered from outside the building by a steam engine. From his memory as a frequent visitor to the shop before it was dismantled, connoisseur and collector of early woodworking machinery Walter Clement made these drawings to show how the workshop was arranged.

Above, Cullars workshop and its layout. Below, a molding machine.

Some of the machinery was quite elaborate and up to date, other pieces quite ordinary but necessary and serviceable, including many hand tools that dated from the Cullars brothers' earlier years. The Cullars collection of powered woodworking tools is believed to have begun when J. A. Cullars acquired certain machines from the Langdon Hall basement when James Smith, the Sparta, Georgia, contractor, dismantled his workshop there after completing work

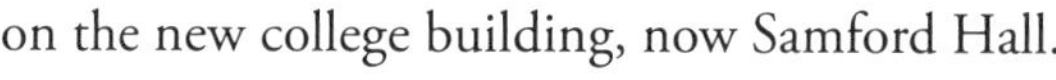

on the new college building, now Samford Hall.

With these and many other tools, the shop was able to turn out elaborate wood effects, most prominently the showy gable and porch decorations they featured on most of their framed residential projects.

The two Cullars family houses on South College Street show the characteristic exterior decorations in their gables (sometimes referred to as "gable pediments") and in their elaborate brick chimney tops. Their designs were at least inspired by, if not directly copied from, those found in drawings widely available in books and journals of the day, of which several from J. A. Cullars's papers have survived. Cullars stored wooden patterns for these designs in the loft portion of the shop, available for reuse—for example, in restoring damaged elements of the Yates-Ingalls house around the corner from the shop.

Top, gable and chimney at 421 South College; below, Cullars Haynie (Carter) House porch decoration.

From a design point of view, there is nothing particularly original or innovative in these effects. But considering the volume of this work, the variety in the effects distributed over the town, and the fact that none of the work was "off-the-shelf" of some commercial distributor, the achievement of the Cullars enterprise was arguably the equal of any large building firm in any large city. Although many of the Cullars-built houses in this style have been destroyed, those that remain serve to document the claim.

The bulk of J. A. Cullars's early house building business arose from the acquisition of building sites in the neighborhood near his shop. Two photographs of the same house built in this neighborhood by the Cullars brothers demonstrate the evolution of some of these buildings. The image of

Two iterations of the original Auburn home of the M. L. Cullars family at 358 South Gay Street.

the renovated building shows how one might develop and preserve such a house, even for rental purposes as, in this case, was accomplished by the longtime owners, Lynda and Joel Tremaine.

The Samford Avenue Cullars-built house that once faced toward town at the end of Gay Street was moved slightly to the east in order that Gay Street might be extended southward as the town expanded. Now located on the southeast corner of Samford and Gay and a rental property, 204 East Samford Avenue has lost its gable decoration and its chimneys have been rebuilt but the fine woodwork of decorative details under the eaves of the front porch remains. One block to the east, on the corner of Samford Avenue and Wright's Mill Road, another Cullars project, locally known as the Williams house, is no longer easily recognized as a Cullars effort because so much of the characteristic Cullars decoration has been lost, very likely due to maintenance difficulties as the house became mostly a collection of rental spaces.

Cullars, of course, built houses outside his own neighborhood, such as the Zuber-Tatum House at 305 East Glenn Avenue. Though now obscured behind a high wall and greatly altered, the house was built as a small-town showpiece in 1899.

Top, 204 E. Samford; center, Williams House, 210 E. Samford; bottom, 305 E. Glenn.

There is no evidence that Cullars designed any of the structures he built. He occasionally worked with architects, some with national reputations, such as William Warren and the Lockwood brothers, and others only locally known. The family homes, for which J. A. Cullars is best known and remembered, however, show originality only in his ability to produce a wide variation in assembling well-known elements into decorative effects. To judge from what is known of the journals he read, he would have been familiar with the popular architectural styles of the day. His clients apparently relied on him for up-to-date if not original designs and certainly for the quality and tastefulness of his work.

The Hulse House.

Although J. A. Cullars was actively working in the early years when "kit" houses were being offered to the public and gaining some popularity, no such house built by Cullars has been authenticated. There is one good candidate, however: the Hulse House at the corner of East Samford Avenue and Wright's Mill Road, which is often called a "Sears house." Neighbors across Wright's Mill Road recalled its having been built from a kit, and one former owner claimed to have found Sears imprints on uncovered house parts during renovation, but no such imprint has been found in recent examinations of the building. Though most kit houses were frame buildings, Sears also provided kits for houses to be built of locally obtained masonry.

A catalog of kit houses offered by the Aladdin Company was found among J. A. Cullars's papers, but no record of a purchase by any Auburn party has been located in the Aladdin Company's archive. However, designs closely resembling Hulse House may be found in catalogs of most companies that produced kit houses.

The claim that Cullars was the contractor for Hulse House is certainly arguable on circumstantial grounds because of the close, longstanding relationship between Frank Hulse and Cullars. The Hulse lot was part of the property on the south side of Samford Avenue that Hulse, professor of civil engineering, had surveyed for Cullars. It is not far-fetched to imagine that Hulse would engage Cullars to build his house. On the other hand, Cullars built no other solid masonry houses, though the old Cullars Bank of Auburn building was of masonry. The Toomer House and the Bottoms House were brick veneered. The A. L. Thomas House, on North College, recently identified as Cullars-built, was stucco over concrete block.

All of the frame houses remaining in Auburn that can be reliably attributed to the Cullars brothers are presently either rental or commercial properties save one—the house at 429 South College Street, recently acquired by Linda and William Dean. With each loss of a house designed and built by the Cullars, and many have been lost and many more are now threatened, Auburn loses a part of the "loveliness" that once distinguished the village and the history of the town is further diminished. Even though the grander Auburn houses are preserved and cherished, they were only a part of what Auburn came to be. Arguably, builders like J. A. Cullars and his brothers—smart, ambitious, industrious, talented, far-seeing—were the people who gave Auburn just the architectural usefulness, stability, and charm that made it the delightful and livable town that once so pleased its residents and visitors.

AUBURN ICE & COAL CO.

The difference between building as an occupation and building as a business is the difference between J. A. Cullars—for whom contracting was a way to make a living—and Auburn Ice & Coal Co.—for which it was a way to make money. The corporate model that Auburn Ice & Coal introduced to the Auburn building scene was the culmination of a development pattern encountered often in American business history. Typically logging gave rise to sawmills, sawmills to lumberyards, lumberyards to purveyors of general building supplies, and building suppliers to corporate building contractors.

Three Auburn businessmen organized the Auburn Ice & Coal Company in 1925 with $16,300 in capital. According to their incorporation application, the nature of the business was to "buy and sell coal and ice." The three incorporators were S. L. Toomer, W. L. Long, and Homer Wright.

Sheldon Toomer, an Opelika native, graduated from the Alabama Polytechnic Institute in 1892. Thereafter he played many roles in Auburn, both for the college where he was a member of the board of trustees, for the town as a founder and president of the Bank of Auburn and as a pillar of the Episcopal Church, and for Alabama as a member of the state legislature representing Lee and Russell counties. His business interests were centered in the legendary Toomer's Drug Store, in the bank, and in the Auburn Ice & Coal Company.

Walter L. Long's place in Auburn revolved around his dedication to two institutions, the Auburn Ice & Coal Company and the First Baptist Church. Following W. L. Long through the U.S. Census from 1920 to 1940 provides information about Long, about the Auburn Ice & Coal Company, and about social and economic mobility in small-town Alabama generally. In 1920, W. L. Long lived in Wacoochee, a small settlement on the Columbus Road

From top, S. L. Toomer, W. L. Long, and Homer Wright.

A DAUGHTER'S MEMORY OF WALTER LONG

He was always a man of business and [there is] hardly an image of him that he wasn't dressed in a suit and tie and his shoes polished. The family lived in the house directly across the street from the Auburn Ice & Coal office, but [he] drove to work. In the mornings he'd get in his black sedan and back across the street to the office; he'd drive back to the house for lunch at noon; and again drive back across the street for the afternoon's work; and at night, here he'd come driving home from across the street.

It was somewhat funny this thing about him backing across the street for work each day, but he said he was trying to use his time efficiently by keeping his car near the office door for when he might be called away to a meeting or to a job site. My father was totally dedicated to his work.

near Salem. He was twenty-seven years old then, renting a farmhouse for his wife and three children. His education had ended at the eighth grade, when his father died, and he went to work to help support the family. Nonetheless, by completing a bookkeeping course he was able to move off the Columbus Iron Works production line into an office job at that company.

By 1930, Long and his family, now grown to five children, were living on Bragg Avenue in a home, valued at $3,000, built by a predecessor to the Auburn Ice & Coal Company. According to the census, this home included a radio set! Long's occupation is recorded as "operator" for a "lumber company," i.e., the Auburn Ice & Coal Company. In 1940, the last available census report, Long still lived on Bragg Avenue, was employed as "proprietor" in a "retail lumber business," working eighty-four hours a week and earning $3,600 a year. Records of the Baptist Church, various civic groups, and campaigns for charitable causes in Auburn show that Long had become a prominent community presence, while the records of the Auburn Ice & Coal Company reveal him to have been a dependable and imaginative director of that enterprise and, no doubt, one of the principal reasons for its success.

Homer Wright must have been the junior partner in the launch of the Auburn Ice & Coal Company. He was only a small stockholder, and the company records do not show that he made any substantial contribution to its decisions or projects. Still, he was a notable presence in the town. During and after his education in A.P. I.'s pharmacy program, he assisted Dr. Steadham, physician and pharmacist, at the doctor's drugstore on North College Street, just about where the Lipscomb Building is located. When Steadham decided to give up the drugstore, he sold it to Homer Wright. Later Wright had built the drugstore building on the corner of North College and Tichenor, designed by W. N. Womelsdorf, that is today the home of the eatery known as Cheeburger Cheeburger. Under a high canopy along Tichenor, Greyhound buses loaded and discharged passengers for many years before their stop was twice moved farther out of town and ultimately to Opelika.

Homer Wright is remembered as an entertaining figure by the students and townspeople who frequented his drugstore on North College Street and, it seems, as a reliable source of financial help to those among them whose usual funds ran short. He served as a member of the Indian Pines Recreational Authority, which developed the Saugahatchee Country Club (now the Indian Pines Golf Course). Wright's geniality may have been the key to his appointment as postmaster in 1935, to be succeeded after his death in 1943 by his wife, Katherine.

The genesis of Auburn Ice & Coal was in North Carolina, and the company proceeded successively to Harris County and Columbus, Georgia, then across the Chattahoochee to the Salem-Wacoochee-Bleecker area, and finally to Auburn. Claude J. Young, lumberman and mill owner, Charles Haynes, "lumber mill saw filer," and John A. Cook, "lumberman planer," as they were described in the 1920 census, all came from North Carolina. In Harris County, Georgia, the Bland-Cook Lumber Company was chartered in 1917 by Haynes and Cook with a Georgian partner. After some negotiations in court, Bland-Cook and other petitioners managed to settle claims against the United States government for compensation after their timber leases were interrupted by condemnation proceedings involving the expansion of Camp (now Fort) Benning.

By 1923, the Bland-Cook Lumber Company was operating in Bleecker, Alabama, and dissolved its Georgia corporation altogether in 1927. The teenaged Walter L. Long, who was living in the Bleecker area, found employment at the Columbus Iron Works across the Chattahoochee River. Only a few records track the movement of W. L. Long from the Columbus Iron Works to his employment as accountant for the Bland Cook Lumber Company, and only a few records track the transition from Bland-Cook to the C. J. Young Lumber Company (sometimes known as the Auburn Lumber Company), or of their move from Bleecker to Auburn. The sale of the C. J. Young Lumber Company to the Piedmont Lumber Company is recorded in a Lee County deed book. Although the A.P.I. Board of Trustees' minutes for 1932 record two purchases of lumber from C. J. Young Lumber Co., "for bleachers" and "bleachers for parade," the name change from Young

Piedmont Lumber Company.

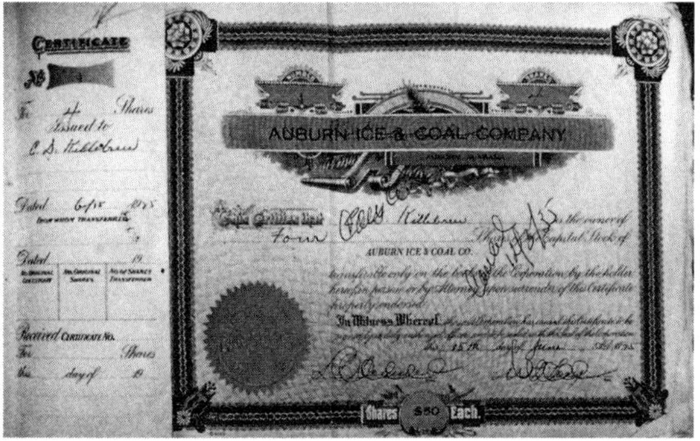

Auburn Ice & Coal Company; its stock certificate.

to Piedmont seems to have occurred much earlier.

When the Piedmont Lumber Company was registered in Alabama in 1920, the names on the registration were Charles H. Haynes, C. J. Young, and J. A. Cook (all originally with North Carolina roots); W. L. Long was its chief operations officer, in fact if not in title.

A tract of land to the north of early twentieth-century Auburn, through which the tracks of the Western Railroad of Alabama passed, was the site of J. G. Beasley's coal and wood yard, featuring both a sawmill and a rail spur that ended on a trestle, so that rail cars of coal could dump their loads there. Later, Bragg Avenue, originally Ridge Grove, would be developed through the Beasley tract, paralleling the railroad for some distance and offering convenient access for dealers in commodities such as lumber and coal. This was the location of Piedmont Lumber Company (formerly C. J. Young Lumber Co., successor to J. G. Beasley), whose property extended along Bragg Avenue west as far as an alley that became Brant Street, running south to the railroad right of way. The Auburn Ice & Coal Company set up its business—an assortment of buildings and tanks—on the Piedmont site, with access off Brant Street, next to the railroad spur that served both its coal storage bin and Piedmont's planing mill.

The relationship of Piedmont Lumber to Auburn Ice & Coal is not entirely clear. The Sanborn Fire Insurance Map of 1928 shows the titles of both companies on a single plot of land, as if they are two parts of a single company. As early as November 1923, two years before he organized the Auburn Ice & Coal Company, S. L. Toomer sold timber rights on eight hundred acres of land north of Auburn to Piedmont Lumber Company for $4,500. Perhaps, then, the ice and coal business, originally just an adjunct to the lumber business, expanded to market the products of the lumber mill, until finally becoming a single corporate entity under the name Auburn Ice & Coal Company. That W. L. Long was the single largest stockholder in the combined company suggests that his stake in Piedmont was the basis for his owning the largest part of Auburn Ice & Coal. No available records show if

Long, Toomer, and Wright had intended to acquire Piedmont Lumber. In any event, Auburn Ice & Coal Co. completed the acquisition of Piedmont Lumber Co. in 1929, thus adding lumber and later general building supplies to the ice and coal that it offered the Auburn community.

Capital to launch the new venture was raised with a stock issue that attracted buyers for the four hundred shares offered at $50 par value. In company records dated 1935, forty-nine investors are named. The largest shareholders were C. Felton Little (thirty-six shares), W. L. Long (eighty-six shares), Sheldon L. Toomer (thirty-seven shares), and Emil F. Wright (twenty-seven shares). In the First National Bank of Montgomery, "Baldwin & Co." held twenty-three shares on behalf of clients named Dunstan and Glenn. These larger investors comprise a clear majority and, as minutes of the company show, they made all decisions without complaint from the minor stockholders. Founder Homer Wright, it should be noted, held only five shares of the initial offering. A board of directors, headed by Toomer as president, Little as vice-president, and Long as secretary-treasurer and manager, and including Emil Wright, W. O. Jones, and Alonza Meadows, among others, was the official decision-making group, though minutes of their meetings show that they always approved whatever Wright and Long suggested to them.

Below, 152 Bragg Avenue, and bottom, 146 Bragg.

The property that Auburn Ice & Coal Company acquired from Piedmont Lumber included land on the north side of Bragg Avenue, some of which had been divided into building sites, at least one of which already was already built upon. Auburn Ice & Coal's contracting era began on this property when W. L. Long, who became the company's business manager, acquired 146 Bragg Avenue for his own residence and built next door a house at 152 Bragg Avenue, where Thad Pratt, who had followed Long from Bleecker to become bookkeeper for the company, lived.

Auburn Ice & Coal began to acquire vacant properties in the town and to build modest houses on them. Many were rental units that provided a steady income for the company over the years. Some were

houses built on spec and rented to Auburn newcomers and sold to investors. A typical effort was the row of four rental properties built along the east side of North Gay Street above its intersection with Opelika Road. The first two building sites were already occupied, one (now destroyed) by a house that J. A. Cullars built for B. C. Pope, later the home of the Tippins family, the other (also destroyed) by a masonry building, the Sibley Apartments.

The remainder of that side of the street toward Drake Avenue was unimproved. Auburn Ice & Coal built modest, more-or-less bungalow-style rental houses on these lots in the 1930s. Early on, some of them became the homes of young Auburn families, including Blackburn at 432 North Gay and Hughes at 438 North Gay.

The expansion of Auburn to the south, when Gay Street was extended past Samford Avenue, afforded contractors new building sites to develop. Auburn Ice & Coal built houses along that street, on the corner of South Gay Street and Virginia Avenue, for W. G. Simpson in 1939 and for L. E. Shotts in 1940. In the same period the company was contractor for a house for John Whatley on East Thach and for a two-family house for Miss Etta Majors and Mrs. Burson in Pineview.

Top, Sibley Apartments; above, the Pope-Tippins House; below, Shotts House.

Auburn Ice & Coal was most conspicuously at work in downtown Auburn when it was given contracts for two major projects on the south side of Magnolia Avenue between College and Gay Streets. Toward the east, the prominent Hitchcock Brothers, Jake and Jimmy, had engaged Auburn architect William Womelsdorf to design a new downtown building that would hold two businesses. One of these was the A&P grocery store, a business that had served Auburn customers in several earlier locations and that would move on to several more from the Hitchcock Building. The other space was leased to a drugstore that would become a minor Auburn institution for some years, Markle's Drug Store. The upper floor of the two-story brick building that Auburn Ice &

Coal Co. constructed for the Hitchcocks was student dormitory space. The structure extended sixty-five feet along East Magnolia and opened for business in March of 1941.

On the other corner of the block stood a large two-story building that had been a fixture in downtown Auburn for years, next to the longstanding home of Burton's Bookstore to the south. Over time it accommodated the Kandy Kitchen, Benson's Confectionary, a variety of other businesses and offices, and then the First National Bank. The property—sometimes known as "Benson's Corner," in competition with "Toomer's Corner" across the street—belonged to the Thomas estate. The Thomases were early large property owners in downtown Auburn; they owned the first building on what became Toomer's Corner, and their Thomas Hotel was one of the principal institutions in the village. The Thomas heirs decided to renovate the Benson's Corner property and secured plans for doing so from Walter Burkhardt. In May of 1941, the owners let the contract for renovation to Auburn Ice & Coal Co., which had entered a bid of $23,000 to do the work. A variety of tenants were relocated to other places in town, and the remaining space was to be devoted exclusively to Burton's Bookstore and the First National Bank.

AUBURN FIRMS TO GET NEW HOME

Now home of the First National Bank and Burton's Book Store will be this structure on the corner of College and Magnolia Sts. Expected to be opened officially by Sept. 1, the building formerly housing Benson's Confectionary is being completely remodeled in a most modern manner. The improvements, to cost approximately $23,000, are being made by the Thomas Estate, owners of the property.

Top, Markle's Drugstore interior; above, proposed Benson's Corner renovation; below, hangar for Naval Aviation planes at the Auburn-Opelika Airport.

Though the contracting business of Auburn Ice & Coal is best remembered for the houses it built, the company was involved in a few other non-residential projects. Two from the 1940s are still standing. In 1943, at the Auburn-Opelika Airport, Auburn Ice & Coal built a concrete block hangar with metal roof to shelter training aircraft for Naval Aviation cadets in training there. The contract was for $9,659.

Somewhat grander and much more remunerative was the 1948 expansion of Auburn's First Baptist Church. W. L. Long, described in a church history as "one of the most active and influential lay leaders in

Top and center, Auburn First Baptist during renovation and complete; above, Glanton House.

the church," offered Auburn Ice & Coal's winning bid of $109,890 to the Baptist congregation. The renovation extended the building front toward the East Glenn Avenue sidewalk.

Aside from one renovation project for a campus building, Auburn Ice & Coal is recorded as having secured only a single major construction project from New Deal building programs. The Federal Works Agency, created in 1939, subsumed many of the construction programs that President Roosevelt had created since the beginning of the New Deal. Warren, Knight & Davis, architects who had a continuing association with the Alabama Polytechnic Institute and long afterwards with Auburn University, were commissioned to design a practice house for the college's home economics department.

A publication of the college's Building and Grounds Department recorded that the building contract was given to Auburn Ice & Coal, who completed construction in 1939. (Construction has since then sometimes erroneously been attributed to the Murphy Pond Co. of Columbus, Georgia.) For some years the facility was known as Georgian House, presumably a reference to its style. By resolution of the Auburn University Board of Trustees it was renamed the Louise Glanton Home Management House in 1961. Presently, it is the home of the Auburn University Marriage and Family Therapy Center.

As World War II intruded, New Deal construction slowed and stopped; military requirements redirected manpower and building materials toward the war efforts. At war's end, however, Auburn Ice & Coal Company resumed its role as one of Auburn's leading building contractors and was ready to take advantage of federal financing opportunities. Just as the New Deal had provided pre-war financial assistance for new housing, the GI Bill offered financial assistance for housing and education to returning veterans, who were flocking to Auburn to enroll at A.P.I. Typical instructions to the Auburn Ice & Coal Company's management read:

> The manager presented a plan for doing some speculative building of dwellings provided they can be financed through the F.H.A. or G.I. bill. On motion by W. V. Jones and A. Meadows the plan was approved and the management to start as soon as possible.
>
> BE IT RESOLVED, that S. L. Toomer, the President, and W. L. Long, the Secretary, of Auburn Ice & Coal Company, Incorporated, be and they are hereby authorized and empowered in the name and on behalf of said corporation, and under its corporate seal, and within their own discretion, to buy vacant lots, improve the same, construct buildings or dwelling houses thereon, and to sell said property or any other real property now owned by the corporation, at such prices as they deem reasonable and profitable to the corporation. [Minutes and Resolution of the Auburn Ice & Coal Board of Directors, 9 October 1952.]
>
> The manager raised the question of buying some lots and building dwellings on them for sale. This question was discussed and was approved by the directors provided we could secure the lots. [Minutes of the Board of Directors, Auburn Ice & Coal Co., 1 February 1955.]

Before the '40s were over, the town was expanding by subdividing the large properties surrounding its traditional core. Auburn Ice & Coal, in partnership with B. C. Pope, a prominent Auburn realtor, and Alonza Meadows, a member of the Auburn Ice & Coal Company board, developed the North Park Subdivision that lay west of North College Street, for example, which adjoined the Cary developments of winding streets, large lots, and upscale houses with rectangular street and lot lines, small building sites, and more modest houses.

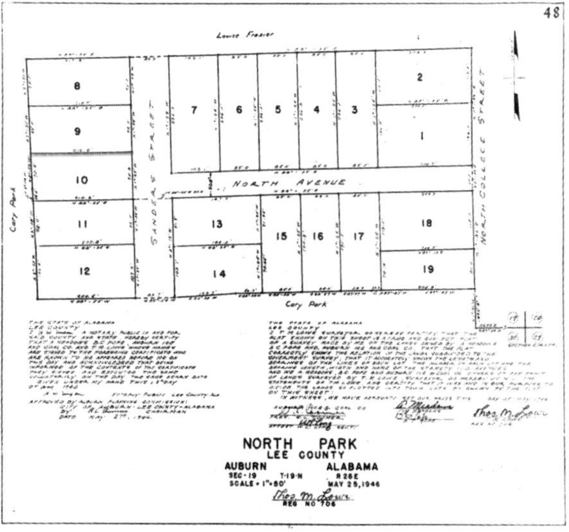

North Park subdivision plat.

Auburn Ice & Coal was the principal in transactions involving thirteen of the nineteen North Park lots, some improved with company-built houses and some unimproved. (North Avenue is now West Norwood Avenue.)

Auburn Ice & Coal was also a player in other Auburn developments from the 1950s on, particularly the Ridge Crest subdivision (the large development along the extension of South Gay Street past Samford Avenue) and the Williamson (Foster) subdivision (on the west side of South College Street before it intersects Woodfield Drive).

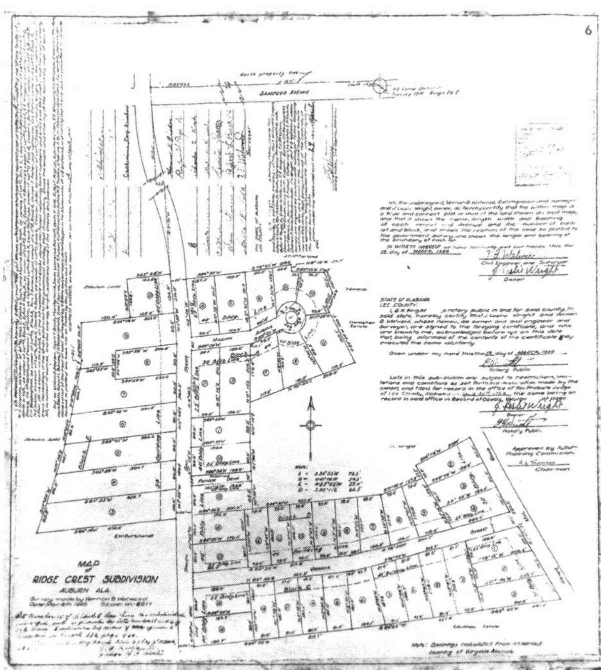

Plat for Ridge Crest subdivision.

Euel A. Screws, Builder-Developer

Euel A. Screws's contributions to the town's built environment is little known in Auburn, though he is regularly and fondly remembered in Opelika as a property developer, building contractor, building supply entrepreneur, innovative civic leader, and pioneering city building inspector.

In his hometown, Blountsville, Alabama, young Euel Screws was duly registered for the military draft at age seventeen, but flat feet kept him from active military service. With the First World War looming, the United States government and the navy in particular was preparing by beefing up its fleet, offering young men opportunities in the Mobile shipyards, to which young Euel Screws headed. There his talent and industriousness were recognized by an invitation to train as a shipbuilding supervisor. In adjacent illustration, he can be seen in that class, rear far left at the table, in overalls. Members of the Screws family believe that the skills he later put to use in non-naval construction projects were first learned from his shipbuilding experience.

Euel A. Screws Sr.

The Auburn part of Screws's story began when the Armistice of 1918 ended the immediate need for a beefed-up fleet. The Screws family moved from Blountsville to Auburn around 1920, likely, as many families did, to ensure access to affordable higher education at the Alabama Polytechnic Institute. Euel's father, Albert G. Screws, worked in Auburn as a grocery store clerk. Euel became a member of the college's cadet corps and a member of the college's architectural club. For reasons not thus far uncovered, his enrollment at the college lasted only two years (1919–1920).

Euel Screws, second from left, in a Mobile classroom, 1912; below, one of his houses in the "Screws Addition."

In their Auburn years, the Screws family were committed Presbyterians. The pastor of the Auburn church during this time was the Reverend J. T. Hutchinson, who is remembered not only for his service to that congregation but also for his work on behalf of education for the African American children in and around the community. Notably, he was a leader in raising funds for a school for them, built just outside the western town limits. No direct evidence has been found to establish the influence of the Reverend Hutchinson on Euel Screws, but the possibility ought not to pass unremarked that Screws's sense of public obligation reflected the minister's in respect to treatment of minority members of the community.

Screws set up his building supply business and, in time, married and established the family home in Opelika. He developed there what was recorded as the Screws Addition to the Alta Vista subdivision, building several houses in the so-called "Spanish bungalow" style with walls of white or pastel stucco and red clay tile roofs—a style much more popular in California than in east Alabama.

Screws first appears on the Auburn building scene, so far as is now known, as a building contractor using the company name Eureka Construction Company. The contract he signed with Miss Annie Heard in 1922 to build the house that until recently still stood on South Gay Street is remarkably detailed and probably unusual for the time, when building projects of this type were often done more informally. The contract shows the precision of the principals, both owner and contractor, in specifying not only dimensions and materials but also sources of parts to be obtained from out of town suppliers, with catalog parts numbers included in the specifications. Next door to Miss Annie Heard's house, Eureka then built another, in similar style, for her sister, Miss Ella Heard.

Annie Heard house; below, her Eureka contract.

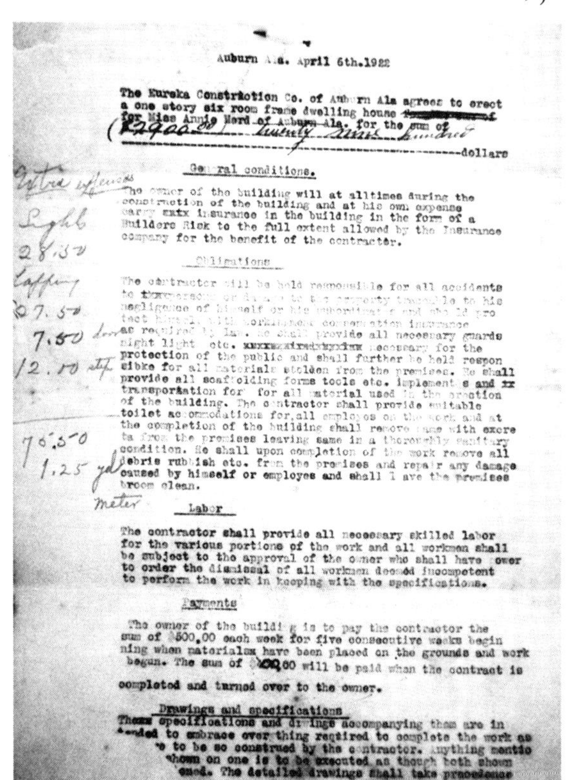

Auburn Ala. April 6th.1922

The Eureka Construction Co. of Auburn Ala agrees to erect a one story six room frame dwelling house for Miss Annie Herd of Auburn Ala. for the sum of ($2900.00) twenty nine hundred ---dollars

General conditions.

The owner of the building will at alltimes during the construction of the building and at his own expense carry insurance in the building in the form of a Builders Risk to the full extent allowed by the Insurance company for the benefit of the contractor.

Obligations

The contractor will be held responsible for all accidents to persons or damage to the property traceable to his negligence of himself or his subordinates and should protect himself with workmens compensation insurance as required by law. He shall provide all necessary guards night light etc. necessary for the protection of the public and shall further be held responsible for all materials stolen from the premises. He shall provide all scaffolding forms tools etc. implements and transportation for for all material used in the erection of the building. The contractor shall provide suitable toilet accommodations for all employes on the work and at the completion of the building shall remove same with excreta from the premises leaving same in a thoroughly sanitary condition. He shall upon completion of the work remove all debris rubbish etc. from the premises and repair any damage caused by himself or employes and shall leave the premises broom clean.

Labor

The contractor shall provide all necessary skilled labor for the various portions of the work and all workmen shall be subject to the approval of the owner who shall have power to order the dismissal of all workmen deemed incompetent to perform the work in keeping with the specifications.

Payments

The owner of the building is to pay the contractor the sum of $500.00 each week for five consecutive weeks beginning when materials have been placed on the grounds and work begun. The sum of $400.00 will be paid when the contract is completed and turned over to the owner.

Drawings and specifications

These specifications and drawings accompanying them are intended to embrace everything required to complete the work as ... to be so construed by the contractor. Anything mentio... shown on one is to be executed as though both shown ...ened. The detailed drawings shall take precedence

Just as he was in Opelika, Euel Screws was a property developer in Auburn. Today, townspeople hardly remember that Payne Street was originally Screws Street—even though some maps even today superimpose the name Screws over the general Payne Street area. The original plat of the subdivision of the property that Euel Screws acquired shows its division into seventy-nine lots on both sides of the street, each having a thirty-foot front, though some are offered as two or three adjoining lots. One intersecting street ("Hare Street") allows access to and from the west; the north and south limits of the subdivision are Thach and Samford avenues, just the same as the boundaries of Payne Street today. Chains of title for Payne Street properties produced today all include the information that the property had earlier been owned by W. F. and S. L. Samford, sold to I. M. Payne, inherited by his daughter, Mary I. Morris, and then purchased by Euel Screws. Notice the unusual orientation of the accompanying drawing. North lies to the left; present Thach Avenue is labeled "College Street"; Samford Avenue is shown vertically at right.

So far as yet discovered, only one other project occupied Euel Screws in Auburn—a major one, which had an impact for many years and on many lives. As in many Southern towns, when agriculture no longer seemed able to provide an adequate livelihood or for other reasons no longer seemed desirable, many African Americans saw better opportunities in the towns and often clustered at their edges, just inside or just outside them. So it was that Euel Screws bought a large tract of land from Phillip and Annie Foster, on which he developed a subdivision. We may be sure, though it was not announced, that his intention was that it would be an African American enclave, for he named it Lincoln Heights. The project was developed in two stages, the first in 1923 of some one hundred lots on thirty-seven acres and the second in 1929 of about fifty lots on thirty-seven more acres. Lots were slightly narrower than those on Payne Street, twenty-five feet rather than thirty, but about 150 feet deep, for surrounding land was much less developed at the end of West Glenn Avenue, the access artery into Lincoln Heights, and the possibility of a backyard garden would be an attractive opportunity for homeowners there.

Although most of Lincoln Heights has lately been swallowed up by cash-heavy developers buying out original homeowners with irresistible offers in order to put up garish student apartment buildings, some records of the early development of the Heights and some memories of what happened there are recorded. Invaluable accounts have recently been published in *Lest We Forget: A History of African Americans of Auburn, Alabama* by the Committee for the Preservation of Auburn's African American History. In one account Mr. Dewey Bedell remembers E. L. Spencer Sr., a prominent Auburn lumber dealer and banker who had purchased a number of lots in the Lincoln Heights subdivision.

> "There weren't any houses to rent . . . Nobody had a need to build many houses for Whites to rent, much less Blacks. Those who had to move off the farm were glad to live in a cowshed . . . E. L. Spencer, Sr. was in the lumber business . . . and he'd mark off a small lot and build a little hut on it and let the family pay him so much a month until it was bought.
>
> "That's why there are so many small lots . . . Mr. Spencer was doing a good deed because he did make it possible for them to get a roof over their heads." (*Lest We Forget*, 96)

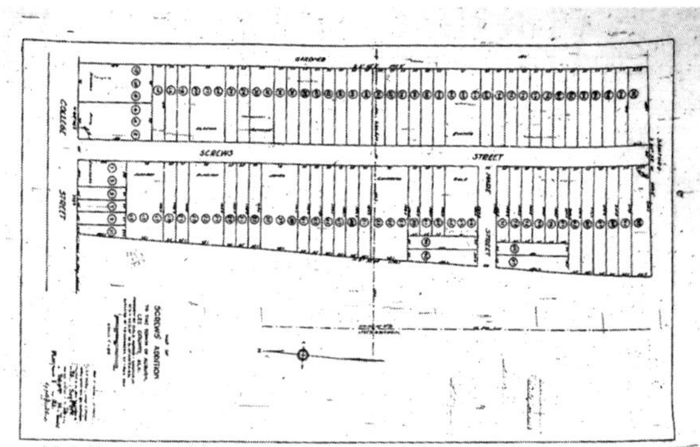

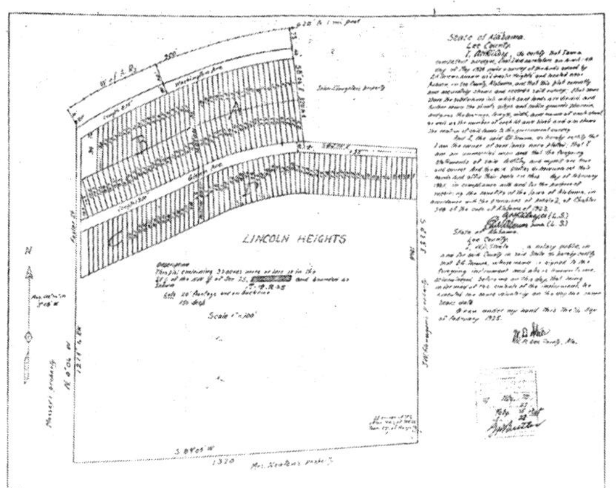

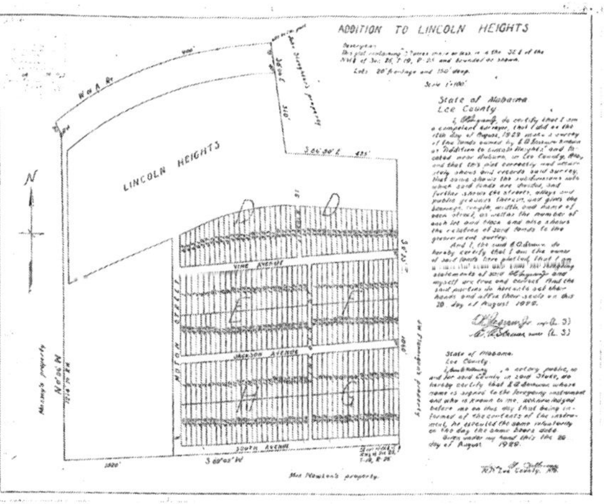

Plats for Screws Addition, Lincoln Heights, and Lincoln Heights Addition subdivisions.

The last chapter in Euel Screws's history in Auburn is perhaps the most

Lee County Training School, under construction, top, and completed.

dramatic and noteworthy. At the northwest corner of the Lincoln Heights subdivision lies one lot, larger by far than any of the others—the plot of land that Screws reserved for a school and donated to the Lee County Board of Education for that purpose. The Lee County Training School, as it was called, was brought into existence through several uncommon circumstances, in addition to its having been built on a gift of land for a school for black children from a white donor. The donation was accompanied by an unusual arrangement stipulating that the contractor would be Euel Screws and that all the workmen would be African American.

> "An agreement was made that the donor of the property [Screws] would be given a contract to build the school and that skilled Black workers would be hired. [The account continues with names and trades of the workers.] School children helped the builders with the labor; girls cooked and served the meals without cost to the builders . . . The workers ate well." (*Lest We Forget*, 88–89)

Lesser-Known Auburn Builders

The surge of building that took place in Auburn and throughout the United States toward the end of the 1930s was, without question, due to the stimulus applied by the Roosevelt administration's New Deal programs. In Auburn that boom was regularly, extensively, and more or less accurately reported in the *Lee County Bulletin*, though, as was the case with newspapers everywhere, the *Bulletin* was much more interested to report for *whom* a building was built than to report who was hammering the nails or pouring the concrete. Still, the *Bulletin*'s occasional reports of contractors is the only source of information about many of Auburn's construction projects, especially about the smaller, house-building jobs, in the years from 1937—when the paper began publication—until the outbreak of World War II in 1941. The *Lee County Bulletin* reported the names of thirteen contractors who obtained building permits in that period.

Auburn Ice & Coal Co. and Opelika Lumber Construction Co. were two of the major builders during those years. The great builders celebrated in this volume worked in the company of scores of others, little known or even unknown today. The names of many are unrecorded in the memories and documents that underlie this history, but there are a few that are little remembered and who deserve whatever attention can be paid. One of these is Ab Chrietzberg, whose own home is one of the "sole survivors" recorded elsewhere in this volume. While it is certain that he was contractor for other Auburn houses, no record has been found to identify which they are.

Isaac S. Newton is another insufficiently recognized Auburn builder. He is associated with the Newton House—later called the White-Harris House, originally located on Warrior Court, also sometimes known as Drake Court and College Court. He made substantial improvements to the original house, which is the construction project most often attributed to Newton. The Newton house once was one of the premier antebellum buildings in the town. It was much photographed, studied, and limned, as can be seen in the adjacent study by an Auburn college student.

Below, study for the Echols-Newton House; bottom, the Ruffin House.

A recently remembered clue suggests one further building that could possibly be attributed to Newton—the greatly admired Ruffin House. Though the design is sometimes attributed to the college's Building and Grounds Department architect, Milton Hill, the dates make that unlikely. The house stands next to the Samford Avenue school building that has served variously as the Lee County High School, Auburn Junior High School, Auburn Middle School, and most recently East Samford School. One source is remembered to have supposed this was the house Newton built for himself. Now it is certain that this was not his own residence; his actual residence through the years is listed in public documents. The probable connection is that Newton was the contractor, and Jerry and Verna Ruffin were his clients.

Just a block east on the other side of Samford

From top, Coppedge, Forte, and Pope houses.

Avenue is a house definitely constructed by Isaac S. Newton, the Frank Orr-designed home of Mr. and Mrs. William H. Coppedge (see p. 110). A complete set of specifications for the house, saved by the family, attests that Newton was a skilled contractor and artisan. Orr's instructions were numerous and detailed. The project was large and complicated and as up-to-date as any of Professor Orr's more elaborate designs.

By far the leading contractor, judging by the number of projects reported in the *Bulletin*, the most prolific Auburn builder among those "lesser sung" is Jesse J. Hodges. He is not a familiar figure in Auburn history. Hodges had been a carpenter for Alabama College in Montevallo and an active contributor to the social and civic life of that community. According to census data, neither he nor his wife, Maggie, was formally educated beyond the ninth grade. Not surprisingly for an upwardly striving family, he sent his son, James, off to Auburn, where he graduated from A.P.I. in 1939 with a degree in pharmacy. While James was still attending A.P.I. his parents and sister moved to Auburn, thus explaining why the college listed James's residence as Auburn. In 1940, Jesse Hodges was a busy Auburn builder, and Maggie Hodges was a "rooming house proprietress" in their home on East Magnolia Avenue.

The *Lee County Bulletin* listed J. J. Hodges as contractor on the following projects between 1938 and 1942: the Iverson Caldwell House on Pinedale, the A. W. Jones House on Nelocco, the Paul Rudolph-designed Atkinson House on East Samford, the Cowert House on Cox Street, Delony House on Hare Avenue, Austin House on Brookwood Drive, a house for B. C. Pope on the corner of Chewacla Drive and East Samford, and the Gray House on Dumas Drive. The house he built in 1940 on Samford Avenue for Mr. and Mrs. Forte was typical, fitting appropriately with neighboring houses, in two of which Mrs. Forte, the former Louise Kreher and the future Mrs. Allen Turner, had once lived.

Further evidence for the extent of his impact on the local built environment is found in Lee County deed books, where numerous property transfers both to and from J. J. Hodges are recorded.

The Kerrs

Before moving to Auburn, Louis Reaves Kerr Sr. was a builder in Roanoke, Alabama, responsible for several residences and churches in Randolph County and in Heard County, Georgia. The Kerr family moved to Auburn from Roanoke in the mid-1920s, building their home in the 1800 block of Opelika Road, just east of the current Red Lobster restaurant location. Their son, Louis Jr., later built his family's home next door. The Kerr family homes remained on the Opelika Road property until the property was sold in about 2014.

Louis Kerr Sr. is especially remembered as contractor of the Pi Kappa Alpha House on North Gay (see p. 179) but is also remembered by his granddaughter as contractor of the post office across the street from the Pi Kappa Alpha house on the corner of Gay and Tichenor. This was earlier the location of the Auburn Public School. Louis Kerr Sr., it was said, moved the swings, which were once on the playground, to the house on Opelika Road, where his granddaughter "grew up swinging on those swings." It would be easy to imagine that Mr. Kerr was responsible for razing the old school building and perhaps was a subcontractor for the post office. However, the contractor of record for U.S. post offices is the U.S. Treasury Department.

The Kerrs.

Louis Jr. followed in the footsteps of his father as a building contractor of both residential and commercial properties in both Auburn and Opelika. His contracting work, however, was interrupted by a serious accident, a fall of two stories off a ladder. Landing on a hammer in his back pocket, his back was broken, and he was bedridden for a year.

Louis Kerr Jr. had a reputation as a "working contractor," that is, in addition to supervising the manual work

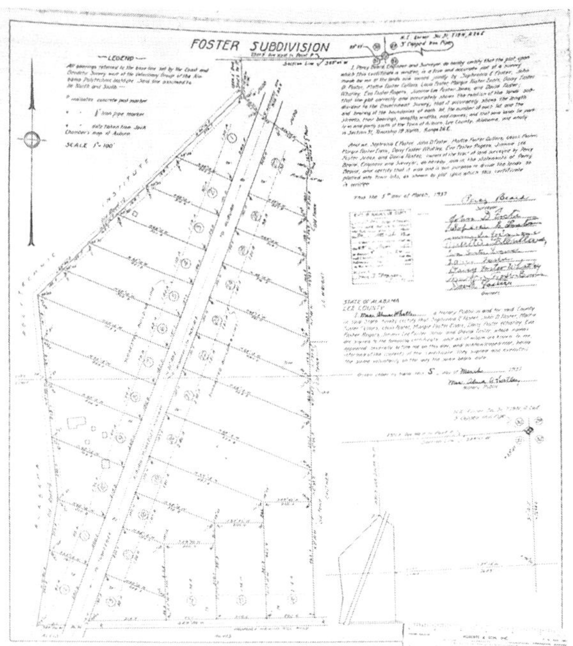

Foster subdivision plat.

of others, he was himself a manual laborer. When Auburn mayor Louie James developed Terrace Acres, Kerr built the homes of Mayor James and Lamar Ware. He worked with the architect Earl Lancaster on a number of projects.

On the A.P.I. campus, Kerr Jr. was contractor for the building at the corner of Donahue and Thach, which was shared by the federal credit union and the campus police department and is now named the Millard Dawson Building. He did renovations on Broun Hall on Magnolia. But arguably his most challenging project was the conversion of Mary Martin Hall from a three-story building to one of four stories. He supervised the work on Mary Martin Hall when it was converted from a library to an office building, a conversion accomplished during cold enough weather to require portable heaters to ensure proper curing of newly poured concrete. In downtown Auburn, Lewis Kerr Jr. was responsible for building the extension of the Baptist church to the sidewalk bordering East Glenn Avenue and for erecting the Village Theater on North Gay Street, now an Auburn bank building.

Builders like J. J. Hodges and Louis Kerr Jr. were very much in demand when subdivisions opened farther and farther from the center of Auburn. One of these, the Foster subdivision, was platted on what may have been Auburn's first city-approved plan. This subdivision was developed on land purchased in 1869 by James Douglas Foster and his wife, Sophronia Elizabeth Lee, who lived on the property in a log house along the road to Tuskegee. With an inheritance from the estate of her father, Levi Lee, the Fosters built a house located at what now is 750 College Street.

James Douglas Foster died in 1919, but Sophronia and other family members continued to live in this house. In 1938 the Foster family developed a twenty-six lot subdivision of the property extending from today's Donald Davis Arboretum southward to the present Woodfield Drive. According to the family's account, this step was taken to fund college educations for all of their children and to set aside a home site for every Foster child who wished

The Foster-Bannister-Ham House originally faced west and the present rear (left) was the front of the house; when the main road was moved, the house was reconfigured and the former rear is now the east-facing front (below).

one. Jimmie Lee Foster and husband Dan Jones built a house directly south of the original Foster home and another further south was built for Sophie Foster and her sister Mary Foster Sellers.

The original Foster house of 1870 (lot #8 on the plat) did not follow a common practice of building around an original log house but was a new structure. The house faced west toward the original track of the Tuskegee Road, with a long back porch toward the east. After three years in a rented house in Auburn, Turpin Bannister, dean of Auburn's School of Architecture, bought the house and lot #8 from the Foster estate in 1947. Soon after the purchase, however, Dean Bannister accepted a position at another university, selling the property to Bill Ham, a prominent Auburn businessman. The house was substantially altered by the Hams with a long series of windows; the former back porch became the front entrance. A pool and pool house were added to the western side of the property, and a breakfast room was added to the northwest side.

4

Materials

WOOD

Historians of the founding of Auburn agree that the first buildings in the village were made of logs. Beyond that, little has been recorded, possibly because the pioneers were more interested in building than in writing about building, so we know little about what species of logs were used, how they were joined (that is, the notching techniques builders employed), or what sizes of structures were put up in the village.

In some places, pioneer log buildings received a weatherboard layer and thus were preserved over long periods of time. This seems not to have been the case in Auburn, for the original logs were probably not oak or chestnut or walnut but more likely pine. Were these first log buildings simply undivided spaces or were there several rooms in the building? In a later phase, were log structures replaced or added to, as double pen houses with dogtrots, for instance?

Log cabin at Old Alabama Town.

Even under weatherboarding, the humidity typical of the area encouraged rot and depredating insects, further threatening log buildings. The upshot is that few, if any, original (that is, antebellum) log buildings still stand in the village. Auburn's first log houses must have resembled the one pictured here, an 1820s cabin built in the Montgomery area and now preserved in Old Alabama Town in that city. Rather than the brick piers and chimney seen here, original masonry would have been rubble stone.

Omitting local instances of log attic framing

in a few existing houses and modern buildings of logs prepared commercially, only one later building, the Ebenezer Baptist Church (now the Universalist-Unitarian Church) built on East Thach Avenue in 1869–70, can be authenticated as an original log building. It was early covered in weatherboard, thus ensuring its survival for a century and a half until today. No careful examination of the underlying log structure is possible without disrupting the modern use of the building, so no photographs of the original log construction are available.

Chancey's Mill.

Early in the development of building in Auburn, wood was the construction material of choice because it was abundant, easily available, and easily worked and because it was a byproduct of clearing land for farming. As the town's population grew, demand for dimensioned lumber argued for the introduction of sawmills where water could power them—at Wright's Mill, Moore's Mill, Shelton's Mill, for instance—and ultimately within the town where steam engines might power them, as in Chancey's Gin and Mill, north of the town, photographed here.

Although the forests of eastern Alabama did not lack hardwoods, pine forests were usually the choice, being more available and easier to mill. The long-leaf pine, it is sometimes claimed, built antebellum Alabama, and as any owner of an antebellum wood structure is certain to tell visitors, "heart pine" (heart wood as opposed to sap wood) was that part of the trunk more prized and more often chosen for the best buildings. A lamentable result of the preference for long-leaf pine, because of its greater ratio of heart wood to sap wood, has been the disappearance of the great long-leaf pine forests, now replaced by less desirable varieties of pine trees.

Timber frame buildings succeeded log construction in many places as the American colonies developed. So far as is known, timber-frame or post-and-beam construction was not used in Auburn, although mortise-and-tenon joinery, particularly in roof framing, exists in some older frame buildings. Since lumber in smaller dimensions was plentiful and more easily handled than larger, heavier timbers, Auburn builders looked to modern techniques and, just as everywhere else in the United States, adopted the balloon frame

method for wooden buildings. A photograph of the construction of Auburn Hall has been preserved. As in any two-story building at the time, studs run from (bottom) sill to (top) plate. Balloon framing, it is thought, developed in the early nineteenth century but became widely popular only as sawmills produced standardized small dimensioned lumber in quantity and as wire nails became widely available and inexpensive.

The modern technique for the construction of two-story wood-frame buildings is platform framing, which does not require studs the length of two stories and which has some advantages in fire suppression in wall cavities. In this process, the first story is completely framed on the foundation, a subfloor for the second story is placed upon it, then the frame for the second story is constructed on that subfloor. Roof construction proceeds just as for a balloon-framed building.

Above, Auburn Hall under construction, 1937; below, early view of Noble Hall; bottom, rubble stone masonry at Noble Hall.

MASONRY—STONE

In locations where native stone was plentiful and easily worked, stone construction was the material of choice when pioneer attention turned from an immediate need for shelter to a desire for more permanence. Stone may also have been the choice when aesthetic considerations came into play. There is only one remaining early stone structure in Auburn. One of the area's most important buildings—Noble Hall (Frazer-Brown House)—is a rubble stone plantation mansion, though the original columns were wooden. The stone core thickness measures about twenty-two inches bonded with lime mortar and covered with plaster painted white. Some outbuildings on the property were erected with the same materials and construction method, more roughly finished outside and unfinished inside where the rough stone may be examined.

In more modern buildings, stone surfaces are left exposed for aesthetic effect. An example of the use of stone in an otherwise concrete structure is the Shelton Mill Road building originally used for processing milk on the Gardner farm. Unfortunately, the building is abandoned and has been threatened with demolition even though the structure is sound.

Two stone houses that have been destroyed were significant contributors to Auburn's built environment. In the process of razing them, the structure of the buildings was revealed.

The Gosser House stood on Cedarcrest Circle, a one-story house designed by Walter Burkhardt and constructed, it is said, with stones collected by the family from the Chewacla Creek area. The house was rustic, with large exposed beams inside and craftsman-style hardware. The stonework was left exposed on some interior walls, in others covered with rough planks attached vertically, as are the interior partition walls.

Professor Burkhardt designed a quite different stone building for the Lowry family, built on a more exposed site on South Gay Street. It, too, has recently been demolished to clear the way for further depredations of the neighborhood of family houses once considered major contributions to Auburn's reputation as a lovely village.

The exterior of the house here is stone veneer over structural clay building tile, which was not often used in domestic building in Auburn. The source of the stone is not known, but by the time the Lowry House was constructed (ca. 1940), stone of appropriate thickness to use as veneer was readily available from commercial suppliers.

The universal appeal of building in stone is perhaps due to the fact that stone conveys values of sturdiness

From top, stone-sheathed dairy building; the Gosser House, from as-built to abandonment to present-day ruins.

and permanence, of taste, even of class and economic success. But impressions of these sorts do not necessarily require an actual stone building, only an impression that the building is made of stone. Stone veneer is the usual method for doing this. Nor should it be necessary to veneer the whole house in stone. On Payne Street, only the first story of the R. G. and Dorothy Arnold house is veneered in stone. Around the corner in Pinedale, the Burkhardt-designed house originally built for the Iverson Caldwells used a stone veneer only on the front side of the main block of the building.

Top, the now-demolished Lowry House, 2009. Below, the Arnold House, and bottom, the Caldwell House.

Perhaps the best remembered stone buildings in Auburn before World War II were known to townspeople as "the three little pigs," presumably in some slightly skewed reference to the children's story of the big bad wolf. These three small houses were all built at about the same time (1930s) on the north side of East Samford Avenue. Neither architect nor builder has so far been discovered. Like almost all other stone buildings of this period, the construction is stone veneer over wood frame. We have no record of the source of the stone, but presumably it was not local, for local stone is not found in thin enough layers to be used as veneer, and machinery for slicing stone was not available in Auburn at this time. The east-most of the three houses has unaccountably been stuccoed and is now a distracting presence alongside its two siblings, and the front of the middle little pig has been decorated with an out-of-scale portico.

Before those alterations, the three houses had been homes for a number of well-known Auburn families, especially those whose children attended the nearby Lee County High School. Their names will be familiar to long-time Auburnites: Gibson, Carnahan, Cannon, Kreher, Groth, and Culver. The legendary Louise Kreher-Forte-Turner taught physical education at the high school for a time, as well as at the college, and is especially known for instructing other Auburn children in the art of modern dance. Mrs. Turner lived in three different houses in this section of Samford Avenue—first as a tenant of Mr. and Mrs. W. H. Coppedge in the large house that Frank Orr had designed for them just west of the three little pigs, then in the house at the east end of the row, and finally in a house she had built to the east of the three little pigs.

Substantial stone resources are found in Lee and Macon counties along Chewacla Creek and the streams that feed into it. The Chewacla area that supported the nineteenth-century Chewacla Lime Works attracted the attention of the New Deal as a site for the development of a public park by the Civilian Conservation Corps. The project began in 1933 and ultimately resulted in six stone cottages, a stone bridge, a stone dam and spillway, and various auxiliary structures of stone, as well as other buildings constructed in wood. The complex is now part of the Alabama State Park System.

In the summer of 2015, the present owners of the Cullars-built former Bank of Auburn building on the corner of North College and West Magnolia began a renovation project in the main downstairs space. In the course of removing modern surface materials they discovered that the interior party-wall was constructed of rubble stone plastered over to produce a hard, smooth surface. No further examination of the building structure is possible without disturbing surfaces that the owners and tenants wish to retain. It was clear that Cullars had constructed the exterior walls of brick. What is the explanation for the stone construction on the interior? Thus far, architectural historians have no answer.

From top, "three little pigs"; Chewacla stone cabin; Chewacla stone bridge; rubble rock partition wall in Bank of Auburn building.

A longtime landmark and entertainment venue in Auburn, the Graves Center Amphitheater still stands even though the buildings that were originally around it have been removed. The amphitheater was constructed with Belgian blocks said to have been originally used as paving blocks for Commerce Street in Montgomery. Belgian blocks are not, in fact, from Belgium, but stones cut, usually from granite, in small sizes for use in curbing or paving. Surfaces are rough rather than polished. On a

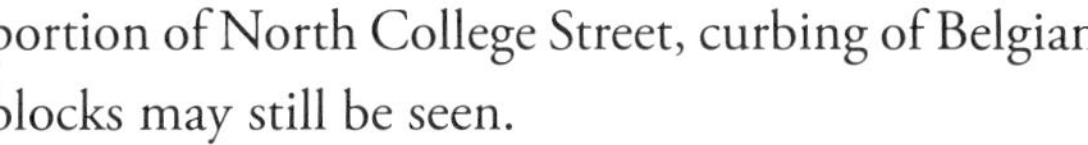

portion of North College Street, curbing of Belgian blocks may still be seen.

MASONRY—BRICK

In early Auburn, brick was most often the material of choice when permanence was desired because stone was not easily gathered and worked in quantity and because the clay soils of the area were much easier to obtain and prepare for use. At the same time, the rampant accounts of bricks molded and burned on the grounds must be considered with skepticism. The early brick buildings in Auburn were few; only one can be documented with any confidence—the 1850s Presbyterian church (now Auburn University Chapel). The illustration shows the chapel's handmade brick with modern repointing of joints.

From top, Graves Center Amphitheater; repointed original brickwork, Auburn University Chapel; original brickwork, Samford Hall.

The first college building, Old Main, was likely constructed of local, handmade brick, some of it reused in constructing its replacement, Samford Hall. But the face brick of all the standing early campus buildings are clearly pressed brick (or press brick)—that is, made by machine in a process that dates from the mid-nineteenth century in many places, somewhat later in this part of Alabama— probably produced in a factory setting in Opelika or, even more likely, in Columbus, Georgia. Pressed brick produced a noticeably smoother face to the buildings, in more uniform color, and with sharper edges allowing narrower mortar joints. The lower photograph is 1888 brickwork on Samford Hall.

With factory brick easily available, delivered from Opelika or Columbus at first by mule and wagon, later by motorized transport, and from Montgomery, Columbus, or even farther away by rail, building in brick became widespread. For commercial building, brick was less vulnerable—though not immune—to fires which threatened the business districts of many small towns, including Auburn. Thus the town gradually replaced

its wooden businesses with brick. When the Cullars family replaced its clapboarded general store on the corner of Main (now College) and Magnolia with a new brick one in the late 1890s, they expected it to last. And it had to be fireproof enough to convince a security-conscious client, the Bank of Auburn, to move in (see p. 78). The building has lasted through several clients to the present day. Except for recently introduced metal buildings, virtually all of the downtown business buildings are now of masonry, though not all of brick.

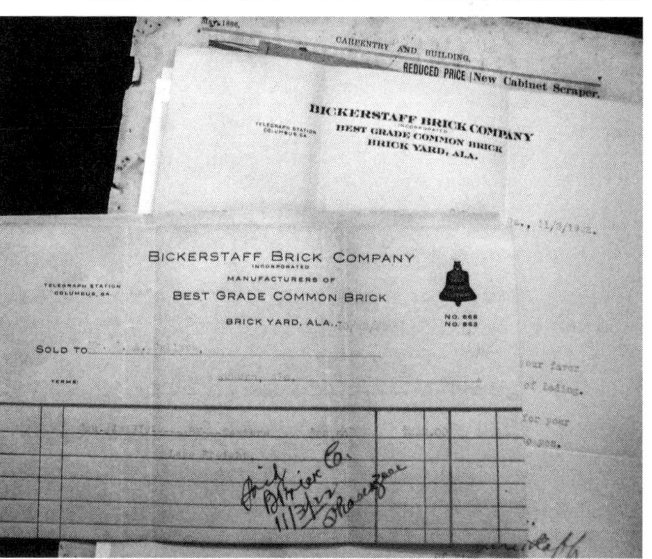

CARPENTRY AND BUILDING.

REDUCED PRICE | New Cabinet Scraper.

BICKERSTAFF BRICK COMPANY
INCORPORATED
BEST GRADE COMMON BRICK
BRICK YARD, ALA.

TELEGRAPH STATION COLUMBUS, GA.

BICKERSTAFF BRICK COMPANY
INCORPORATED
MANUFACTURERS OF
BEST GRADE COMMON BRICK
BRICK YARD, ALA.

TELEGRAPH STATION COLUMBUS, GA.

NO. 668
NO. 863

SOLD TO

TERMS:

Top, Toomer's Chateau; above, the builder's invoice showing the source of its brick.

While Auburn's masonry business buildings were originally constructed of solid masonry, new construction today, particularly in large buildings, is more likely to be masonry veneer over a framed skeleton. That frame, however, is seldom wood; today it is more likely steel or even aluminum. Thinking that solid masonry structures were more likely than others to encourage problems with humidity and cold temperatures, homes of modern commercial brick, even early ones, were typically brick veneer.

The house that locals referred to as Toomer's Chateau featured a brick veneered ground story under a beam-and-stucco second story in Tudor style. The invoices that the builder, J. A. Cullars, left among his papers show that he obtained the brick from Bickerstaff Brick Company of Columbus, Georgia. A recent surprising discovery is that in an inventory of his shop, which was prepared in order to apply for a loan, J. A. Cullars listed a brick-making machine. It is likely that this referred to a machine to make concrete "bricks" or concrete blocks since Cullars is not known to have had a kiln. Such machines were widely available, and their products required no kiln to burn (or dry) them.

MASONRY—TERRA-COTTA AND BUILDING TILE

Other than brick, clay-based building materials used in Auburn were mainly terra-cotta and hollow building tile. The difference between the three media results from different methods of preparation, specifically the temperature at which they are fired. Because terra-cotta is prepared with a lower temperature than brick, it is more porous and fragile; for this reason, terra-cotta is considered a decorative material rather than a structural one.

Older Auburn campus buildings are rich in terra-cotta—busts on the main facade of Samford Hall, decorated columns at the entrance to Hargis Hall, rosettes within squares inserted high on both those buildings and copied widely in ornamental gates through the campus. In the town, the 1899 Methodist church now known as the Founders' Chapel is especially well decorated with terra-cotta. Domestic architecture in Auburn, however, shows little of it, one reason being the dearth of early masonry houses and the difficulty of attaching terra-cotta decoration securely to frame buildings.

From top, Samford Hall bust, rosettes; Hargis Hall colonette. Below, AUMC Founders' Chapel Magnolia Avenue facade.

MASONRY—CEMENT

To build in stone, at least in cities and on estates of some pretension, was to claim a certain status, whether by intention or not. Stone was more expensive, more difficult, and thus more costly to work. The stone house or church or courthouse would say to an observer, *this family or congregation or county is wealthy*, and by implication *is owed some deference*. The next step, obviously, is to find a way to build a stone house or church that is not so expensive, the materials cheaper to acquire and work. That material is cement-based concrete.

Cement, an ancient material, famously used by Roman engineers to construct some of the wonders of their empire, was introduced to the Auburn building scene as concrete block (first solid block and later hollow block). Auburn's introduction to dramatic domestic architecture of concrete came by way of the Dillard-Lawson House.

The imposing 1894 Dillard-Lawson House, located at the eastern end of Magnolia Avenue, now operates as Greystone Mansion, a commercial hospitality enterprise. Its size, its materials, and the decorative elements of its street front were surely meant to call attention to the house and its occupants, to compete with its understated, elegant neighbor, Pebble Hill, and to put to shame the dowdy neighbors that lined other parts of east Magnolia (before The Castle was built). Online accounts report that this was the first house in Auburn to include indoor plumbing and electricity.

The original owners and reputed builders of the house were the family of A. L. Dillard, a prominent grocer and sometimes amateur actor who appeared onstage with the Auburn Dramatic Club when it presented its first plays, *A Regular Fix* and *Terrible Tinker*, with musical accompaniment by Miss Allie Glenn at the piano. Dillard, related by marriage to the builder of Pebble Hill, Nathaniel Scott, may have hoped to outshine Scott's creation, but for architectural and historical importance, Pebble Hill is clearly the winner. Mrs. Dillard, it is said, was ever eager to be in the forefront of progressive movements. Accordingly, she was the first woman in Lee County registered to vote.

The Dillard-Lawson house is in most ways a traditional house yet built of non-traditional materials. While concrete has an ancient lineage, concrete block in the modern sense is a late nineteenth- to early twentieth-century innovation, and the development of patterning techniques on concrete block is an especially significant clue to understanding some aspects of American social and technological development. Social historians now conclude that people like the Dillards did not build in imitation stone materials instead of real stone just because it was more economical, but rather because they judged it was actually "better" than real stone, just as patterned tin ceilings were actually "better" than

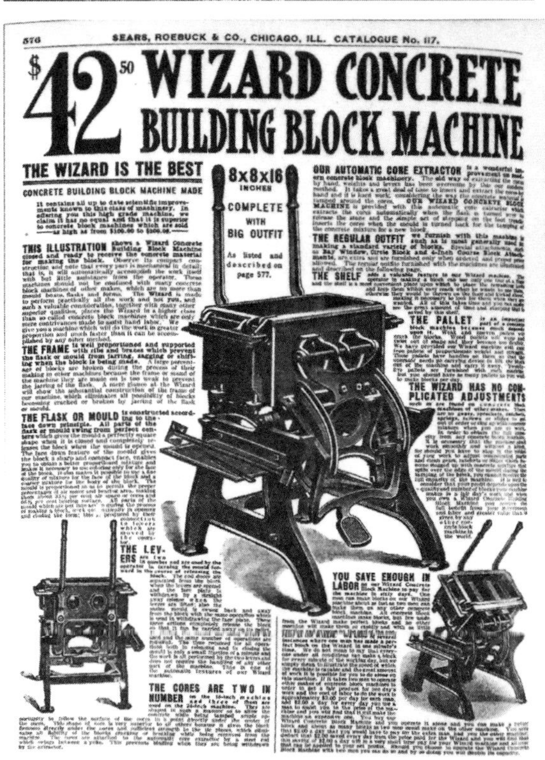

Top, Greystone Mansion; above, ad for machine to make concrete blocks.

plaster ones, not merely cheaper and easier to install.

According to Dillard and Lawson family lore collected by Ann Pearson, manufacture of the concrete blocks for the house was a do-it-yourself effort by A. L. Dillard himself. Commercial manufacture of concrete blocks was not usual in small towns since they did not provide a large enough market to support a whole business making blocks. However, for the do-it-yourself crowd, Sears, Roebuck and other companies marketed backyard block-making machines that were efficient and sturdy, so that any able-bodied workman could conveniently turn out the blocks for his own house and even some more to sell to his neighbors. Most of these machines had interchangeable plates to provide a variety of molded block faces. The dozen different designs that one of the Lawson children reported counting among the Dillard house blocks, along with the plainer units for the columns of the portico, were probably produced with a single machine.

Mr. Dillard claimed to have a secret formula that rendered his blocks waterproof; though he may have claimed they were, he probably relied on the instructions that manufacturers of the block machines distributed with their products, which explained how to render concrete blocks *less permeable*. It was a matter of ensuring that the finer aggregates were at the block surface, coarser ones deeper inside—not a secret formula.

The portico itself leaves the observer with at least one mystery because the whole ensemble suggests that it was intended to support a full-length gallery across the upper story, presumably uncovered except for the middle section. Why else build those truncated end pillars that are attached to the front wall and portico with what might have been rim-joists?

The Dillard house changed owners a number of times, becoming fraternity house and boarding house along the way, and then came into the possession of the James Lawson family—James Lawson Sr., an Extension Service executive, Mabel Lawson, a university professor of English and licensed lawyer said to have been the first Alabama woman to win a criminal case, and their three children. Following the Lawsons, the building has been home to commercial enterprises.

After restoration work by the present owner, Mary Ann Stiles, the Dillard family home, now called Greystone Mansion, serves as an event center, primarily a wedding venue. Interestingly, the house once was the scene of

Above, front and side detail views of Heard House.

an earlier, widely reported wedding in 1917, with the bride's mother, Mrs. A. L. Dillard, attending her daughter as matron of honor! An account of the event was reported in the October 21, 1917, *Montgomery Advertiser.*

In Auburn, as in most sections of the United States, the homemade concrete block fad sprouted everywhere. A fascinating local example is the AME Zion Church on Martin Luther King Drive (see p. 144).

Another eye-catching example is the Heard House located at 310 West Glenn Avenue. The house was completed early in the twentieth century to be the home of the John Frazier Heard family. However, after it was completed, as his descendants remember the story, Mr. Heard's family refused to leave their home on Moore's Mill Road. The house then became rental property, as it has remained, housing students as the influx of student renters has spread to that area of the city.

The house displays interesting surface features that indicate a careful consideration of the decorative possibilities of the medium. The rock-faced blocks are more elongated than is common with this material; they project beneath the windowsill level to form a pronounced belt course. At corners the blocks have smooth faces, and at the window level courses of rock-faced block alternate with courses of smooth block. The overall impression is that careful planning and an experienced builder were responsible for this house, and possibly that the concrete materials were commercially produced rather than homemade.

Concrete blocks proved just as useful in commercial applications as in domestic architecture. A downtown Auburn photo illustration from the

Concrete block application in downtown Auburn, as depicted in a 1940 children's book.

1940 children's book *The Runaway Train* pictured one rock-faced concrete block element of the North College street scene. In this case, the purpose was apparently only to close an original gap between buildings. The structure still stands in downtown Auburn.

Architecture and building construction offer little opportunity for irony, but if they did, we might look to this opportunity: patterned concrete block that imitates stone is itself imitated in metal. Sheet steel, stamped to resemble the three-dimensional surface of a rock-faced concrete block surface, appeared along with the growth of mobile homes that ordinarily did not move. The space beneath a trailer was often enclosed with such faux-rock-faced concrete sheets. On framed buildings as well, a deteriorating or porous wall surface could be and many times was covered with such patterned metal sheets, sometimes painted, in an effort to spruce up appearances and keep out wind and rain.

Concrete block—variously called "cement block," if composed only of sand, cement, and fine aggregate, or "cinder block," if the aggregate is slag—has proved to be a versatile and exceptionally sturdy building medium. A variation on the original products had added the category of "hollow" to describe the introduction of vertical openings through the material to lighten their weight for easier handling, increase their insulating qualities, and provide channels through which electrical and plumbing materials may be run. One Auburn house stands out for its color or its blocks and their unusual size, but even more for its reputation as a "Sears House." The house was built for Frank Hulse and his wife on the southwest corner of Samford Avenue and Wright's Mill Road. Professor Hulse, a civil engineer, prepared land surveys that may be found in the Lee County courthouse, including a survey for his own property and the Cullars holdings from which it was purchased. Hulse had been at one time a tenant in one of the Cullars family houses on College Street. Various attempts have been made in recent years to confirm the local assumption that the Hulses bought their house in pieces from Sears, Roebuck & Co.

Skeptics suggest that could not be the case because it is a masonry house.

Sears, however, did design and sell kits for masonry houses, but the homeowner still had to acquire the masonry for such a house locally. The upshot is that no evidence in the house connects it to Sears. Nonetheless, the design, and the local story itself, suggests that it *was* a kit house, but from another of the many companies that followed Sears in the business—Montgomery Ward, Aladdin, etc. The house's concrete blocks measure four-by-four-by-twelve inches, smaller than today's standard eight-by-eight-by-sixteen-inch block dimensions, and it was manufactured in a dark brown color and laid in white mortar.

Above, top, commercial use in downtown Auburn of concrete, and below, of chamfered-edge concrete blocks.

Concrete block has played an essential part in commercial and institutional building in Auburn as elsewhere. The interior block walls of schools, hospitals, and other office buildings are often simply painted and otherwise unmodified. The drab and institutional appearance of exteriors, however, has sometimes elicited builders' ingenuity. One of the older downtown Auburn buildings demonstrates such an attempt. Three separate businesses now occupy what may have originally been the Dillard Block. However, the surface of the upper floor shows that the building was originally constructed of blocks molded with chamfered edges, as an examination of the exposed sides and rear of the building confirms.

Buildings constructed for purely utilitarian purposes may not require any decorative approach to the concrete blocks of their walls. The Little Cotton Warehouse, explored further at p. 127, may be a good example. But for retail businesses or restaurants or entertainment venues, something more than the unadorned basic concrete block might offer an advantage. One advance in block technology—the split-face concrete block—has proved popular for this reason. Auburn is full of split-face concrete blocks. Look for any recent Walmart store or Waffle House restaurant and you will find them. The technique is simple. Mold two concrete

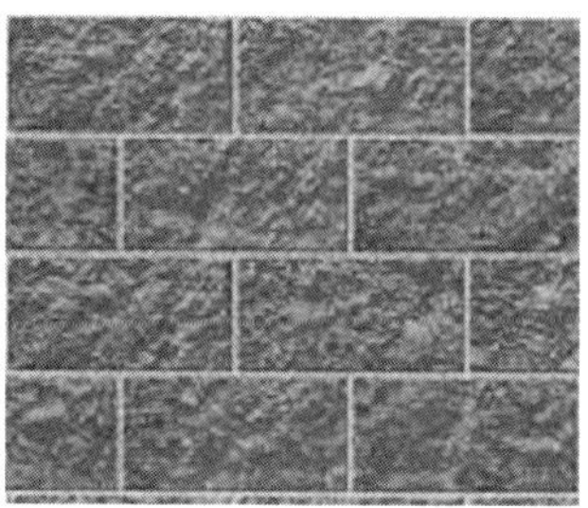

Split-face block wall; a split-face block

blocks together as one, then split it into two pieces. The result is that each block has five conventional concrete block faces and one irregular face. Each block is then unique, for the random distribution of the aggregate governs the details of the split surface. This, then, reproduces one (but only one) of the desired characteristics of rubble stone—the unique surface of each unit in the wall. It remains for the mason to build from *inside* the wall in order to lay the blocks plumb and straight, which he cannot do from outside the wall, where edges are irregular.

METAL

As a building material, metal is a latecomer to Auburn. No cast iron building fronts are recorded. At least two building thresholds are known to have been cast in iron, serving both as an advertising medium and wear-resistant entry point. By and large, however, the principal use of metal in building was as a roofing material, both as sheet metal applied with a standing-seam technique and as metal shingles. (Neither, properly speaking, was actually tin, though the generic description "tin roof" was generally used.)

World War II first brought metal to the Auburn building scene. Although that era lies barely on the edge of our scope, three buildings will serve to represent the use of architectural metal in Auburn. Earliest was the aircraft hangar built at the Auburn-Opelika Airport by A.P.I. for military training purposes. The arched roof is laid on steel trusses to produce a clear span under which aircraft could conveniently be stored. The sides, including doors at each end, are sheathed in corrugated steel panels.

A.P.I. benefited substantially from wartime development of metal construction techniques with its acquisition of, among other things, the Student Activities Building, another corrugated metal structure that proved difficult to heat and ventilate and which was acoustically imperfect as a concert venue. The university broke ground for the new Student Activities Building in 1982.

In downtown Auburn was—and still is, in disguise—one of World War II's lasting innovations: the Quonset hut. The advantage of this type of building is that it affords a clear span of great length without trusses to support the ceiling—just what would be required for a theater, which is just what it became: the War Eagle Theater of 1948. By definition, a Quonset hut is "a lightweight prefabricated structure of corrugated galvanized steel having a semicircular cross-section." This image of the building shows that the structure was supported on walls that enclosed the auditorium seating area, and the semicircular feature provided a large screen area above it as well as ample ceiling height. The theater entrance also enclosed a part of Athey's Café, which was included in the ensemble of entertainment there and marked by an unusual downtown Auburn use of glass blocks.

From top, A.P.I. Activities Building; metal hangar at Auburn-Opelika Airport; Quonset Hut that served as the War Eagle Theater.

The War Eagle Theater, one of three downtown movie palaces, closed—as did its cinematic neighbors downtown—perhaps because in-home television entertainment became more popular and as a grander picture palace was built far from downtown. The War Eagle Quonset building is still in place, now used for another entertainment venue, the Skybar Cafe.

5

Purposes

BUILDINGS FOR COMMERCE

Of the many reasons to build, utility is one quality that encompasses all of them. Some buildings, however, are "useful" in an almost figurative sense—memorials and monuments are toward the end of a continuum of building utility. Toward the other end of the range are buildings that, at least theoretically, are only utilitarian. If utility is a consideration in the typical, architect-designed family home—useful in affording shelter, physical comfort, privacy—in the more figurative sense it may also be useful in impressing the neighbors—establishing reputation and status, demonstrating sophistication, and the like.

Recognizing that the gradations are not precisely described and that categories are flexible, here is a record of some buildings that are useful in the more literal sense, built with little or no intention to compromise utility with considerations of beauty or status or self-promotion. Auburn's earlier commercial buildings fit neatly in the category of those designed principally for utility. For that reason, they easily adapt to a variety of uses, some commercial and some not. Consider the neighborhood grocery store, for example.

THE GROCERY STORE SAGA

From Auburn's early days, Auburn folk were able to pull their buggies up to any one of several general stores for the purchase of basic food staples. By the twentieth century Auburn boasted several of what came to be known as grocery stores—Byrd's, Dillard's, Foster's, C. A. Jones, Moore's Meat Market, J. W. Allen, W. A. Cullars, Taylor's, Zuber's, Brittain Drake's—and today it is difficult to claim "Old Auburn" status if you can't talk about the kindness of Hudson's Grocery and Moore's Meat Market during the Depression years when the college paid in scrip, or about how Vick's Grocery extended credit to its customers during the rationing stamp years of World War II, or about how Mr. Wright of Storey's Southside Grocery was one of the best meat cutters in town.

Auburn's first grocery stores were in the center of town. Some, like S&S Grocery, even delivered your phoned-in grocery order. Neighborhood stores began to appear; the grocery chains added to the mix, including A&P, PigglyWiggly, Kwik-Chek, Big Bear, Kroger, Publix, Walmart, then a Walmart Super Store, and now Auburn can even boast a Sam's Club Discount Warehouse store. And the ultimate irony: Auburn has returned to the neighborhood grocery store concept with five new Dollar Generals, two Walmart neighborhood stores, and one new Family Dollar store, all built in 2017–2019. Of course, this is not actually a *return* to the "neighborhood" concept because these convenient and perhaps economical stores are not exactly neighborhood friendly. But, alas, it's all about how you adjust to the inevitable fact that times change and life moves on.

Outside of the downtown Magnolia and College Street area the neighborhood grocery stores were mostly small establishments that sold canned foods and basic non-perishable staples. They also sold candy, tobacco products, cold bottled drinks, and most certainly hoop cheese and crackers. A surviving structure typical of these neighborhood stores is the late 1920s building on the southeast corner of Ross and Harper. The small rectangular building is brick with a stepped front facade, windows only on the front except for one small, high window on the side wall near the rear of the building, and a thick heavy back door. It has a concrete floor and a pressed steel sheet ceiling. The store was first operated by Jere Williams, a bachelor who lived only a couple of blocks away on East Glenn with his unmarried sisters, Sarah and Annie. Neighbors remember Mr. Williams as a small, quiet man who always wore

Williams-Richburg Grocery.

khaki pants and long-sleeved khaki shirts. His cash register consisted of his shirt pocket for paper money and his pants pockets for the change. After Mr. Williams closed the store it remained empty for a number of years before it was purchased and operated by Mr. Richburg from Opelika.

From the 1970s to the 1990s the building was home to Jenny Pierce Antiques. Mrs. Pierce rented the building from Jim Strickland, and she said when they opened the door on her first visit to the building there were so many large roaches running for the walls that it looked like they were hosting a soccer match. Jenny and her husband, George, painted the concrete floor Jamestown Grey and stamped it with a pineapple print and added an antique pine front entrance door and a latticed porch on the back stoop. George spent many days and nights cleaning what Jenny referred to as the "punched tin" ceiling.

Most of Auburn's commercial buildings that have survived from the late nineteenth and early twentieth century have ceilings commonly referred to as tin ceilings, but they were never made of tin. They are stamped, pressed sheet metal—zinc, copper, and by 1900, steel. Scholars and historians explain that the derogatory term "tin" suggested that the cheaper mass-produced pressed metal products were of lesser quality than traditional wooden or decorative plaster ceilings, when in actuality the pressed metal sheeting was an attractive, durable, practical, and economical improvement in building construction, as Pamela H. Simpson makes clear in *Cheap, Quick, and Easy, Imitative Architectural Materials, 1870–1930.*

Today the simple brick building at 238 North Ross is home to Spinks and Son Tailoring. It survives not because of any architectural significance but because for many years it had a purpose—serving its neighborhood's needs—and in later years the owner found positive ways to reuse this simple building and to continue profiting from his investment. Most likely it continues to survive today only because the development "chips" have fallen in other directions, but with the new mega multi-family development one block away on Ross and Glenn, more redevelopment is likely "in the cards" for North Ross Street.

Carter's Grocery, North Gay Street.

Other examples of useful neighborhood grocery store buildings that survived include Carter's grocery store building at 236 North Gay Street. This neighborhood grocery, built in the mid-1930s, has continued as a retail building and had several incarnations through the years, including one as Auburn's first pawn shop. At the time of publication, however, this property has been sold—from Mitcham Avenue to Glenn Avenue—for redevelopment to yet another group of investors with little interest in preserving the Old Auburn and great interest in lining their pockets even further.

Surviving at 476 Opelika Road is the building that housed Brittain Drake's Grocery. The grocery, which served northeastern Auburn, opened just prior to World War I and was later operated by Velma and Dewey Bedell, Mr. Drake's daughter and son-in-law. The adjoining building, also owned by Mr. Drake and later the Bedells, has been used as apartment, office, and retail space.

Foster's Grocery (and its neighbor to the left, Van's Lounge) typifies the fate of many such establishments—declining demand for neighborhood grocery stores in the face of price competition from fairly accessible grocery chain stores. And, as Auburn has expanded, these neighborhood stores, as real estate, are increasingly desirable to developers, who make tempting cash offers to owners.

This is particularly the case with retail and service establishments in the traditionally African American neighborhoods on the outskirts of Auburn, such as, for example, John Byrd's Grocery, which opened in the mid-1930s on the northwest corner of Byrd and Martin Luther King Drive. The building fits easily into the category of "southern/rural vernacular" in that it was built as a functional and unpretentious structure without a trained architect and using available materials (stone foundation piers in original part and a thin plywood attempted stepped facade on the street side). An addition on the western side uses concrete blocks for pillars and

From top, Drake-Bedell Grocery, Opelika Road; Van's Lounge and Foster's Grocery; John Byrd's Grocery, Martin Luther King Drive, and, below, its rock-pier foundation.

Southside Commercial Row, South Gay Street.

standard steps. Altogether a serviceable commercial building built to fill a need, not to impress with style.

Even well-funded and carefully planned neighborhood grocery ventures ultimately fell victim to the even better funded and even more carefully planned corporate grocery businesses, spelling the demise both of downtown and neighborhood competitors. Storey's Grocery (PigglyWiggly) occupied the gabled north end of this south side strip. Its neighbors were the second Markle's Drug Store and the Williams Flower Shop, among others. (The flat-roofed structure at extreme right, the Amsterdam Cafe, is a later addition.)

As the demise of the neighborhood grocery story was proceeding, opportunities to make a living with this type of business still attracted some entrepreneurs, though their successes were few and typically short lived. One was in a concrete block building on the corner of Dean Road and McKinley Avenue. Shortly after the business was operational, around 1950, it was purchased by Mr. and Mrs. Eugene Waller, whose dreams had outlived their employment at Pepperell Mill and who were focused on the prospects of owning a business of their own. Reportedly, the business was a success, in part, so it is thought, because it was the only place within the city limits selling beer. More conventionally, the Wallers stocked milk, bread, and other basic food items. As with many of the neighborhood grocery stores, this building has accommodated a number of businesses that succeeded the grocery store; one of the longest lasting is the pet grooming salon, its current occupant.

Waller Grocery, McKinley Avenue and Dean Road.

BEYOND THE NEIGHBORHOOD GROCERY STORE

The commercial buildings in Auburn's downtown, just as in most urban landscapes, are adaptable to almost any retail purposes, proved by a constantly changing mixture of fast food, boutiques, personal care, and souvenir shops, mixed with an occasional bookstore and professional office and still a very few, long-lived stores—a famous corner drug store, a barber shop, a hardware store, a bank. It hardly pays the observer to try to puzzle out any symbolic character in the buildings that house them. There are, however, some business structures on the periphery of the downtown that deserve a little more notice by virtue of their histories or accommodation of unusual uses.

One of these is the Little Warehouse. Auburn may have boasted one or two cotton warehouses and cotton gins and grist mills, but there were never any great cathedrals built to agriculture and industry other than structures where first young men and then, by 1892, young women studied the agricultural and mechanical sciences. Today there remains only the C. E. Little Cotton Warehouse from the 1890s to attest to any agricultural endeavors. The warehouse is located directly south of the railroad tracks from Auburn's old train depot and situated halfway between the Charles E. Little home on Gay Street and student apartments on North College Street.

Little Warehouse; detail of its roof ventilation structure.

In the 1870s the brick building was a cotton warehouse with a loading platform built across the front side of the building facing north towards the train station. In later years, when there was a concrete rock factory on the western end of the Little family property facing College Street, the structure was used as a lime and cement storage facility. In 1928 the Littles fitted the building out as a steam and pressing room to be used by Young's Laundry, once fronting on North College Street.

Today, after standing considerably more than a century, it provides meeting rooms and office and storage space for small business needs. The original rectangular cupola, aiding ventilation of heat and moisture and providing natural lighting, remains atop the roof; a stepped facade was added when the brick was covered in stucco. Why the building has survived most likely has to do with the good judgment and business acumen of the two families who have owned and managed the property since the 1890s. Charles E. Little, the first owner, surely saw to the sturdy original construction of the building, but it was C. Felton Little who, in managing his father's estate, continued his father's work. In his 1929 report to the heirs of the C. E. Little estate, son Felton explained, "The old brick warehouse has been fitted up for a dry cleaning plant. These improvements consist mainly of concrete floor, windows, doors, electric lights, ceiling, and plastering the inside walls, the cost of which was $635.00. This building now rents for approximately $22.00 per month." In his 1930 report to the heirs he added, "The windows in the dry-cleaning plant had to be fitted with iron bars because the plant has been burglarized three times in the past year."

The brick warehouse was under the care of Felton Little, as executor of the C. E. Little estate, until the time of his death in 1972, and after that it was purchased by James May, who fortunately shared Little's respect for property. May continued the Little business legacy of good property maintenance, adaptive reuse, and appreciation of the past. Today the building remains a part of the May estate.

In 1913, the Claude Jackson Young family moved to Auburn from North Carolina. Mr. Young owned and operated a lumber mill, C. J. Young Lumber Co., on Ridge Grove Road, and several nearby properties in the North College and Mitchum Avenue area. His grandson, Guilford Evans "Buck" Young Jr., opened a business in the two-story brick building at 214 North College Street, which William Womelsdorf designed as a general store with upstairs space for student housing. A Gulf Oil pump in front of the store emphasized how "general" the store was.

Young's general store, Ridge Grove Road.

As a military reservist, Evans "Buck" Young was called to active duty immediately after the Pearl Harbor attack, making it necessary that he close the store. The family opened Young's Laundry in the building, a business that proved a great success, at one time employing a staff of over seventy. Except for the college, it was reputed to be Auburn's largest employer. When the laundry closed, the building was rented by other business tenants, one of which, Freewheeler Bicycle Shop, left a large advertising mural painted on the brick south side. The building, which today is nearly swallowed by high-rise student housing, is owned by Young descendent Margaret Young Brown, who conducts her law practice in the second-floor office space.

The building that W. N. Womelsdorf designed at 124 Tichenor Avenue for the *Lee County Bulletin* (see early photo, p. 51) was in one sense a commercial building, but that description seems too limiting for an enterprise that not only offered printing services but also produced, sold, and distributed newspapers, providing an invaluable record of the town's history and developments. The Bulletin Building, financed by Felton Little, was obviously adaptable for purposes greatly different from its original use. Here it is shown as a coffee shop.

Top, the Bulletin Building as a coffee shop; bottom, the *Lee County Bulletin* staff in the 1960s: from left, J. C. Woodall, pressman; Alma Schaffer, society editor; Neil Davis, editor; Henrietta Davis, associate editor; and Graham McTeer, managing editor.

The *Bulletin* was an integral part of life in Auburn and in the county. A brief look at those stalwarts who worked inside this building will more nearly complete this view of the outside.

Auburn's first twentieth-century newspaper, the *Lee County Bulletin* (which became the *Auburn Bulletin* in 1968), was brought to life in February 1937 by the founder, Neil O. Davis, a 1935 journalism graduate of Alabama Polytechnic Institute. In 1938, Davis married his classmate Henrietta Worsley. During World War II, while Neil was stationed in Washington, D.C., Henrietta made frequent trips back to Auburn to assist the wartime editor with publication of the paper. The Davises returned to Alabama with their three children, Katherine, Lee, and Owen, in 1945 and began rejuvenating the *Bulletin.*

Neil and Henrietta, as editor and associate editor, produced the *Bulletin* for almost forty years until the paper was sold in 1975 to the Boone newspaper chain (begun in Tuscaloosa). Katherine Savage, daughter of the owners, said of her parents, "Mother and Daddy were hard-working and dedicated individuals. They both stayed up all night when they were 'putting the paper to bed.' Daddy had a recliner in the press shop where he could take short naps. I remember them working so hard physically that they would wear out the soles on their Hush Puppy shoes and have to send them off to be resoled."

All of the printing was done in the Bulletin Building from the early days, when a linotype machine cast type from hot metal, with a big stove used to melt the metal to be poured into the plates. The floor in the entire building was concrete; underneath the stove was a circular pit to catch hot metal that spilled. There was also a huge pit below the presses. When printing technology evolved to a cold-type offset press method, the Davises sent J. C. Woodall for the necessary training to operate the presses. Mr. Woodall, the son of Sarah and Sam Woodall, had grown up in Auburn and was responsible for the presses until the paper was sold.

Graham McTeer was managing editor for the *Bulletin* from the early 1950s until the paper was sold. He died of cancer shortly after. He and the Davises worked closely together. Graham's beat was the city council and Henrietta's was the school board.

Alma Schaffer began working at the paper in 1947, writing feature stories and a weekly column, "About People You Know." The column included Auburn's social "essentials," featuring news like—"Mrs. W. W. Hill and Mrs. O. C. Medlock alternated at the silver service . . . Miss Marianne Jackson attended a weekend retreat at the University of Alabama . . . Mrs. Roy Staples and little Charlie Tune recently returned from an excursion to Columbus." Neil Davis wrote of Alma at the time of her death, "She wrote about thousands of Auburn people and in so doing did more to create a feeling of community in this town than anybody."

The work of the Davis family was a vital part of the Auburn community. Their paper focused on the interests of the Auburn community but also challenged local citizens to see themselves in a state and national context. It was said of Neil Davis that his was a true voice of Southern liberalism. His editorials during the civil rights era never shied away from calls for calm, justice, racial equality, and social reform. He not only wrote about but also lived his beliefs by serving as an Auburn Presbyterian Church elder, teaching Sunday school, working in 1969 to establish the Presbyterian Community Ministry, and in numerous other ways.

274 WEST BRAGG AVENUE

The commercial building at the corner of West Bragg Avenue and Frazier Street once was the center of an active business and entertainment area for Auburn's African American community. While cultural changes in the South have made many other opportunities for business and entertainment available, another result has been the disappearance of most of the structures that hosted similar business and recreation venues. Most, but not all—274 Bragg Avenue, long neglected, remains. Over the years, the sturdy brick building at various times sheltered a grocery store, clothing store, night club, pool hall, café, cab company, and perhaps other enterprises no longer easily remembered.

From top, 274 Bragg Avenue survived neglect; center, after adaptation; restored as a residence.

The building has come to life again through the efforts of an ingenious renovation/restoration architect, David Hill, who has given the interior of the building a gleaming industrial look, retaining and adapting enough touches of the old surfaces (such as a tin ceiling) and spaces to produce an efficient, comfortable home for his family and an enviable list of awards for his ingenuity. The exterior of 274 Bragg retains enough of its original texture, while adding enough that is not original, to ensure the passerby that something extraordinary has happened here—an uncommon blending of the commercial and the residential.

BUILDINGS FOR EDUCATION

The campus of Auburn University includes several school buildings of sufficient distinction to deserve praise, along with many others that are quite ordinary. When one looks beyond the campus at the town surrounding it, only a few school buildings deserve a spot among Auburn's architectural survivors, both because they have lived long and because of their important contributions to the life of the community over those years.

For many years, the county school—Lee County High—was located in Opelika. The school moved to Auburn in 1914 when Opelika wished to replace the county school with its own city school and when Auburn offered incentives of land and money to secure its bid for the Lee County High School. In 1931 county authorities concluded that it was advisable to move the school into a new building on a more convenient site (East Samford Avenue), with additional space and more amenities—a dedicated auditorium, cafeteria, and library.

Phenix City's Snellings Lumber Company was chosen as contractor with a bid of $101,000. The plan of the building, sometimes referred to as an E-plan, was one of several recognized by professional educators as suitable for modern educational facilities. The spine of the E was filled on both floors with one classroom at the front of each end and a school office and cafeteria between them on the first floor and a library between them on the second. The outer arms of the E were classrooms on both floors, with the eastern arm for grammar school grades and the western arm for high school. The central arm was the auditorium, with heating plant underneath. Toilets for grammar school girls and boys and high school girls and boys were inserted in the "spine" of the E opposite the cafeteria and the library. For grammar school students, cloakrooms were placed at the rear of their classrooms. Lee County High School, of course, was not wholly a high school since it was partly the Auburn Grammar School as well. It contained another unusual feature in that on the

Lee County High School.

second floor of the grammar school wing, at the end of the hall through the "spine," was a small room in which one of the town's best-known piano instructors, Mrs. Iverson Caldwell, gave private (that is, at the students' expense) lessons.

1926 agriculture class at Lee County High School.

The space available around the former Lee County High School building was filled first by a vocational building behind the school, which housed an agricultural wing (for boys) and a home economics wing (for girls). Next, a gymnasium was built, also to the rear. When the main building was incorporated into the Auburn City School System, the campus expanded greatly, with a city swimming pool facility behind the gymnasium, a dedicated cafeteria to the east, a new classroom building to the west, and other additions. The original building has endured minor changes in its clientele—from K-12 to "middle school" to "junior high school"—but from the street view, the only noticeable change to the building is that modern windows have replaced the originals.

As the city's school-age population grew, the board of education authorized a new high school, still on East Samford Avenue but on what seemed then the edge of town. The older Samford Avenue high school building, though "uninspired" in the opinion of some, proved itself to be a timeless design that has worn exceedingly well as it nears its second century. Its original replacement, on the other hand, was built with a trendy roof line that now appears dated and out of fashion. The further addition to that building is much more attractive and, so far, its postmodern style wears well.

Class in Mrs. Bottoms's Samford Avenue kindergarten.

Another type of school building that has survived, perhaps because of its modesty and adaptability, is the independent private

From top, structures that housed Mrs. Bottoms's kindergarten; Mrs. Meagher's kindergarten; and Mrs. Meagher's speech and hearing clinic.

kindergarten. As in many towns, private nursery schools and kindergartens were an important part of Auburn's educational institutions. A public kindergarten is believed to have operated for a period of time in the Lee County High School building, though formal records of it have not been found. Most preschool programs operated in private homes. Mrs. Lannie Martin opened a kindergarten in her home on Opelika Road; Mrs. Bottoms conducted a kindergarten in her home on Samford Avenue, a modest single-story brick-veneered house, built in 1938 by the Cullars family. The kindergarten was operated in the rear room with louvered windows.

A larger facility was Mrs. Meagher's kindergarten at 235 East Glenn Avenue, near her residence though not attached. Both house and kindergarten building are believed to have been built by her husband, Red Meagher. The two-story frame structure originally had two front entrances and two double sash windows above them serving an apartment. Current memories refer only to the kindergarten use of the building. Seemingly, it was commodious enough to have had multiple uses at the same time. At present, the property has been sold and is scheduled for demolition. Another mega student housing development will replace the beloved home of Mrs. Meagher's kindergarten.

In one of her columns for the *Auburn Bulletin*, Ann Pearson records the origin of the early Auburn speech and hearing clinic organized by Mrs. Meagher in another nearby building. Noticing that some of her kindergarten students needed such services, she prevailed upon the Auburn Pilot Club to support a clinic and A.P.I. staff members to provide the professional services required for it. The adjacent newspaper image from 1982 shows the building at the time Mrs. Meagher was involved both in kindergarten classes and supervision of the speech and hearing clinic.

In appearance, both the Bottoms home and the Meagher building are quite like many other domestic buildings of their era. In addition to its economy of construction that would have been an advantage to women trying to support their own families, a kindergarten building that appeared to be or actually was a house could be an effective pedagogical device to ease the transition of young children from home to institutional education.

The history of education in the years of racial segregation in many places is well-documented, but it includes no information about surviving historic buildings that served the African American community in Auburn. Whether private preschool institutions were available for African American children isn't known. A reasonable assumption is that before any public schools were provided for African Americans, opportunities for education at all levels were created in Auburn, as in most other communities, in African American churches. Probably the Ebenezer Baptist Church was one of those.

Top, Frazier Street Masonic Lodge; above, White Street Baptist Church.

Even after African American public schools were created, early education classes were conducted in non-public, non-school buildings. The Masonic Lodge on Frazier Street was called upon to host first grade classes in 1917. At the White Street Baptist Church, two basement rooms were set aside for first grade classes in the 1940s. Though these buildings were not created as spaces primarily for the secular education of young students, they served that purpose before the town's public officials chose to do so.

BUILDINGS FOR INDUSTRY AND AGRICULTURE

Below, Auburn cotton gin; bottom, ad for manufacturer of coaches.

AUBURN COACH FACTORY

THE undersigned having rebuilt their very extensive establishment, that was consumed by fire, beg leave to announce to their patrons and friends in general, that they are ready to receive and execute all orders that are given in their business in the most workman-like manner; and as for durability and beauty, they flatter themselves that they can be surpassed by none, for they superintend the construction of all vehicles that are made in their establishment, and being competent and practical in their branches of business they can say it with safety, and moreover they will state all work that is turned out from their establishment is warranted for twelve months, with proper usage, and if not satisfactory to the warrantee, they will be amply satisfied after the work is returned.

They will always keep on hand an assortment of Carriages, such as Rockaways, Coaches, Buggies, Waggons, &c. And as they have procured the Patent to manufacture Hubbard's Patent Spring Buggy, they intend to keep an assortment of them on hand to suit the hard times. Persons wishing to purchase would do well by giving us a call and examine Hubbard's Patent Spring Buggy. The ease and simplicity of their construction cannot be surpassed. The proprietors of this establishment have been selling their work as reasonable as it can be procured in either, Columbus or Montgomery, and intend to continue to sell at reduced prices from this time out. Their work is not built simply to sell but to do ample service.

STELTS & ALLAN.

ISAAC STELTS, JOSEPH ALLAN.

Auburn, Ala., Oct. 8, 1852. 34—ly

OLD RAGS WANTED.

To the extent that there was anything industrial in Auburn before World War II—i.e., the manufacturing of products with machine tools or with specialization of function on assembly line organization—it is best represented by only a handful of enterprises, none of which operated in a building that still remains. Earliest would be the gins and sawmills, a few of which operated in the town, but mostly nearby, some continuing in operation for quite a while. The earliest venture in a more ordinary industrial sense was probably the Auburn Coach Factory.

The Cullars shop on Samford Avenue fits the definition well, having a large array of machine tools with which it turned out multiple copies of architectural components (see p. 83).

Another manufacturing facility was the ice plant, still standing, though not in operation, on the grounds of the Russell Company, successor to Spencer Lumber Company, which succeeded Auburn Ice & Coal Co. Modern factory buildings, however, waited until the post-World War II era to appear. And, in case there is any confusion about automobile manufacturing in Alabama, the Auburn automobile was not manufactured in Auburn, Alabama, but in Indiana, notwithstanding some of the clever interior decorations of the lamented Auburn Grille.

While training students in industrial arts did not ordinarily require imitating an entire factory on the campus, the requirements for training students in agricultural arts sometimes did. For that reason, a complement of recognizable agricultural buildings—barns, silos, coops—were constructed on or near the campus quite early in Auburn history, accompanying the more modest private ones that townspeople used to manage their own gardens and orchards and livestock yards.

Auburn is a "cow college." In 1872, operation of the college was transferred from the Methodist Church to the State of Alabama and under the Morrill Act was established as a land grant college and named the Agricultural and Mechanical College of Alabama. Whether known as the Agricultural and Mechanical College of Alabama, Alabama Polytechnic Institute, or Auburn University, the school has a distinguished history of encouraging agricultural teaching, research, and outreach initiatives—a worldwide agricultural heritage.

From top, barn on the A.P.I. farm; early agriculture experiment station buildings on the campus; dairy barns and silos.

This early livestock barn must have been planned to serve more than agricultural utility. What might have been intended with a design so elaborate and height so great? The building was part of the Experiment Station Farm, which Sanborn maps show was part of the town at the time. Other experiment station buildings were nearby as shown in this somewhat fuzzy photograph.

In 1999, the Auburn Board of Trustees, in coordination with the College of Agriculture and the Agriculture Alumni Association, began the development of Auburn's Ag Heritage Park. Barns and residences now form the core of Auburn's work to honor past, present, and future contributions of agriculture to society. The architecture of Auburn's remaining early twentieth-century agricultural buildings in Ag Heritage Park was obviously meant strictly for utility rather than architectural statement, but their contributions are significant. Construction on the dairy barns with silos, a livestock barn, and two dairy farm residences was completed in 1929. The residences were for the herdsman and the creamery manager.

At one time in Auburn history, gardens and pastures dotted the town. Beasley's Pasture was a large area occupying what is now the site of Auburn municipal buildings along Ross Street. The tract was not only pasture but

also garden and recreational playground for town youngsters. Mr. Beasley built this imposing shed to accommodate the preservation of garden produce not only for himself but for other gardeners as well.

As in the case of Mr. Beasley's Canning Shed, few agriculture-related structures remain in the town today. An exception is the early twentieth-century Mule Barn on the Sunny Slope property. The appearance of the building, especially its attractive gambrel roof, suggests that it was constructed with more thought than mules deserve. This barn roof style is often used to increase space to store animal feed. The opening to the upper level suggests it may have been designed to make loading of stores easier.

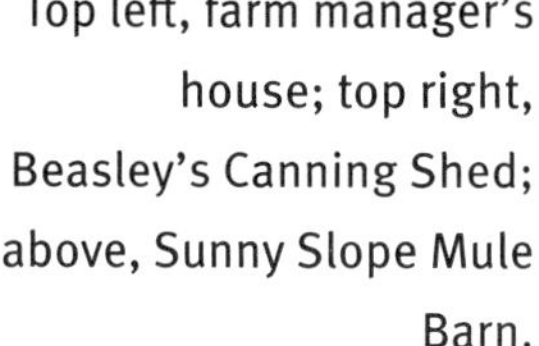

Top left, farm manager's house; top right, Beasley's Canning Shed; above, Sunny Slope Mule Barn.

BUILDINGS FOR WORSHIP

House, church, school—the early building agenda for most pioneer communities—was just what the Auburn settlers recognized as their most urgent construction tasks. One of these early buildings still survives on its original site, fortunate to have been raised in bricks rather than logs. The original Presbyterian Church was sturdy enough, and adaptable enough, to accommodate a variety of uses over the many years it has lasted since the original construction in 1851. The original design was well suited for the simple requirements of Presbyterianism in a frontier community—twin entrances under a narrow portico supported on square pillars on the main facade, truncated steeple with bell on top, unobstructed auditorium space within. The dual entrances beg for an explanation that is not documented. Perhaps one was for men, the other for women, although Presbyterianism is not known to have required or encouraged such separation. Somewhat more likely, each door may have given access to one of two aisles that an interior arrangement of pews made necessary.

The original steeple bell, which called congregations to services, has disappeared, but when the building was reconfigured after the college acquired it, a new steeple over a more imposing major entrance on the southwest corner of the building suggests that a bell was still thought necessary, original or not. After serving as YWCA headquarters, Auburn Players theater, and perhaps other unremembered purposes, the old Presbyterian Church re-emerged as a space for worship and other ceremonies, becoming the Auburn University Chapel in 1976 through a gift from the E. L. Spencer Jr. family. The architect for the renovation was Nick Davis, professor of architecture at Auburn University.

Top, the first Presbyterian Church; above, Auburn University Chapel.

Another long-term survivor among Auburn religious buildings has a quite different history. According to most Auburn historians, former slaves built the Ebenezer Baptist Church (now home to a Unitarian-Universalist congregation) by their own hands and at their own expense, on land donated by a white friend, Leonidas Payne. It is still a formidable presence on East Thach Avenue, with simple lines in the classic church form—a steepled entrance drawing the observer's eye past the small windows in the facade and the lunette decoration above.

The interior arrangement is a simple and straightforward auditorium with a platform for the pulpit in front of the choir against the back wall. The structure is made of logs, covered in weatherboarding painted white. Although the interior is simple, even stark, the ceiling is far from ordinary,

showing the skills of the builders that were presumably acquired when, as slaves, they were building for their enslavers rather than for themselves. Although somewhat hidden by a light fixture, one of the features of the ceiling is a four-pointed star centered above the auditorium.

The history of Auburn's original Methodist church is treated elsewhere in this volume (see p. 11). According to legend, that building, or perhaps just pieces of it, was incorporated into the Methodist Church of 1899. The years of the late Victorian period were a time of sometimes heated debate among churchmen and architects about what style was appropriate for Christian sanctuaries. The argument for classical styles was rejoined by another that argued the classical temple form was a creation of heathen religions and therefore improper for a Christian sanctuary. Some enthusiasts campaigned for Gothic style on the grounds that it was the product of Christian European cultures and embodied Christian attitudes toward the Almighty and, especially in its architectural features and decorations, referenced Trinitarian religion and an authentic Christian history.

Above, Ebenezer Baptist Church, and right, detail of its ceiling; below, Auburn Methodist Church.

The growth of Methodism in the United States associated it with Victorian morality and Victorian style, as diverse and secular as that might be. A Methodist church, therefore, was required by followers to be appropriately up-to-date, unencumbered by the symbols of Roman Catholicism or the Church of England, sufficiently plain to encourage the worshiper's direct attention to his relationship to the deity and not to architectural magnificence.

Auburn's 1899 Methodist Church fit that bill fully, although from a distance of more than a century it may seem to modern observers more "charming" and "picturesque" than plain and reserved!

Auburn's inventory of historic churches has been considerably thinned by a too-eager impulse to replace older structures by newer ones that seem more up-to-date, more commodious, easier to maintain, in better locations, and more welcoming to prospective members. To un-churched wrecking balls have fallen edifices that deserved to be preserved, including: the 1912 Catholic Church of the Sacred Heart; the old Akron-plan Presbyterian Church of 1917; the Methodists' Hamill Sunday School Building, built in 1913; Trinity Episcopal Church of 1887; and the Church of Christ on Glenn Avenue, built in 1940.

Fortunately, some newer churches merit present care and future preservation for reasons either of excellent design or other contribution to the community's built landscape. That list would include the Episcopal Church of the Holy Innocents, now St. Dunstan's. Even though an earlier Episcopal church, a classic board-and-batten Gothic country church, had to be razed to erect St. Dunstan's, it is perhaps as worthy a successor to the earlier church as one could hope. The design by the talented Montgomery architect Frank Lockwood refers to the Tudor period of its English Episcopalian heritage. However, recent descriptions of St. Dunstan's have described its "Norman tower" and its "Gothic nave"—an illustration of the fact that describing buildings according to period styles is often contentious, elastic, or arguable. The church was constructed under the direction of Algernon Blair, the Montgomery contractor well known for the wide reach of his business and the quality of his work.

St. Dunstan's Episcopal Church.

All in all, the church, in recent years updated by Montgomery architect Bobby McAlpine, is a dignified counterpoint to the unremarkable commercial buildings flanking it along the south side of East Magnolia Avenue. Original pews and some windows were removed in the renovation, and spaces were provided upstairs for the "church mice," Auburn students responsible for various tasks in the church. By decision of the Episcopal Bishop of Alabama, St. Dunstan's would be principally devoted to a college ministry, as indicated by its street sign, "The Episcopal Church at Auburn University"—the latest direction for this building that many years earlier had housed the ping-pong table and jukebox of the village's Youth Center on its upper floor.

After many years at its central location, Auburn Episcopalians left the downtown, first for a suburban location on Church Avenue off South Gay Street, then erecting a new edifice next to the earlier structure. That project proved to be a worthy addition to the history of Episcopal building in Auburn. In a postmodern idiom, Auburn once again can boast a Gothic church: Holy Trinity Episcopal. The successful design, the last work of the late Montgomery architect (and Auburn University alumnus) John Shaffer, clearly outshines the rather ordinary classical church buildings put up in Auburn in recent decades, to say nothing of those churches that can be identified as such only by signs out front or by steeples or crosses on their roofs.

Auburn's stock of church buildings also includes two that bear more conventionally "modern" (rather than postmodern) descriptive labels. For innovative appearance and for the histories attached to them, both deserve care and long life. The first in this category is the sanctuary that Auburn architect Walter Burkhardt designed for the Catholic community, St. Michael's Catholic Church, which was raised on the same location as their original church. The one-story building (see photo, p. 40) is circular in plan with a distinctive, if somewhat clichéd, roofline of peaks and valleys focusing on an awkward central cupola that repeats the angles of the larger roof below. The interior must have been a breathtaking experience to first-time worshippers and even later visitors. It is entirely open, and although relationships between parts of the traditional Catholic furnishings in a conventional auditorium plan are not abandoned, they have been modified enough to deemphasize hierarchy and encourage inclusiveness of parishioner

Holy Trinity Episcopal Church.

participation in the liturgy. When the Catholic congregation moved on to a new and larger suburban facility, they sold the Burkhardt building to their Methodist neighbors, who used it for adult Sunday school; a food pantry; children's, youth, and college activities; and a number of other ministries.

Auburn Church of Christian Scientists.

Another striking modern church building in Auburn—the Christian Science Church—was designed by James Prestridge. Christian Science has a long history in Auburn. The small congregation, including several prominent and well-to-do members of the community, at one time met in college buildings. A Christian Science reading room once operated above the Bank of Auburn in the building owned by the Cullars family. Old photographs show an exterior stair on the Magnolia side leading to the second-floor reading room.

Mrs. Emma Heck Cary, a member of the church, donated a site in the Cary Woods development for Auburn's first Church of Christian Scientists. From the street, the building is almost unnoticeable. The narrow two-story facade is the only visible part of the building. By tradition, Christian Science churches include large gathering spaces, furnished almost as domestic living rooms, in addition to conventional auditorium spaces for worship services. Even within the modest dimensions of this building, that tradition was observed. By the early 1990s, the number of congregants had dwindled to the point that it seemed prudent to give up the building. It was sold to Congregation Beth Shalom of East Alabama and is now in service as the Beth Shalom Synagogue, dedicated in 1992.

No systematic study has recorded the extent to which, in the post-Civil War years, members of churches built their own sanctuaries, but there are two examples in Auburn—Ebenezer Baptist Church, previously discussed, and the AME Zion Church on Martin Luther King Drive.

The AME Zion Church was built by its members, of materials largely created by them, to their own design, and to symbolically reflect elements of their faith as well as their hopes for respect and a dignified life within

AME Zion Church, Martin Luther King Drive.

a larger community that did not often offer them respect and dignity.

The church was constructed to replace a small frame building that once stood on Cox Street on the western edge of Auburn. With the leadership and participation of the pastor at the time, the Reverend Butler Williams, parishioners themselves produced and laid the rock-faced concrete block for the building. The Reverend Williams may have designed the building as well. The principal facade features an open portico with double arches behind which are double doors into the sanctuary. Let into the front gable block work above the portico are crescent moon and star symbols important to the denomination. Small windows in the front wall are fitted with stained glass, repeating the appearance of the large ones featured on both sides of the building. The windows appear to have been repurposed from another building, perhaps the church's earlier sanctuary on Cox Street.

THE CHURCH BUILDINGS DESCRIBED here are distinguished by substantial age or commendable design or importance to the history of the town. In applauding their survival, Auburn may hope to advance the possibility that they will continue to enhance the city's built environment for many years yet.

6

Residential Buildings

THE OLD GUARD

Auburn's reputation as the "loveliest village" rested especially on its homes, for at the time the sobriquet was first applied the village contained only a few commercial structures and only one college building. The nineteenth-century homes featured here took pride of place in the village, and, in the main, they still do, though one is sadly neglected and another disfigured.

Five of the historic nineteenth-century homes—Noble Hall, Pinetucket, Sunny Slope, the Allen-Gregory-Shaw House, and the Webster House—were raised on the outskirts of the town, although Auburn's town limits have expanded to include them today. Two others—Pebble Hill and the Ogletree-Wright-Ivey House—were built facing the town center on elevations at the ends of perpendicular streets meeting at the intersection of Gay Street and Magnolia Avenue. The sixth, the Halliday-Cary-Pick House, easily the most celebrated early house in Auburn, surveyed Main Street (now College Street), on which visitors traveling south entered the town.

Just as in much of America, the Greek Revival style captivated home builders in Auburn who could afford to pay attention to style in the antebellum period. Except for Noble Hall, a true plantation mansion, the others are best described as cottages, even if they are not as modest as the modern sense of "cottage" might suggest. The Halliday-Cary-Pick House is more properly described as a "raised cottage," having a partially below-grade ground floor beneath the principal level. The other "cottages" are single-story structures.

Noble Hall

Unlike the other antebellum homes still standing in Auburn, Noble Hall is a plantation house rather than a "cottage." Its site, though now within the town limits, once stood what must have seemed a goodly distance away when the estate included about two thousand acres, many outbuildings, and accommodations for Addison Frazer's family, his wife and three children in the 1850 census, and for his slaves—forty-two according to the 1860 census.

The in-town "cottages" are one-story buildings, though some perch on raised basements that offer a second floor of living space, and all show their principal porticoed entrances toward the access roads that lead toward the town. Noble Hall, by contrast, has two full floors above ground and columned entrances front and back, as if to address both the road to the town and the supervision of the plantation.

On the other hand, Noble Hall shares with its other antebellum survivors around Auburn an attachment to Greek Revival style, a preference thoroughly associated with the South in the antebellum period, though by no means ignored in other parts of the United States at the time. But within the general partiality toward the Greek, Auburn showed a distinct predilection for an almost stripped version, simple to an extreme degree, eschewing the more decorative embellishments that an authentic Greek Revival canon permitted. This version of the style may have been a local aesthetic idiosyncrasy, but at least two other factors surely played a part—economic considerations and the skill level of local artisans.

Clearly plainer was less expensive than fancier. Even when large landowners experienced boom times (and all owners of antebellum homes featured here had large land holdings) all were familiar with the uncertainty of agricultural prosperity in the South. It behooved anyone in that period—even before war approached—to lean to the side of modesty in home-building, no matter what their associates in cities were up to. Another aspect of this phenomenon was the impermanence of actual residence in a county like Macon or a town like Auburn. Unless they had academic reasons to come to Auburn, the spirit that drove newcomers here was just as likely to later drive them even further west for yet more fertile and cheaper land.

Noble Hall, as of May 2015.

As to the ability of artisans to produce more

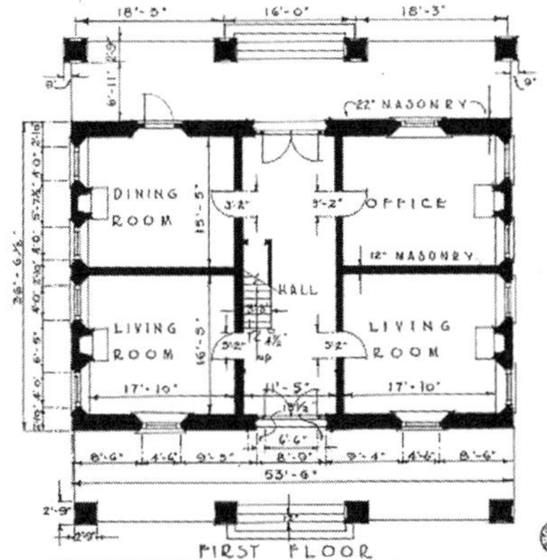

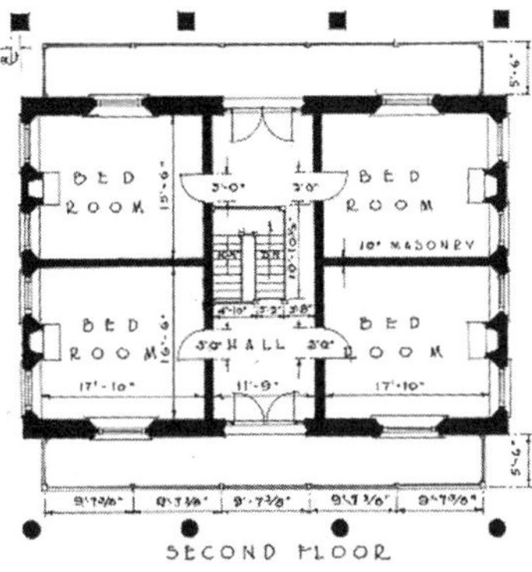

Left, Noble Hall floor plans; below, a tennis party, date unknown.

elaborate versions of Greek architecture, there are few instances of it in Auburn, though many instances of it in other rural places and cities in Alabama were often a product of the efforts of artisans trained elsewhere, particularly in areas outside the Southeast. Although the pattern books that purported to teach local artisans how to build in the Greek style were widely available by the 1840s and '50s, the attention both of prospective home owners and available labor was directed much more to agricultural production than to building design and construction.

Through its history, Noble Hall exemplified the typical interplay of these forces. Its original general conception was grand enough, even though the execution was restrained. The plantation owner, Addison Frazer, engaged a Kentucky builder, Henry Foster, whose crew of carpenters, plasterers, and rock masons constructed the building. The plan would typically have been devised by the builder in consultation with the owner. As shown in these drawings from the HABS survey in 1934, the dimensions of the plan are generous, the arrangement of rooms conventional.

The builder covered the house, including the front and back tetra-style verandas, with a shallow-pitched hipped roof. In a modified Doric, the simplest Greek order, the front round columns and the rear square ones stand on pedestal bases. During renovation the wooden columns were replaced by brick masonry, plastered over. Second-story balconies on both the front and rear porticoes running the full width of the house are cantilevered rather than supported on the columns. Openings in both front and rear elevations are similar: on both levels, single windows of the style sometimes known as jib windows, holding two sashes with nine over nine lights, reach to the floor on each side of the doorways. All four entrance doors are double-leaved and framed in sidelights and transoms. As shown on the plans, each room has a single window on the side of the house, and each is served by a side fireplace with flush chimney. On the interior, plaster returns from walls to windows are rounded rather than square or slanted. The entrance hall is dominated by the reverse-flight hanging staircase.

Even though the most available and most easily worked building material in the area at the time was timber, Noble Hall was constructed of rubble stone. Though durable, the medium was hardly compatible with the refinement that Greek Revival style required. To bring the structure up to standard, Foster covered the rubble with plaster, producing the smooth surfaces that were needed. Stone construction was used both for the eighteen-inch thick outer walls and for the thirteen-inch thick inner walls.

Addison Frazer was an active Methodist churchman in Auburn. According to church records, he played some part, as a member of the church's board of trustees, in the ultimately successful campaign to locate the East Alabama Male College in the town. Addison Frazer's son-in-law inherited Noble Hall, which then became known as the Casey Estate ("Casey" being pronounced "KAY-zee").

The modern history of the house may be said to have begun with James V. Brown, A.P.I.'s superintendent of Buildings and Grounds, who acquired the property in 1932 not long after he arrived in Auburn. According to town legend, the house had stood abandoned for some time and had become a popular gathering and picnicking destination for Auburnites. Brown, whose name still attaches to the house (earlier known as the Frazer-Brown House), began restoration of the building, work still in progress when, in 1941, Brown sold the property to Dr. Luther Noble Duncan. The purchase price of $15,000 included the house and 250 acres of surrounding land.

In 1872, as the Agricultural and Mechanical College of Alabama (later

"Alabama Polytechnic Institute" and later still "Auburn University"), the school was designated Alabama's land grant college under terms of the Morrill Act. It was to be expected that members of the college community associated with agriculture would be among the faculty's stars, including Dr. Cary in veterinary science, who had acquired the Halliday-Cary-Pick House, and Dr. Duncan, who had served agricultural interests statewide as director of the Alabama Extension Service. He was named president of the Alabama Polytechnic Institute in 1935 and served until his death in 1947.

Although Dr. Duncan himself never lived in the house, three generations of his family have supervised the restoration and maintenance of the property to the present day—Dr. and Mrs. Duncan, their daughter and her husband, Dr. and Mrs. A. M. Pearson, and now Dr. Duncan's granddaughter, Ann Pearson. Noble Hall was placed on the National Register of Historic Places in 1972. Later the property was known as the Frazer-Brown House, after later owners. It was renamed Noble Hall by Mrs. Pearson, using the middle name of her father, Luther Noble Duncan.

PINETUCKET*

Pinetucket, a Greek Revival house, including surrounding outbuildings, is located on Wire Road on a rise at the southern edge of Auburn. Lewis Allen Foster, a New Yorker, developed the estate beginning in 1835. Foster was born in 1812 in Marcellus, Onondaga County, New York, coming to Auburn from Talbot County, Georgia, soon after marrying his wife, Dorinda Long, in 1835. His father, Clark Foster (b. 1790), and brother, David S. Foster (b. 1814), later followed him and settled in Auburn. David S., the great-great-great-grandfather of the present owner, Mary P. Norman, built his home on a large acreage near the present-day intersection of South College Street and East University Drive. Lewis

Pinetucket.

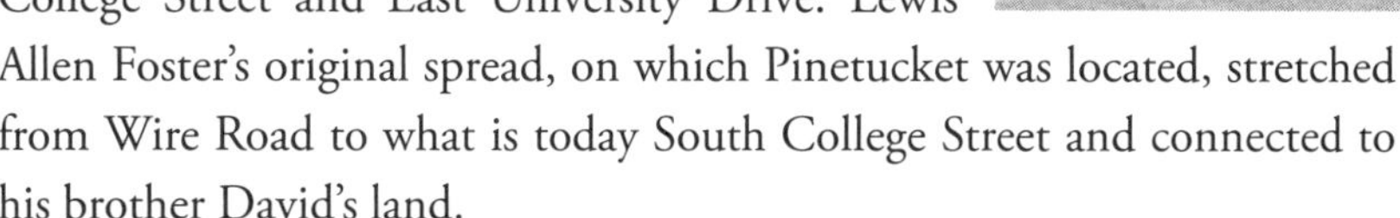

Allen Foster's original spread, on which Pinetucket was located, stretched from Wire Road to what is today South College Street and connected to his brother David's land.

Pinetucket was built of heart pine on side sills measuring twelve by twelve

*Based on *The History of Pinetucket* by Mary P. Norman.

inches and front and rear sills measuring sixteen by sixteen inches. Interior sills under the center hallway and under the perimeter of every room measure twelve by twelve inches as well. The mortise-and-tenon joints of the house frame were secured by wooden pegs, some of which are visible through the paint on the door frames inside the house. Square iron nails were used to join board and batten features in the house. The four front rooms of the house measure sixteen by sixteen with twelve-inch ceilings. The center hall is nine inches wide and thirty-three inches long. Original features of these rooms are: one-inch thick wall plaster, one-inch by twelve-inch baseboards and, in most rooms, original chair railings. Pinetucket, like many of the finer homes built during this period in the Auburn area, is intentionally simple, without elaborate moldings or ornament. It is an unpretentious Greek Revival cottage.

A wide breezeway, enclosed in 1946, connects the house to a rear portion noticeably different from the front. Quite like a New England "barn-style" building, the rear two-story structure with shed roof might be older than the front four Greek Revival rooms. The original dining room, with pantries on each side, was located in the rear downstairs room. Upstairs, above the dining room and breezeway, are two rooms once used as bedrooms.

The brick root cellar under the dining room includes an arched support for the dining room fireplace above it at the rear of the house. Speculatively, the archway may originally have been an opening to the well. Subsequent owners found a large hand-tooled five-ounce solid silver spike, three inches in diameter, embedded in a sill in the root cellar. Two competing legends about the spike have persisted—one, that the spike is where the Christmas ham hung; the other, that it was the first spike nailed into the house. (As Mr. Foster was in the iron foundry business, it is believed he smelted other precious metals as well.)

While all of the doors in Pinetucket are original, including the front doors, which have the original lock and key, some other features of the house are out-of-the-ordinary for the period, for example, the closets in two rooms at the front of the house. Opening on each side of the fireplaces, their doors measure two feet and six inches by five feet and nine inches. The doors are assumed to be original in that they match the original interior doors that open to the hall. Though not unusual, but still somewhat ingenious, the front entrance to the house is recessed by two and a half feet, perhaps to minimize introducing colder air in winter. The sidelights at the front door are operable windows, opening vertically, instead of fixed windows, as is more common in Greek Revival houses. The most surprising inclusion in the house is the zinc-lined indoor shower closet. Family members remembered showering in this closet and left descriptions of the material and the experience in their recollections of the house.

Pinetucket is in virtually its original form, although several outbuildings were removed in the 1940s. Until 1947, Pinetucket had no indoor plumbing or electricity. However, two of the original oil lamps were converted and are still used in the house. During the 1947 "modernization" of Pinetucket, the original ten-inch wide pine flooring was covered with hardwood oak floors. Acoustical gypsum tiles were removed from the original ten-inch butted board ceiling. The asbestos siding that covered the weathered lap board was removed to reveal the original weathered lap board, with the original square-headed nails in the siding, which is in remarkably good condition. In 1992, the 1940s porch was removed, and a gabled portico was constructed, similar to what the Alabama Historical Commission advised was probably the original design.

Pinetucket is one of the area's last antebellum Greek Revival homes that includes original outbuildings. The property now includes five acres of land, on which the original brick carriage house, barn, corn crib, and art studio remain. The photographic studio/art cottage, built for artist Dorinda Foster, and her husband, L. A. Foster, a photographer, has plastered walls and its original fireplace in the middle room. Historians believe the photographic studio to be one of the largest freestanding photographic studios surviving in Alabama from the period.

The carriage house and barn are in fair condition. The original mortise-and-tenon barn, held together with large wooden pegs, sits on a rock foundation. Since the main barn was almost a mile away, this barn may have been some type of manufacturing storehouse. The brick for the thick walls of the carriage house was made on the property. Also on the property was a collection of buildings for the manufacturing and sale of threshing machines and rubber belting, a sawmill, brickworks, ironworks, and a variety of agricultural buildings. For his tinware business, L. A. Foster included smelting works and even built a dormitory for the young men who came to Pinetucket to learn the business before he sent them out on the road selling his handmade pots and pans.

Pinetucket has been passed down through the women of the Foster family, preserving ownership in the same family for 170 years. When Lewis Allen Foster died in 1894, he left the house to his wife, Dorinda. When Dorinda died, she left it to her niece, Mary Jane Foster, and her husband, Leonidas Warren Payne. Florida Mae (née Foster) Cherry, wife of George Nicholas Cherry, purchased the house from her Uncle Warren Payne in 1900. In 1941, Florida Cherry willed the house to her daughter, Leda Cherry Foster, grandmother to the present owner, Mary P. Norman, who acquired the house in 1988.

It is said that Pinetucket was in the path of Wilson's Raid in 1865. Many houses in the area were pillaged and burned, but Pinetucket was not. Family legend has it that when the Yankees came to the house, Mr. Foster gave General James H. Wilson a Masonic sign, and the house was not burned. It is more probable that the house was saved because Foster was a born Yankee and was able to talk the Yankees out of destroying his home. Foster also had a fine stable of horses and purportedly gave them to the invading union officers, traveling to Ohio after the war to regain possession of them. According to family lore, two Confederate soldiers are buried in the adjacent Foster Family Cemetery. The story is that the soldiers were on their way home from the war, contracted the measles, and died at Pinetucket. Their graves were never marked.

Restoration of the original gardens is underway. The teardrop garden, with its original daylilies, iris, crepe myrtle, snow belles, and cherry laurels, outlined in liriope, is still there. What is believed to be the largest and probably oldest crepe myrtle tree in the state is located on the property. The original pecan orchard planted by George Nicholas Cherry is directly behind the house. Pinetucket was placed on the Alabama Register of Landmarks and Heritage in 1977.

Sunny Slope*

Now well within Auburn's town limits, Sunny Slope sits on a partially wooded five-acre tract a short distance southeast of the intersection of

South College Street and Kimberly Drive. The tract is a remnant portion of the 1700-acre Samford plantation that existed here in 1857. Irregular boundaries enclose the main dwelling, which is approached off-axis by a long driveway leading east from South College Street. Surviving dependencies include a well and well house and a barn/stable. Contiguous land, no longer part of the Sunny Slope tract, was devoted to agriculture and pasturage.

Sunny Slope, restored.

The dwelling is a one-story clapboarded residence on a brick-pier foundation (now in-filled with concrete block), under a shallow hipped roof. The west (front) elevation measures forty-six feet across and is distinguished by a full-length, six-columned veranda recessed beneath the main roof slope. The veranda screens a three-bay entrance elevation centering on a broad main doorway framed by sidelights and transom, with a single nine-over-nine sash window to either side. (The superimposition here of a five-bay portico over a three-bay facade is an unusual departure from classical canon, which dictates that window and door openings should align with the open bays defined by a porch or portico.) A molded baseboard running from either side of the doorway to each end of the gallery reinforces the traditional Southern concept of the porch as a kind of outdoor living space. Square-molded caps obviously derived from a Greek Revival-era pattern book—probably by Minard Lafever—embellish each of the portico's square columns, two of which are modern replacements for the originals. The three-part entablature above continues the theme of extreme simplicity. A low, half-hipped central dormer (ca. 1910) punctuating the roofline is the only significant visual change to the original facade.

Double-leaf doors open into the anticipated central hall, divided midway by a secondary partition through which a wide, single-leaf glazed door leads into a rear passage. A pair of rooms to either side is served by back-to-back interior fireplaces, now flanked by shallow closets. Recent renovations have reconfigured the rear additions to the original house for kitchen, dining, bath, and bedroom spaces. Structural evidence suggests that the house originally

* Based on the National Register nomination prepared by Kitt Conner.

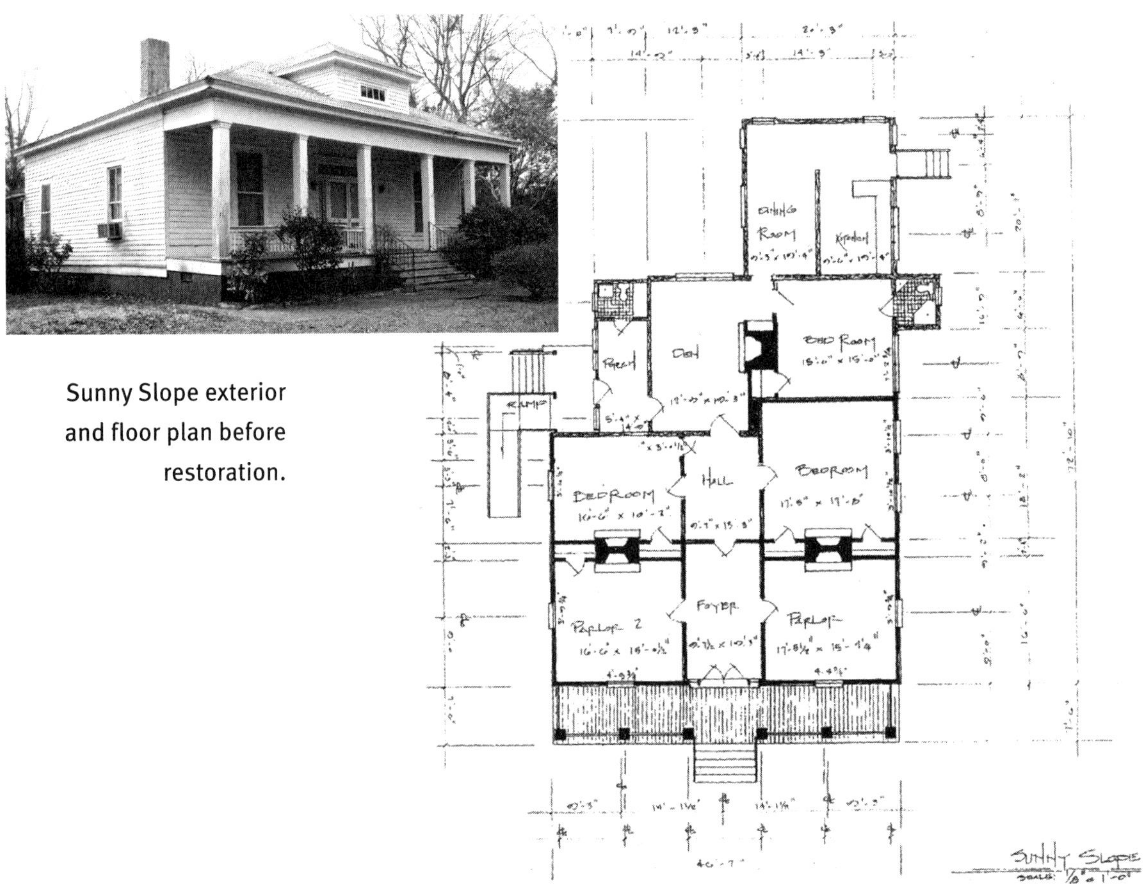

Sunny Slope exterior and floor plan before restoration.

may have been L-shaped, embracing only the colonnaded front porch, the main hall, and large flanking front rooms, plus a single ell room (now the room on the south side of the rear hall). The rear hallway itself appears to have been an open porch. The house arrived at its present configuration with a large turn-of-the-century extension across the back. Two-over-two sash windows on both the north and south side elevations probably date from the time of enlargement.

Woodwork throughout the main body of the house is largely original and adheres to the pattern of almost puritanical simplicity typical of the late antebellum period in the Auburn area. These include Greek Revival-derived two-panel doorways encased by narrow and idiosyncratic eared architraves, as well as unadorned post-and-lintel mantelpieces. Some of the mantelpieces

Sunny Slope mantel detail.

retain a certain delicacy of proportion more characteristic of the Federal period of the 1820s and 1830s than the heavier and plainer Grecian treatment of the 1840s and 1850s. Particularly notable is the mantel in the northwest front room—presumably the original parlor—with its narrow, molded overmantel. This is a feature seen elsewhere in the Auburn area.

Away from the main house is a gambrel-roof barn (see p. 138) allegedly dating from 1904 and used as a mule barn when sharecroppers tilled the surrounding acreage. The barn is clad in weatherboarding except for the east elevation, which retains an earlier sheathing of wide vertical boards. A hand-dug well at the northern edge of the property is believed to date from the mid-nineteenth century. Its covering well house, dating from about 1950, has been removed.

Before the Civil War, Sunny Slope was the seat of a 1,700-acre plantation situated a distance south of Auburn, in old Macon County. After the carving up of Macon County during the Reconstruction era and the expansion of the "loveliest village of the plains" in the twentieth century, the old plantation house now lies within the corporate limits of Auburn in what is today Lee County.

Macon County's land title records offer only a few clues about the origin of Sunny Slope. The large Macon County landholdings acquired by brothers Lewis Jefferson Dowdell and James Dowdell were in the vicinity of, but apparently did not include, Sunny Slope. Yet the Dowdell inheritance was firmly attached to the plantation when Lewis Dowdell's daughter, Susan Lewis Dowdell Samford, became the first mistress of Sunny Slope. As her father's estate finally was settled in the mid-1850s, her husband, William Flewellen Samford, received on his wife's behalf $32,257.57 from the estate, an enormous sum in those days. The Dowdell inheritance obviously helped to fund not only Sunny Slope but also William F. Samford's other activities as pamphleteer, newspaper editor, and political candidate. As if to underscore the connection of Lewis Dowdell to Sunny Slope, Susan Dowdell inherited two pieces of his furniture, a heavy mahogany card table and a massive mahogany sofa, and both of these articles adorned the parlor of her little plantation house outside Auburn.

There can be little doubt that William F. Samford named Sunny Slope. He had a literary bent, an erudite style, and a knack for words. He provided striking names for his other residences, including Monk Barnes, Hybla, Eyrie, Cedre Villa, and The Hills. Sunny Slope is indeed situated on a gentle slope where it catches the western sun, but the name also may have some literary derivation.

William and Susan Samford came to Sunny Slope around 1857. Immediately prior to that time they lived at Eyrie, near Little Texas and outside Tuskegee, where Samford owned and edited the *Tuskegee True Union.* With characteristic restlessness and changeability, however, Samford decided to sell the newspaper soon after purchasing it. He considered moving to Texas, where his aged parents had migrated, and he also had in mind Montgomery, where he hoped, in vain, to acquire the *Montgomery Advertiser.* Instead, his granddaughter wrote, ". . . [he] moved his family to a charming home, 'Sunny Slope,' near Auburn."

As pamphlets and articles emanated from William Samford's pen, Sunny Slope quickly became a center for the strident advocacy of Southern rights. At the same time, it functioned as a plantation. The 1860 United States agricultural census and slave schedule for Alabama offers insight into Samford's agricultural activities, which he himself admittedly neglected in favor of political and polemical concerns as the nation headed toward war.

Although in 1860 Samford continued to own agricultural properties near Tuskegee, the census figures appear to address only Samford's location near Auburn and apply only to Sunny Slope. They reveal that he owned sixty-five slaves. Historians consider five slaves a "substantial" holding and twenty-five slaves a "large" holding in 1860, so by these measurements Samford would be considered a large slaveholder indeed.

Ten people (Mr. and Mrs. Samford and their eight children) occupied the Sunny Slope plantation house, which was not at all large in its original configuration. Furthermore, the Samfords had living with them for a time a boarder who was teaching the children penmanship and writing.

According to the census, Sunny Slope had seven hundred acres of improved land while a thousand acres remained unimproved. The cash value of the farm was listed as only $1,500, which was low compared to its neighbors. Furthermore, the plantation produced only a hundred bales of cotton annually, which also was low considering the large labor force Samford had at his command.

In published writings, Samford objected vehemently to the Southern planter's rule of thumb that each field hand should be responsible for the cultivation of twenty acres. To Samford, the supposed guideline did not take into account a slave's age, gender, or physical condition. As he said, "We ought to consider the claims of humanity." Had he put the guideline into effect at Sunny Slope, he would have required only thirty-five slaves to take care of his seven hundred cultivated acres. It therefore appears from the limited available evidence that he practiced what he preached and refused to apply at Sunny Slope a guideline that he considered to be too onerous for his slaves.

During the Civil War, the plantation became a recruiting center for Confederate soldiers who received basic training before being shipped out to fields of conflict.

Sunny Slope was placed on the National Register of Historic Places in 2009. Ann Pearson purchased the property in 2014, restored it, and donated it as a living trust to Auburn University. At present, it is the administrative center for Auburn University's Osher Lifetime Learning Institute (OLLI).

Pebble Hill*

In both its form and style, Pebble Hill is typical of antebellum plantation houses in east Alabama. The house is a square one-story frame dwelling that is set atop a raised brick foundation and covered by a low pitched, hipped roof. A small porch shelters the front entrance, while a full-width porch or gallery is located on the rear elevation. On the interior, the house features a wide central hallway with two rooms of equal size on each side of the hallway. The wide hallway with doors at either end, the tall ceilings, and the full-width porch helped cool the building in the hot Alabama summers. This basic form is repeated, with some variations, in plantation houses throughout the Chattahoochee Valley. The form persisted well into the twentieth century. Although a few historians and architectural historians have investigated this form as a distinctive regional building type, further

* Based on the National Register nomination prepared by Kitt Connor.

Pebble Hill.

research is needed on its geographical range, as well as its origins and architectural legacy.

Like many other houses constructed in Alabama before the Civil War, Pebble Hill displays architectural details that reflect the Greek Revival style, which was immensely popular in the United States in the 1830s and 1840s. The house's symmetrical facade and floor plan, as well as its low-pitched roof, are characteristic of the style. Other Greek Revival features include the wide frieze below the cornice, the columned front porch, and the rectangular lines of the woodwork and windows surrounding the front door. Many of the antebellum Greek Revival houses in Alabama that are preserved and interpreted for the public are grand, high-style residences with ornate architectural details; Pebble Hill is a more typical example of how members of Alabama's planter class applied the Greek Revival style to their dwellings in the 1830s and 1840s.

For much of its history, the house likely stood within a complex of outbuildings. One of the original outbuildings remains intact and is currently attached to the southeast corner of the main house. Built at approximately the same time as the house, the building has several exterior design elements that mirror those found on the main house, including the wide frieze at the roofline and a low-pitched roof. Originally the outbuilding stood elsewhere on the property and may have served as a kitchen; in the early twentieth century, it was moved to its present location and connected to the main house. Members of the Yarbrough family who lived at Pebble Hill in the 1920s and 1930s remember a barn and chicken house on the property. Archeological work may uncover additional information about the placement of outbuildings and the landscape of the area immediately surrounding the house. A greater understanding of the outbuildings and landscape can shed light on domestic and agricultural production at Pebble Hill in the nineteenth and early twentieth centuries.

Nathaniel J. Scott came to east Alabama in the 1830s, part of the wave of settlers who poured into the area after the United States acquired the territory from the Creek Indians. For Scott, the move to Alabama was part of a gradual movement westward. Born in northeast Georgia, he migrated to Harris County in the late 1820s. In 1829, he married Mary King Embree of Columbus. In 1836, the Scotts, their young children, and their African American slaves joined Nathaniel Scott's brother and half-brother in moving to Macon County, Alabama. Nathaniel and Mary Scott quickly accumulated land and more slaves, becoming prosperous planters and slaveholders.

The Scotts helped build the town of Auburn, which was founded by Nathaniel Scott's half-brother, John J. Harper. They were early members of the Methodist Church in Auburn, and in 1839, Nathaniel Scott was appointed a town commissioner. In 1841, he became the first Auburn resident to represent Macon County in the Alabama House of Representatives. In 1844, he was elected to that office again and in 1845 was elected to the state senate.

In 1846, the Scotts purchased approximately one hundred acres of land just east of Auburn for $800 and likely constructed Pebble Hill soon after buying the property. Situated close to town, Pebble Hill was the Scotts' primary residence, though they continued to own farmlands in the area surrounding Auburn. While living at Pebble Hill, they actively supported the development of schools in the growing town. In 1847, Nathaniel J. Scott helped organize the Auburn Female Institute, which was later renamed the Auburn Masonic Female College. In 1850, fourteen students who were attending schools in Auburn lived with the Scotts at Pebble Hill. In 1856, Scott and other Auburn Methodists established the East Alabama Male College, and he served on the college's board of trustees from 1856 until 1863.

During Scott's first term in the state legislature, he became acquainted with Alabama politician and writer William Lowndes Yancey, a leader of the secession movement and an ardent defender of slavery. By 1860, Scott, like Yancey, supported secession. After the Civil War began in 1861, two of Nathaniel and Mary Scott's sons—Embree and John—joined the Confederate Army. In 1862, Embree Scott died of illness following the Battle of Seven Pines in Virginia. Nathaniel J. Scott died the following year, leaving Mary Scott and her grown children to manage the family's plantations.

Mary Scott sold Pebble Hill during the tumultuous years that immediately followed the defeat of the Confederacy in 1865. Absentee landowners managed the property until 1876, when Mary Virginia Riley purchased it. The little information available about Riley raises tantalizing questions about her identity and about how she supported herself and her family as a widow in late nineteenth-century Alabama. Born in Washington, D.C., in 1828, she married before she was twenty years old, but the name of her husband remains unknown. By 1860, when she was thirty-two years old, she was a widow living in Montgomery, Alabama, with three young children. The 1860 census did not list an occupation for her, she owned no real estate, and her personal estate was valued at $200. By 1872, she had likely moved to Lee County, where her daughter Amelia married Frank A. Hodges, a cotton buyer and son of a wealthy Mobile merchant. In 1876, Mary Riley's son, John Milton Riley, married Jennie Clower, the daughter of an Auburn farmer. Her children's marriages into well-educated and well-to-do families suggest that Mary Riley herself was educated and came from the middle or upper class.

It is unclear how Riley raised the $2,250 to buy Pebble Hill in 1876 and to what extent she used the property as farmland. In 1880, only seven of her ninety-seven acres were under cultivation, and Riley produced only five bales of cotton. No records of the farm's operation or products after 1880 have been located; she may have later rented the land to tenants or sharecroppers. Mary Riley lived at Pebble Hill until her death in 1907.

The Yarbrough family owned Pebble Hill from 1912 until 1982, after Dr. Cecil S. and Bertha Mae Yarbrough purchased it from Mary Riley's daughter. Cecil Yarbrough was born in Orion, Alabama, in 1878 and studied medicine at the University of Tennessee. Born in Auburn in 1881, Bertha Yarbrough was the daughter of Oscar Grout, a farmer who owned land on the outskirts of Auburn. She graduated from Alabama Polytechnic Institute in 1900, just eight years after the college first admitted women. They married in 1903 and settled in Auburn, where Dr. Yarbrough established a medical practice. Cecil and Bertha Yarbrough had five children, three of whom were born after the family moved to Pebble Hill in 1912. In 1927, Bertha Mae Yarbrough died at the age of forty-five. The following year, Dr. Yarbrough married Mary Strudwick of Demopolis, Alabama. Dr. Yarbrough died in Auburn in 1946, and Mary Yarbrough died in Mobile, Alabama, in 1967. Clarke S. Yarbrough inherited Pebble Hill from his mother and owned it until 1982.

Dr. Yarbrough served several terms as mayor of Auburn and a term as representative in the Alabama House of Representatives. He first held the office of mayor from 1916 until 1918, when he joined the navy as a medical officer following the United States' entry into World War I. After returning to Auburn in 1919, he was soon reelected mayor and served in that post until 1928. In 1922, in cooperation with other local politicians and powerful alumni of Alabama Polytechnic Institute, Yarbrough successfully fought an effort to move the university from Auburn to Montgomery, the state capital. He again served as mayor again from 1936 to 1944. During his terms as mayor he led efforts to improve the town's roads and infrastructure, and he welcomed President Franklin Delano Roosevelt during his 1939 visit to Auburn.

In the seventy years that the Yarbrough family owned Pebble Hill (1912–1982), A.P.I. grew from a small land grant college into Auburn University, one of the state's leading research institutions. Like many Auburn residents during this period, the Yarbroughs' lives were closely intertwined with the growing university. Most of the Yarbrough children attended A.P.I., and Dr. Yarbrough served as acting director of student health services at the university in the last year of his life. For much of the time that the Yarbrough family owned Pebble Hill, they rented at least part of the house—as well as some of the outbuildings—to students at the university.

The setting, visible from the center of town, on a slight rise at the head of East Magnolia Avenue, is one of the striking aspects of Pebble Hill. The expansion of the university contributed to the transformation of the landscape surrounding Pebble Hill from farmland into part of the town of Auburn. When the Yarbroughs purchased the property in 1912, it encompassed ninety-five acres of farmland. Particularly after World War II, the areas east of Pebble Hill became more densely populated as the number of students and town residents grew. Between 1945 and 1980, the Pebble Hill property itself was subdivided. Student apartment complexes as well as single family homes were constructed along Magnolia Avenue, while much of the land to the east of the house was subdivided, as were other town properties, for residential and commercial development. The transformation of Pebble Hill and the surrounding land during this period reflects the growth of the town during the last half of the twentieth century.

The house is of frame construction with overlapping six-inch-wide white pine boards and rests on a six-foot-high brick foundation. The main block of the house is nearly square, measuring forty-six by forty feet, and is symmetrically divided by an interior central hall. Two bedrooms attached to the southeast corner of the structure appear to have been added not long after the house was completed.

A central portico, now enclosed with screens, is raised on brick piers and originally had curving double entry stairs. Two square columns support a simple entablature. The well-proportioned central double doors are pine with two long vertical inset panels each. They are framed with lights, five on both sides and three above. The framing has been grooved, and the vertical sections are topped with stylized capitals. The effect is that of attenuated pilasters. The windows on the front and sides of the house have two sashes, with six panes per sash.

The interior walls are plaster over lathes; the floors are of heart pine with six-inch-wide boards running the entire length of the room. With the exception of a few replacements, all doors have two long vertical inset panels on each side. The four main rooms have simple wooden mantels of similar design, and the two interior chimneys are flanked by fireside closets, which are unusual for this period in Alabama but are found in several small houses in the vicinity. The closet on the northern side of the house has a window matching those in the rest of the house. With the exception of the room on the northeast corner of the house, all ceilings are faced with twelve-inch-wide boards with battens. The hall and the two rear rooms open onto a twelve-foot-wide gallery, which has been enclosed. The two rooms on the southeast corner of the house have similar door and window treatments and a similar ceiling. Access to these rooms is by a door that opens from the gallery and by two exterior doors. A stair to the rear of the central hall leads to the attic, which in recent years was expanded with dormer windows that will be removed during restoration.

The Hollifields, who rented the house briefly in the postbellum period, seem to have originated the name Pebble Hill. Mollie Hollifield Jones alone referred to it by that name, which is not antebellum and which was not commonly used in postbellum Auburn. Recent construction on the grounds has not discovered any pebbles, so the origin of the name remains puzzling.

Pebble Hill now is home to the Caroline Marshall Draughon Center for the Arts and Humanities, made possible by support from the Draughon family—Ann Draughon Cousins, her husband, Tom Cousins, and her brother, Ralph Draughon Jr.

OGLETREE-WRIGHT-IVEY HOUSE

One of two remaining houses built in Auburn by an original founder of the town, the Ogletree-Wright-Ivey House overlooked the village from a slight rise where Drake Avenue intersects North Gay Street. James B. Ogletree built the home for his family in the late 1840s on twenty acres that spread to the north of the house site. The style was the fashionable Greek Revival interpreted in a manner characteristic of east central Alabama; that is to say, the house expresses the essence of the Greek primarily in its proportions, plain surfaces, and symmetrical volumes, not in embellishment and decoration. The history of the house, the history of its principal owners, and the history of Auburn meteorology are so entwined that separating them is hardly possible.

As the cotton culture spread west from Georgia, James Ogletree, then thirty-six years old, traveled with his large family, his slaves, and his brother-in-law—the town's founder, Judge Harper—to the future site of Auburn in what was then northern Macon County, Alabama. In Macon County, Ogletree farmed extensive holdings as well as his twenty-acre home site. Although the group of Auburn settlers had arrived in 1836, not until the late 1840s were financial conditions stable and prosperous enough that Ogletree could build his new house. The United States census of 1860 records that Ogletree's slaves produced cotton and corn on the one thousand acres he cultivated, while another six hundred acres remained unimproved.

Ogletree-Wright-Ivey House.

Everywhere in the South, political and economic instability loomed by the 1860s. James and Mary Ogletree sold the Auburn property, townhouse, and twenty acres to Adam Hardin in June of 1860. Hardin, in turn, sold the property to W. S. J. Lampkin after owning it for only a year and a half. The Hardin transaction in 1860 produced $4,000 for the

Ogletrees; the Lampkin transaction brought only $2,700 to Hardin in 1861 when early wartime tensions began to depress values in Southern real estate.

Where the Ogletree family lived after moving from their Drake Avenue home is not recorded, but presumably they moved to another of their lands near Auburn, for James Ogletree remained a presence in the town until his death in 1866. He had been a mainstay of the Auburn Methodist Church and a founder of the East Alabama Male College. His remains undoubtedly lie in Pine Hill Cemetery, though the grave is unmarked.

The house that Ogletree built passed from Lampkin to William Wilmot Wright in 1887. In the early 1870s, Wright bought the grist mill that stood south of Auburn on Chewacla Creek. Becoming, then, Wright's Mill, the enterprise lent its name to what later developed into one of Auburn's main arteries, Wright's Mill Road.

The house as built contained only four rooms, two on each side of a wide hall. Expanding the house seemed an obvious solution to the problem of accommodating the large family that Wright brought to live in it. As additions proceeded, two rooms were added to the northwest corner of the building and, most dramatically, a second story was built atop the first.

Today, adding a second floor to a house is viewed with some trepidation. Modern construction techniques ordinarily require strengthening the house frame, particularly the ceiling joists of a single-story house, before adding another floor on top of it. The next dramatic incident in the history of this house, however, suggests that the hefty original construction required no bolstering.

Ogletree-Wright-Ivey House before 1953 tornado.

William Wright's family continued in the now two-story house for many years, populating Auburn for generations with many of its most prominent citizens. The last of William Wright's children to live in the Drake Avenue home were two unmarried sisters. At their passing, Professor William Ivey of the university's zoology department bought the property. The Iveys did not have long to enjoy the whole house after they bought it in 1950, for the disastrous tornado of 1953 took down the second story, though it left the original first story almost intact. Neighbors to

Ogletree-Wright-Ivey staircase.

the east along Drake Avenue suffered even greater damage. Dr. Peacock's house, not old but grand for Auburn, was a total loss, as was the quite old and celebrated antebellum Perry-Cauthen House next door to Peacock. For the Iveys, the tornado provided an opportunity to restore the house to its original one-story configuration. The rather grand staircase to Wright's second floor, though not in keeping with the Greek mode of the original house, was left in place and provided access to the half-story above. The restored roof was given side gables though it may have been hipped originally.

In more recent years, the building was host to a kindergarten, run by the next owner, Russell Wilson, and for a short time served as home for a fraternity that had been temporarily banned from the Auburn University campus. Most recently it was acquired as an investment opportunity by Yonhua (Tommy) Tzeng, retired Auburn University professor of electrical engineering. Dr. Tzeng had the building divided into apartments to rent to students. Regrettably, from his present residence in Taiwan, the absentee landlord, Dr. Tzeng, has not exhibited steadfast attention to Auburn's historically important Ogletree-Wright-Ivey House. These days, this once proud home with a grand view of the community from a slight rise at what formerly was the head of North Gay Street now provides the community with a view of a house in general disrepair and a front yard often littered with beer cans and trash.

Halliday-Cary-Pick House

Arguably the best-known house in Auburn is the Halliday-Cary-Pick House at 360 North College Street; it may be the most admired house as well. Through the years since its construction (ca. 1848), it has been carefully tended by a small number of owners, so that even some imprudent changes to the building have been reconsidered and removed, and some others thought helpful for maintaining comfortable accommodation have been retained where unobtrusive. The house is a framed building of the raised-cottage type, so that two full floors of living space do not overpower the neighbors

along its block of North College Street, now one of only two historic districts in the town. The ground (basement) floor is of brick, while exterior surfaces of the main floor are clapboard, except that flush boarding is used on the street facade.

The composition of the face of the house seems exactly right. The porch is supported on four heavy square brick piers rising from ground level and framing the three upper level openings to the interior of the house—the central double-leaf doorway with transom and sidelights surrounding it, flanked by triple sash windows with the same vertical dimension as the door. Even though the rear elevation of the house is more modest, but again, carefully composed, it should be noted that this was once the main entrance to the house and originally overlooked a large lawn extending eastward to North Gay Street.

Above, Halliday-Cary-Pick House; below, HABS drawing and floor plan.

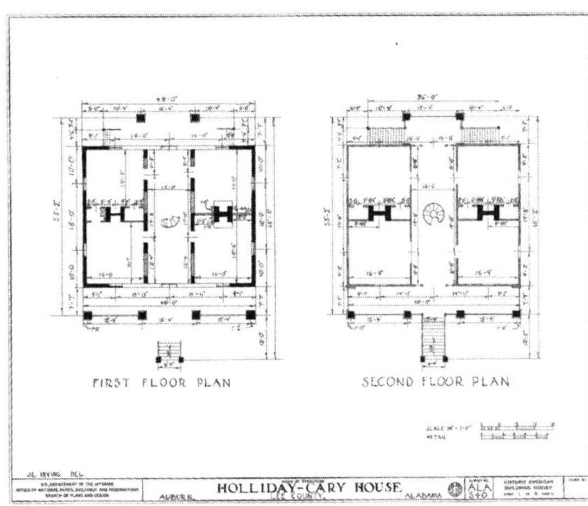

The most photographed and studied interior feature of the house is the staircase rising from ground floor to the center hall upstairs. The tight corkscrew shape of the stair is, so far as is known, unique in east Alabama, and certainly the work of a talented, if still unidentified, builder who apparently was gifted with a fine sense of geometry and engineering and extraordinary woodworking skills.

In addition to its fine architectural presence, the Halliday-Cary-Pick House is notable for the prominent citizens who have owned and lived in it. Dickerson Thomas Halliday, who lived in the house for most of the second half of the nineteenth century, was not the original owner. A prosperous county planter, Matthew Turner, had engaged the builder James Kidd to erect the house. It was to be a wedding present for Turner's son and new wife. However, after deciding not to live in Auburn, they sold it to another party, who, after two years, sold

HABS documentation of Halliday-Cary-Pick staircase.

it to Halliday, who, according to an obituary in the *Columbus Daily Enquirer*, was "one of the most valued citizens of the Auburn village, and a popular and most accommodating merchant."

Dr. Charles Allen Cary, who became prominent in the affairs of the town, in the university, and in the nation, bought the house in 1897 not long after he came to Auburn with training in veterinary science from his native Iowa, with further study in Missouri and Germany. Hired to teach veterinary science and serve as veterinarian for the college's Experiment Station, he eventually founded and became the first dean of the school's new College of Veterinary Medicine. Dr. Cary served as Alabama's state veterinarian and is remembered for various initiatives in that office. He pioneered meat and dairy inspection systems in the United States and was widely recognized for his campaigns to eradicate two serious threats to beef production—bovine tuberculosis and Texas tick fever—by dipping the cattle in prophylactic solutions, a technique he is said to have developed out of experiments in the fish pond in his own back yard on North College Street.

Not only was Dr. Cary a formidable presence, his wife, Emma, seems to have been something of a grande dame of Auburn society, entertaining frequently in the house on North College. Mrs. Cary professed the Christian Science faith, to which, it is said, she credited her recovery from tuberculosis, and was a leading member of the small local congregation. Visiting co-religionists were graciously received at Mrs. Cary's home, according to reports from the Christian Scientist grandfather of one of the authors. After her husband's death in 1935, Emma Cary assumed leadership of her family's development of the land that Dr. Cary had accumulated. She oversaw the development of Cary Park, the area that became South Cary Drive. Cary family lore includes the account that when Mrs. Cary was developing the park, she required potential purchasers to come for tea at least three times before she would consider allowing them to purchase a building lot. Her gift to the local Christian Science community was the lot in Cary Park on which they built their first local church (see p. 143).

After Dr. Cary and Mrs. Cary died, in 1935 and 1954 respectively, the property passed to their children: a son and two daughters. Alice, the younger daughter, married a military officer assigned to the army training program at A.P.I., Capt. Lewis Pick. In time, Captain Pick became General Pick, winning renown and reward as builder of the Ledo Road in India and Burma during World War II. Although Alice remarried after the death of General Pick, the house retained the Pick designation and remained the home of Alice Cary Pick Gibson until her death in 2006 at age 101. In 2011, Fran Pick Dillard, Mrs. Gibson's daughter-in-law, transferred ownership of the Halliday-Cary-Pick House to Auburn University to serve as headquarters for the Cary Center for the Advancement of Philanthropy and Non-Profit Studies.

Allen-Gregory-Shaw House

Once on the outskirts but now securely within the embrace of the city of Auburn, the Allen-Gregory-Shaw House deserves to stand with the few other grand, restored classic homes composing the "Old Guard" of Auburn architecture—evidence of what life in the area once was for a privileged few and what a careful attention to architectural restoration can achieve.

The house, located on Lee County Road 96/Gregory Glenn Road, once commanded a large property acquired by James Abner Allen around 1836 when the former Indian lands were open to acquisition and white settlement. Allen had arrived with a large contingent of slaves to cultivate his new plantation in what was then Chambers County.

Allen-Gregory-Shaw House.

Whatever the configuration of the first Allen house on this property, it was succeeded or perhaps reconfigured as this Greek Revival cottage, the style of choice among the landowning class in the area at the time. The four original rooms in the house were heated with four side chimneys, rather than the two interior chimneys found in most of cottages of this type. That and embellishments of the front portico—the three-part windows, the expansive entrance door, and wainscoting—suggest that Ab Allen, the builder, felt few budgetary constraints when the house went up. The date of construction is uncertain, though family history suggests the late 1840s.

While the house fits neatly into the Greek Revival cottage genre, its special features mark it for closer attention. Notably, the house originally featured two grand porticoes (one now closed in), as can be seen in the adjacent early photograph. One faced the public approach, the other presumably offered a view of major plantation acreage. Another feature, the tripartite window style on the facade, is not unique but certainly not ordinary. Such tripartite windows are very typical of west central Georgia, Troup and neighboring counties, and east central Alabama. The still-unrestored Nunn House on Wire Road near the Macon County line, for instance, is fitted with tripartite windows under the entrance portico.

Above, Allen-Gregory-Shaw House before restoration; below, tripartite window feature.

In the 1930s, after several generations of the Allen family had lived in the home, the property sat abandoned until bought by E. L. Spencer as a source of timber for his business, E. L. Spencer Lumber Co. The house and its condition were virtually ignored by businessmen, other owners, and tenants alike, until 1943 when William Gregory and his wife, Kirk Armstrong Gregory, bought the property. After his graduation from A. P. I., W. H. "Mutt" Gregory served in the university's School of Agriculture as a specialist in animal husbandry and also as an assistant agronomist with the Extension Service. The Gregorys put the large acreage they had acquired surrounding this house in the Gold Hill/Oak Bowery area into pasturage and associated farming for raising cattle.

Restoration of the house began in 1956; after several years of work, the Gregorys moved into it. Nearby the restored house, a small building was erected as the home for the elder Gregorys when their daughter and son-in-law, Mary Elizabeth and Jerry Shaw, occupied the main house and completed its restoration. As of 2017, the Shaws live in both buildings.

The Allen family in front of their home; date unknown.

As all old houses should, Gregory-Shaw has a resident ghost, though a thoroughly benign one. The ghost story originated in the early years of the nineteenth century. Among the several people residing in the house were a baby and a spinster relative named Miss Molly. During a storm one evening, Miss Molly put the baby to bed in a front bedroom, and as she turned the doorknob to the room to leave, she was fatally struck by lightning. Ever since then, but only if a baby is in the house, the spirit, or vapors of Miss Molly, will be felt by the door to the front bedroom. Miss Molly has not appeared in a long time now, since all the Shaw and Gregory babies are grown and gone.

Webster House

A primary example of the local interpretation of Greek Revival style in the mid nineteenth century, the Webster House is among the oldest surviving residences in Auburn. The original house may have been a log structure of two rooms, the kitchen, and what is now called the "English room." The date of its construction is unknown. Around 1840 the house was extended and given a fashionable Greek Revival character. Several additions to the house have been made through its later history.

In the 1840s portion of the house, living spaces and the front porch are covered with a hipped roof, supported at the front by four square columns resting on the porch floor and framing the three bays of the facade. The centered entrance is conventionally arranged with double front doors and side and transom lights. A pair of six-over-six windows flanking the entrance rests on a "chair rail" that extends from a pilaster on each side to the front door frame, so that the sidelights repeat the length of the windows. Porch columns are fitted with capitals and bases appropriate for this vernacular version of Greek Revival architecture and the talents of almost any rural builder.

Walls, both inside and out, are paneled with wide boards laid horizontally. Some of these have been plastered over, but most remained unchanged. These surfaces are now all painted as they may have been originally. Floors

Webster House.

are wide pine planks, but the species of wood in the wall paneling is not known.

Dimensions of the spaces in the 1840s part of the house are in keeping with the style—wide entrance hall, flanking rooms of about twice that width and approximately square, high ceilings. End chimneys serve fireplaces in the two flanking rooms. Woodwork for inside spaces is quite plain. At present, there are no fireplace mantels. Damage from a falling tree demolished one of the chimneys, which was rebuilt to match the chimney and fireplace at the opposite end of the building. There the fireplace is surrounded by brick laid in a decorative pattern rather than a wood mantel.

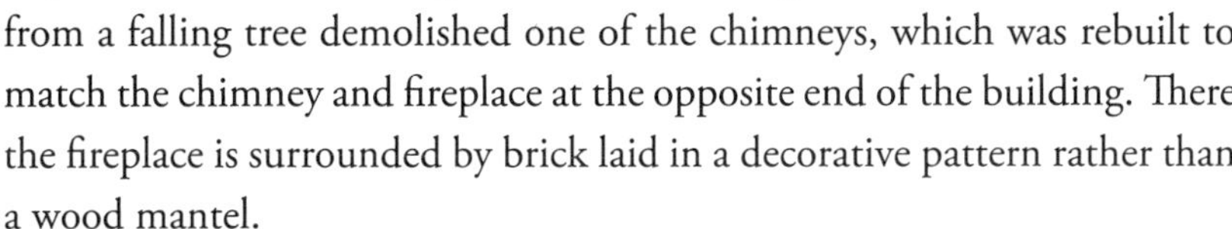

The Webster House is now located on about three-hundred acres purchased after the Indian Removal from Alabama in the 1830s. When purchased by the Webster family in 1922, the property was a large working farm supporting livestock, field crops, and a dairy herd, operated by the parents and six sons of the Webster family and numbers of sharecroppers and field hands.

The property is located on Alabama Highway 14, two miles west of downtown Auburn. The present owner is Mrs. Beverly Webster, widow of Paul Webster, whose parents were the original Webster family. In 1977, Beverly Webster and her parents, Mr. and Mrs. E. C. Robertson, purchased the property from the Webster estate. The house is presently managed by Mrs. Webster as a special events venue. It was added to the Alabama Register of Landmarks and Heritage in 2009.

Hardin-Poucher House (Meadows House)

Another house that could be included among the "Old Guard" under a more expansive definition is the Hardin-Poucher House (Meadows House) on North College Street, by virtue of its age (ca. 1850s) and original conception. Some serious compromises with its original design, however, suggest that it not be included along with the "Old Guard." The Meadows House was built as a genuine antebellum Greek Revival cottage, with a greatly admired full-length tetra-style portico with heavy square piers. Disappointingly, later

Meadows House.

owners shrank the width of the portico floor and shortened the full-length jib windows that once allowed one to walk through the openings onto that porch.

An even more recent owner persuaded the city authorities who oversee such things to allow the building to be moved forward a short distance toward the street it faced (North College) in order to provide space behind it to build apartments. The outcry from concerned citizens about the desecration of one of the town's historic buildings in its historic district might have led to that plan being abandoned and the building being sold to the Catholic church, with the understanding that the seller would complete the restoration agreed upon in his earlier negotiations with the city. The building is to be used for religious services, and the space behind it, rather than being filled with apartment buildings, will become parking space for those attending the services. The property adjoins the Catholic-owned house around the corner, facing Mitcham Avenue, and both facilities are connected with the Catholic campus ministries in Auburn.

7

Sole Survivors

"Stranded populations," a common term in ethnology, is a concept borrowed here to describe stranded houses. These are houses of some distinction because of who built or lived in them, their architectural significance, or simply because they have stubbornly refused to give in to the economic forces that have gobbled up their neighbors. Sadly, these reminders of Auburn's transformation from a lovely residential village into an ordinary city are not the only stranded houses in Auburn but a representative sample.

Little House, 225 North Gay Street

Best known of these sole survivors, perhaps because it has managed to survive longest, is the Little House. It was built in 1892 for a former Auburn mayor and was the home of one of Auburn's first three coeds and later one of the town's most eligible (and prosperous) bachelors. The former mayor, Charles Little, died in 1928; the early Auburn coed, Willie Little, married and moved away; the eligible bachelor, Felton Little, never married. After his death in 1971 at the age of eight-six, forty heirs, none living in Auburn, inherited the considerable estate, which included the house and immediate grounds, an adjacent warehouse, a narrow footage that ran by the railroad tracks over to North College, and properties in other parts of the town and the county.

Felton Little House.

James E. May, Auburn alumnus, purchased the twelve-room Victorian house from one of Felton Little's heirs and moved his property management business to the small garage that once sheltered Little's Model T Ford, noted for its electric lights and self-starter in place of the usual hand crank.

At the time of May's purchase, the house was

being used as office space. Auburn alumnus Jack Saint, retired from the army, started his law practice there. Associates in Family Therapy, owned by Fran Cronenberg and Linda and Gary Connell, also occupied part of the house. Jimmy Sprayberry, the current owner of the house, continues to practice law there.

At the time of the most recent purchase, the grounds around the house included a locally famous, but somewhat neglected, formal garden, which had once featured a summer house, partially surrounded by several small pools. Preserved in the interior of the main house are the original baseboards and wainscoting, heart pine tongue-and-groove paneling in the foyer, and the beveled panes of the front door. The staircase, fitted with a decorative banister with a knobbed newel post, leads to a landing illuminated by a yellow stained glass window.

The exterior touches, consistent with the Victorian mode of the whole building, include the frosted decorative transom window over the front door and a garland carved in one of the hutches of a front gable. The exterior wooden decorative effects, perhaps unmatched elsewhere in Auburn, include vertical surfaces of fish-scale shingles sometimes alternating with rows of plain shingles, a heavy decorated cornice on the front bay window, as well as more ordinary decoration under the front porch eaves. Damage to the slate roof has been patched with old slates found on the property.

The last Little to live in the house, Felton Little, donated the land for Auburn's first park, Felton Little Park on East Glenn Avenue. He and his father were both longtime supporters of Auburn's First Baptist Church. Father, mother, and son are all buried at Pine Hill Cemetery.

CHRIETZBERG HOUSE, 150 NORTH ROSS STREET

The home of the building contractor A. H. Chrietzberg has stood on the east side of North Ross Street since about 1903. Chrietzberg brought his family to Auburn in the early 1900s, when a steadily expanding college and growing town provided plenty of opportunities for a builder. Just as attractive, perhaps, were the educational opportunities for the children in Chrietzberg's large family. The house he built for his family was once surrounded by neighbors in modest frame houses, and even after the west side of Ross Street was completely given over to municipal

Chrietzberg House.

buildings and student apartments and an occasional business, the east side of the block maintained its single-family residential character.

However, the house's neighbors to the north were razed and a stupendous apartment building and parking garage, four stories high, disrupted the scene and outraged much of the town's population. One half of the block bounded by Ross Street on the west, Debardeleben Street on the east, Glenn Avenue on the north, and Magnolia Avenue on the south is occupied by the four-story apartment building and parking deck complex known as 160 Ross.

The Chrietzberg House stands out today, as it always did, as a builder's home, with some originality in the plan and finishes—not glaring, but noticeable. While houses of the period ordinarily would have presented a symmetrical front behind the hipped roof front porch, this one does not. Instead, in addition to the front door to the living space, a recessed entrance is placed to the right. Census data provides an explanation. Mrs. Chrietzberg was "proprietress" of a rooming house (primarily for students) at this location. The front door was for family and guests; the door to the side for her renters.

The recent sale of the building and its conversion into a coffee house promises preservation of the exterior appearance and most of the interior features. Its business success would seem assured in view of the large number of prospective customers living in the adjacent mega apartment complex.

Williamson House, 211 South Gay Street

The Williamson House was fortunate that the first intrusion of nontraditional building on its block did not seem to insult the character of the neighborhood. Next door was Auburn's first really classy private multiparty residence, Wittel Dormitory, on the southeast corner of South Gay Street and Thach Avenue. In succeeding years, the Williamson House was less fortunate,

as its southern flank was gradually developed with student apartment buildings, fast food franchisees, and even high-rise upscale apartments. Now the house stands alone as the only traditional family residence on either side of the first two blocks of South Gay Street. As this is written, the Williamson House has been sold and slated for destruction to provide parking for guests at the "boutique hotel" next door—the remodeled Wittel Dormitory (see p. 212).

Except for its porte-cochere, the house is an unremarkable design; the family it originally sheltered, however, was somewhat remarkable. Mrs. Bessie Wright Williamson pioneered in Auburn as the first woman to sit on the Auburn City Council. Mr. and Mrs. Williamson were parents of two daughters, Mary Lydia and Virginia, for whom Virginia Avenue in Auburn was named.

Top, Williamson House as built; above, as reconfigured; below, 316 North Ross Street.

316 North Ross Street

Though the provenance of this house is uncertain, it bears all the hallmarks of a J. A. Cullars project. Fortunately, it has been well maintained as a residence (though now a rental property), despite the disappearance of similar domestic structures to its north and south and across the street as well. The bric-a-brac in the gable decorations and on the front porch seem exactly right for the volume of the house and its imposing roof line.

Ivey House, Opelika Road

Easily the most fashionable home in Auburn when it was built in the 1930s, the Ivey House was clearly an architectural gem, too imposing to fall to any developer's wrecking ball. In an environment of mostly provincial architectural tastes, the house was bound to attract attention from every passerby, and it still does. Its symmetry, plain stucco surfaces, and restrained decoration, however, save it from seeming pretentious, though to some it still did. But consider that across the Opelika highway at the time was a substantial row of some of the most pretentious houses in any Auburn neighborhood, save its antebellum cottages on North College Street and a few other locations.

Wilkins House, 428 W. Magnolia

In the Wilkins House, one finds a perfect blend of charming design and Auburn history, not even spoiled by its present setting or by garish coloring. It serves today as an entertainment venue under the aegis of its owner, Gameday Centers Southeastern, but just what sort of entertainment is hard to discern. This was the home of Mrs. Pauline Wilkins, whose reputation for superb baked goods is still remembered by Auburn residents of a certain age. Whether supplied by Mrs. Wilkins from her bakery that occupied several sites in town, or from the kitchen in her house, which she bought in 1942, it was clear to her customers that no grocery store deli or donut chain could match her delicacies.

Above, Ivey House; below top, Wilkins House today, bottom, Mrs. Pauline Wilkins in her kitchen.

Ellison-Harper House, 50 Opelika Road

The transformation of Opelika Road from a residential area into an almost completely commercial area was gradual enough that now it seems it must always have been a route strictly for businesses. But the Harper home at 504 Opelika Road was once one of many.

Lewis and Nancy Hill Harper purchased the house from Lizzie Wynn Ellison in 1934. The family estimates the house was built around 1884. Its outside appearance remains essentially unchanged since that time, even the two large cedar trees shielding it from the

Ellison-Harper House.

rush of Opelika Road traffic. Pat Harper Echols, who was born in the early 1950s and grew up in the house, is a proud descendant of the original Auburn Harper settlers. Her description of the house, as included in the 2011 volume *Lest We Forget*, provided these details:

> The house is a three-bedroom house with living room, kitchen, interior hall, and front and rear porch. It was without electricity when it was purchased by the Harpers. The walls were plastered, and the front porch was supported by decorative columns and adorned with gingerbread woodwork across the top. The house still has its original pine molded ceiling in the interior hall and living room. The original metal hook for hanging the kerosene lantern still remains in the hall ceiling, and the original bedroom doors are intact, complete with skeleton key locks.

According to Mrs. Echols, whose own father, Lewis Harper, and uncle, Richard Harper, were skilled carpenters who worked on numerous Auburn homes, the patterned pine ceilings in the house are the exact same design as those found in the Ebenezer Baptist Church on Thach Avenue. She was told that the Perdue brothers, Augustus and Jailous Jr., both of whom held degrees from Tuskegee Institute, did the ceiling work in both structures.

Hawkins House

Hawkins House (destroyed 2018).

It is astonishing that any homes survived the wholesale transformation of Opelika Road into a seething commercial strip as it leaves Auburn, but the Hawkins House did until 2018. The well-proportioned volume of the house, especially the hipped roof, so characteristic of many of the area's traditional cottages, disguised the history of the house, a history that itself replicates that of many area houses, both modest and grand. In 1907, Alex and Susanna Frazier, grandparents of the last member of the family to live in the house, Odessa Frazier Hawkins, bought several acres of land here and engaged a skillful local carpenter, Doc Jones, to help build the house, at first only a one-room shed. Later additions provided a living room, kitchen, bathroom along a central hall, and front porch.

The Hawkins House stood on an elevated site above the traffic and commercialism of the Opelika Highway, providing a well maintained and particularly colorful domestic contrast to the apparently oblivious and often harried drivers who passed below.

Pi Kappa Alpha Fraternity House, 166 North Gay Street

The only survivor of the half-dozen fraternity houses that once lined the east side of North Gay Street is the handsome building that Birmingham architects Warren, Knight & Davis designed for the Pi Kappa Alpha fraternity at 166 North Gay. The local Auburn builder Louis Kerr was responsible for its construction in 1935 (see p. 103). Perhaps it survived because it has a

Pi Kappa Alpha Fraternity House.

more domestic appearance than its now demolished institutional-looking neighbors along the street.

In 1962, the fraternity moved into a new, larger house in a similar style on the other side of town, selling the brick structure to local realtor/developer George Kickliter. Over the years, he rented the numerous rooms in it for a variety of small businesses and organizations, even at one time a beauty parlor. In 2000, Dutch and Betty Higginbotham bought the house, renting the large front area to Alice Henderson, the present tenant, for her realty office. Mrs. Higginbotham hoped to maintain the building as part of Auburn's built landscape indefinitely. The old dorm rooms toward the back of the building are rented to a variety of businesses and other entities, now including a psychology group.

The former fraternity house appears virtually unchanged since the photograph above was taken in the 1980s. Today the entrance portico has been darkened, and a sign is attached to the monumental chimney beside it. Otherwise the exterior seems to have been preserved intact.

Almost any building that has half-timbering would be identified as Tudor, as in the bygone Toomer House. The photographs of the PiKA House show half-timbering on the entrance portico, but there is no half-timbering in gables to the left side and rear. The massive chimney stack and steep roof

Fireplace, Pi Kappa Alpha Fraternity House.

AN INTERVIEW WITH JIM SPENCE, 1952–56 MEMBER OF PI KAPPA ALPHA AND FRATERNITY HOUSE MANAGER

The PiKA house was located on Gay Street. ATO house was across the street, and Kappa Sig and SPE were just north of us, and Delta Tau Delta was south of us where the Auburn Bank is today.

The house had one long hall with twelve rooms, six on each side of the hall, so with three per room we could house thirty-six members. There was one big shower room with four showers. We had only one phone booth with one phone for the entire fraternity. If someone made a long-distance call, they were supposed to write it down on a list in the phone booth, but many times they did not, and we'd have to check the numbers and fine them double for the call.

The house mother, "Mama Lou" Steed had an apartment (bedroom, bath, and sitting room) between the dining room and the dormitory section. She had her own phone. We had two cooks, three houseboys, and we fed 105 per day (six tables with ten per table, so there were two different sittings for meals) six days a week, with a special brunch on Sunday. Sunday brunch was a big deal, and that was when we entertained guests. We always used white tablecloths, china, and silverware. Mama Lou wanted it to be like home, and she wanted us to be gentlemen. On homecoming 1954 we fed one thousand people. The charge for meals was $42.50 per month, and $45 if you got milk. Room rent was $10 per month. [As house manager] I got my room free and $90 per quarter in ROTC money, so my only cost was the $42.50 per quarter tuition.

[From] the front entrance there was the living room to the right with a large fireplace, which was used all the time. The living room had a high vaulted ceiling with heavy wooden beams. At the far end of the living room you would walk into what we called the music room, which included a baby grand piano. The room had windows all the way around, heavy draperies, and sofas along the walls. The rules were that you never were to turn on the lights in the music room!

Outside in back of the music room and living room was a garden area with a fish pond and behind there was "the jungle" where we played volleyball. The fish pond was central to the house because it was used to dunk members when they got pinned or engaged and was very important for icing down beer for big parties. In regards to alcohol, there was no alcohol allowed in the front part of the house except during times like homecoming when alums were present. You couldn't stop alums from bringing alcohol.

The dining room was to the left of the entrance, with the kitchen on the far side of the dining room. There were two rooms upstairs—a chapter room and a make-out room. We all brought our dates to the house. There wasn't anywhere else to go (no one had an apartment), and even if there was some place to go you didn't have transportation. There weren't more than six cars in the entire fraternity; a couple of brothers who came back from Korea had cars. We walked everywhere. When we had our formal, many of us went home and borrowed the family car. Our formals were held in the Student Activities Building, eventually the Foy Union, a hotel in Opelika, the Pitts Hotel in Auburn, and even once on the deck above the airport administrative building. During the formal weekend, the brothers would move out and the girls would occupy the dormitory section of the house. We also had tea parties on Sunday afternoons with the silver service and all.

The fraternity had to go by the rules—the fire and police stations were directly across the street from us. Those were the days!

pitch, in addition to the wooden entrance portico, certainly would fit the Tudor style. Likewise, there are interior elements compatible with that style, especially the dramatic fireplace surround in the large parlor. While the street appearance of this building does not immediately suggest "fraternity house," the architects' plans show how it would accommodate the substantial group of students that lived, took meals, and entertained themselves and their guests in the structure.

8

The Best of the Rest in the Historic District

In addition to houses in Auburn's historic district that are introduced elsewhere in this volume, a number from the early twentieth century described as "contributing resources" add significantly to the charm of this area by virtue of solid design, of typifying an era in Auburn's development, or of connection to notable Auburn residents. Many of these homes stand along the single stretch of North College Street, the 300 to 400 blocks, bounded by its intersection with Bragg and Mitcham avenues on the south and Drake Avenue on the north.

300 Block of North College

At 311 North College Street stands the Lamar House. The Colonial Revival of the first half of the twentieth century drew on a mixture of American architectural roots. In the 1924 Lamar House is a combination of elements that, while not common, is true to the style. The focus of interest for this design is all in the portico and the elements it shelters. The portico roof, mimicking the style and pitch of the hipped roof of the main block, is supported by pairs of slender square columns; the pairing explicitly compensates for their otherwise inadequate dimensions. Under the portico, an elaborate and unusually decorated cornice surmounts the front door, which is flanked by unusually wide sidelights above floor-level panels. At the second-floor level an array of three joined

Lamar House, 311 N. College. The North College Street Historic District records the house as: "Circa 1924. Two-story Colonial Revival influence, wood clapboard with central portico, hipped roof, 6/12 slope (asphalt shingles), four square column porch."

window sashes approximately matches the width of the door ensemble below it. The circular brick stair from sidewalk to portico floor, whether original or not, suits the whole presentation well.

Alma Virginia Lamar, known to all the town as "Totsie," granddaughter of Dr. William Harmong and Ann Marie Glenn Lamar, was descended from a long and distinguished line of Auburn's Glenn and Lamar families. Totsie had the Lamar House built for her family in 1924, having acquired the property from Mitchell Drake, owner of a large house nearby. At the time, she was the main breadwinner for the immediate family group. The job she had secured with the post office made possible the construction of the house and helped provide for the large group of Lamars who lived in it. To help further support the family, her mother took care of boarders and served their meals in this house, as she had done earlier in the neighboring Drake house.

For many years Totsie was a stalwart employee in the Auburn post office and eventually served as assistant postmistress. She was active in the community and especially active in the Methodist Church. She and her sister, Mary George Lamar, a teacher of business subjects at the college, were the last Lamars to live in the house. Mary George died 1981, Totsie in 1990, reportedly the last member of the Auburn Methodist Church who was a descendant of its founders. There is a window, "The Call of the Disciples," in the Founders' Chapel of the Auburn United Methodist Church dedicated to the Lamar family.

The Lamar House is now a company office building for Mary Cho Realty, purchased from the heirs following the deaths of the Lamar sisters. The building appears much as it did when built, though now landscaped to suit modern tastes—a backyard garden surrounded by a latticed brick wall includes a fountain and seating area—and business needs and modified unobtrusively to meet ADA standards as well. The present owner, realtor Mary Cho, is one of the very few business leaders who has been able to maintain the historic qualities of a historic residential property within the business district, an example regrettably seldom followed among Auburn businesspeople.

At 318 North College is the Hardie-McMillan House. Today, in place of its original wooden weatherboarding, this building wears a slick coat of aluminum siding that fortunately does not obscure the original design of the house—a local interpretation of Georgian style—under its hipped roof. The house, built about 1920, was once owned by C. J. Young.

At 355 North College is the A. L. Thomas House, built by the Cullars brothers in the early 1920s. It has been described as "mission style" by some and as "Mediterranean style" by others. Whatever the difficulty of pinning down an appropriate style designation, it is obviously an anomaly among Auburn's domestic buildings. N. C. Curtis, architect of Auburn and later of New Orleans, designed the building for professor of engineering A. L. Thomas and his wife, Delphine. Today it is the home of the A. L. Thomases' daughter-in-law, Beverly Burkhardt Thomas, daughter of Walter Burkhardt (see p. 38).

Below, Hardie-McMillan House, 318 N. College; center, A. L. Thomas House, 355 N. College; bottom, B. F. Thomas House, 365 N. College.

At 365 North College is the B. F. Thomas House, the 1926 Colonial Revival-style home of a longtime Auburn physician. The Thomas house is a conventional interpretation of the genre, excepting perhaps the arched roof of the shallow portico at the front door. Dr. Thomas, a Lee County native, earned his medical degree from Emory University and completed graduate work at the Medical College of New York, where he met and married Olive Bourne, also a medical doctor. The Drs. Thomas returned to Alabama in 1918 just prior to the birth of their son. They lived in Montgomery, where Dr. Thomas Sr. practiced as a state public health officer. Shortly after the birth of Ben Jr., the family moved back to Lee County and in 1926 built the North College Street home where they raised their son and a daughter, Mary Olive. In the 1980s the house became the home of a third-generation Thomas serving as a medical doctor in Lee County, Dr. John Simister Thomas, and his wife Susie. Second-generation Dr. Ben Thomas Jr. received a medical degree from Emory University in 1943. After World War II, he and his father, known as

B. F. Sr., served the Auburn community together for almost forty years.

At 371 North College is the Crenshaw-Hardie House. One of Auburn's turn-of-the-century (ca. 1898) Victorian homes, this one presents a rather simpler version of the style compared, for example, with the Felton Little House on North Gay Street. Embellishments for this house include only the front porch decorations and the bracketed and paneled front bay window, although others may have been removed in the century since the house was built. Bolling Hall Crenshaw, professor of mathematics, was one of the three faculty members (with Professors Luther Duncan and John Wilmore) chosen to lead the college in the early Depression years, said to have been sometimes referred to as "the three learned asses." A reputation for refusing to admit girls to his classes has long been alleged.

Crenshaw-Hardie House 371 N. College.

400 Block of North College

At 406 North College is the Cary-Patrick House. One of the three houses associated with Dr. C. A. Cary (see p. 166 and p. 208), this one was commissioned by Dr. Cary in 1908 to be the home of Col. B. S. Patrick, professor of military science and commandant of cadets at A.P.I. The design could hardly have been improved, for except for the roof dormer it repeats modestly the character of its neighbor to the south, the Cary-Pick House. The roof, it is said, originally was shingled in metal "with finials," a conceit that fortunately was not continued when modern shingles replaced the originals.

At 414 North College is the Fullan-McKenzie House, also called the Drake-McKenzie House. The house as pictured here is a reconstruction of the turn-of-the-century building following serious damage by fire. The original roof, not hipped, was gabled at the left and right sides of the main block with chimneys at both ends. Michael Thomas Fullan served Auburn

Cary-Patrick House, 406 N. College.

for nearly half a century as both student and faculty member. Though his academic specialty was mechanical drawing, he is best remembered in Auburn as founder and longtime leader of the college band.

At 415 North College is the Holmes House. Built in 1912 and originally clad in wooden clapboard, the Holmes House presents an authoritative appearance despite little loyalty to a consistent style. "Victorian with Greek Revival influence" reads its description in the City of Auburn's Historic Preservation Commission's exposition of the North College Historic District.

At 422 North College is the Champion House. From the early 1920s, the house is typical for the town rather than distinguished among its neighbors. Sometimes described as a Craftsman-style bungalow, it has few Craftsman exterior features. Considering the general symmetry of the facade, the off-center placement of the front door and chimney stacks is jarring.

Top left, Fullan-McKenzie House, 414 N. College; top right, Holmes House, 415 N. College; above center, Champion House, 422 N. College; above, Donahue-Knapp House 425 N. College.

At 425 North College is the Donahue-Knapp House. Even with Craftsman features such as the exposed rafter ends, the kick in the porch roof, divided lights of upper window sashes, and the rock-faced concrete block foundation and post bases, it is apt to describe the Donahue-Knapp house as a "storybook" cottage rather than assign it a more conventional designation.

At 433 North College is the Killebrew House, also known as the Allen-Killebrew-Jeane House. For its horizontal impression, in spite of the complex

Top left, the Killebrew House, 433 N. College; top right, the Wright-Nelson House, 447 N. College; above, the Hendricks-Gwin House, 439 N. College.

and imaginative roof structure, the Killebrew House (1904) is one of Auburn's finest Victorian-era designs.

At 447 North College is the Wright-Nelson House, whose array of four double colonettes supporting the front porch is believed unique in Auburn. The house, built about 1920, once was the home of the family of Emil Wright Sr., prominent Auburn banker.

At 439 North College is the Hendricks-Gwin House. A 1929 version of the bungalow style featuring heavy battered brick columns supporting the front porch and a large, front-facing pedimented gable projecting from the low-pitched roof, the Hendricks-Gwin house conveys stolidity and even impregnability.

ON BRAGG AVENUE

Auburn homeowners and builders were no less attracted to the Craftsman bungalow style than the homeowners and builders in most other American cities and towns, where many bungalows have been preserved and showcased as charming, comfortable, and adaptable period houses. Virtual small museums of the style once lined Glenn and Bragg avenues in Auburn as well. Those that once stood near the town's business district are all gone, save one.

When V. Mitchell Drake began to sell parcels of the "White-Drake Place" in 1913, the block associated with Ridge Grove and Main Street (now Bragg Avenue and College Street) quickly became a neighborhood.

In 1922 Dr. Everett Winters and his wife, Ruby Gaston, bought a parcel of land from Mr. Drake and built their home at 121 Bragg Avenue, where they lived for thirty-two years until their deaths in 1954. Dr. Winters was a professor in the College of Veterinary Medicine; Mrs. Winters managed their home, raised their children, taught piano lessons, and was the organist at Holy Innocents Episcopal Church in downtown Auburn. In 2007 the Winters House had been empty for almost ten years and was in ill repair. Thomas Sparrow, whose grandfather was one of the many young college professors, professionals, and businessmen whose families built homes along this street, bought and restored the house.

Students of the style and of this house point to the many characteristics that mark the classic middle-class Craftsman bungalow. Particularly noticeable are features of the clipped gable roof, low-sloped with wide eaves and exposed rafter ends. Corners of the chimney are emphasized with glazed bricks. The off-center gabled porch breaks up the main mass of the house to provide a stepped gable facade with supporting triangular knee braces under the eaves. Exterior vertical surfaces are worked with several Craftsman touches as well: in the gable ends, lattice-work panels contrast with centered windows of an attic or upper story; window panes are oriented vertically; brick piers with concrete caps support the porch posts, including one pier without a post; and a front door in typical Craftsman style.

Below, the neglected Winters-Sparrow House; bottom, after restoration and with Capitol Hill Apartments added behind.

Mr. Sparrow uses the restored house as headquarters for his firm, Commerce Networks. The Capitol Hill Apartments added at the rear of the house were designed to complement the architectural character of the location. Designs for the house and the apartment building were by architect Joe Ruscin of Design Plus; project engineer was Parker Lewis of Civil Design; Thomas

Sparrow and C&S Development were general contractors, and Donald Allen Development was contractor for the Capitol Hill Apartments.

On East University Drive

The Drake-Bedell House, located in the 2300 block of East University Drive, was built for the Brittain Drake family and later owned by his daughter and son-in-law, Velma and Dewey Bedell. The structure, a typical early twentieth-century farmhouse, was situated on a large acreage owned by Mr. Drake. Most of the supplies of fresh vegetables sold in his Opelika Road grocery store were produced by the family on this farm.

The house and property, now part of the City of Auburn, are prime candidates for redevelopment along the rapidly developing commercial corridor of East University Drive, so most likely the days are numbered for this pastoral relic of pre-World War I farm life in Auburn.

Farther Out on North College Street

An early owner of the house that now lies opposite the Auburn University Fish Ponds on North College Street was one R. L. Neighbors, employed as a railroad section boss. Theophilus Pittman purchased the property from him through the New Deal's Farm Security Agency in 1939, a spread of 264 acres with barn, two other buildings, and this house. Before moving in, the Pittmans—parents Theo and Nina and their six children—renovated the house, removing a room at the back of the building and adding a kitchen, dining room, and bedroom.

Below left, the Drake-Bedell House as built; below right, today.

After the deaths of the senior Pittmans, their son Lyman and his family lived in the house. Most of the farm acreage was sold in 2005 for development as the Tivoli subdivision. In 2010, Lyman Pittman's widow, Wilda, sold the house located on Alabama Highway 147 (1910 North College Street). The present owner is Rebecca Powell.

Pittman House, 1910 N. College Street.

Although its porch decorations are more elaborate, its roof is in part hipped, and its plan is apparently reversed, the Pittman house is a close cousin to the Drake-Bedell house. On both, the projecting front gable is rendered nearly as a pediment due to the cornice returns and the plain board at the eave level. The narrow window in the projecting rooms of both houses marks them as dating from about the same time, perhaps even constructed by the same builder.

On Mitcham Avenue

The two large houses across the street from the old train station, at 115 and 121 Mitcham Avenue, share more than just adjoining lots. Both lots were gifts of Mrs. Leila Terrell to her daughters, Annie and Hassie, as they married Cleburne Basore and Charles Hixon, respectively. Before separating these lots from the large tract occupying the corner of North Gay Street and Mitcham Avenue, the property was the site of Mrs. Terrell's boarding house, a local landmark where its proprietress provided accommodations for dozens of Auburn students and meals for other Auburn residents as well. Mrs. Terrell had acquired the house around 1901 from the dentist, Dr. Gachet, whose father built it. A sprawling structure with several additions, it stood out from many others on the north side of town by virtue of its gambrel roof—uncommon in the town to that point—and the gigantic camellia japonica, said to have been the first of that species in Auburn, that flowered in Mrs. Terrell's yard in view of the train station across the street.

To the west of the boarding house property was enough unimproved land to accommodate two later houses for Mrs. Terrell's daughters. The first improvement was construction of the Basore House, now numbered 121 Mitcham Avenue, which lies immediately adjacent to the site of the

boarding house, now lamentably replaced by an undistinguished bank building.

A largish Colonial Revival-style dwelling, the Basore house is clad in gray clapboard and offers a quite plain appearance to the street. The portico at the entrance is supported by thin posts under a substantial pediment. The entrance ensemble, including the panels beside the front door, is painted white, except for the door itself and the tympanum of the pediment, which is filled with gray clapboard to match the rest of the house.

Terrell-Basore House, 121 Mitcham.

Mrs. Annie Basore and her husband, Dr. Cleburne Ammen Basore, head of the university's chemical engineering department, designed the house, calling in, Mrs. Basore recalls, a "young professor of architecture at the university" to assist with technical construction details.

In the Basore house downstairs are three rooms in front—dining room, living room, and glassed-in sitting room—and a spacious central hall, kitchen, sunroom, and bathroom at the rear. Upstairs are three bedrooms and two baths. In the house, built in 1926, fireplaces first supplied much of the heat. The fireplaces are still usable, but gas heat was later added.

Mrs. Basore, who had served as advisor to the college's Chi Omega sorority for more than thirty years, spearheaded the sorority's fundraising campaign for renovating the historic 1850s Auburn Presbyterian Church, now the University Chapel. The Basore house was renovated in 2019 and is now a residential property.

Next door to the Terrell-Basore House, at 115 Mitcham Avenue, Mrs. Terrell's other daughter, Hassie, and her husband, Charles Hixon, built their house in a similar Colonial Revival style, but in brick. Even though the genre is the same, the execution is different enough to satisfy some advocates of the style but dismay others. Dismay would be occasioned by the double sashes on the street facade, satisfaction by the elaboration of the classical-styled entrance—sidelights at the front door, fluted columns for the portico, and a properly rendered pediment and entablature.

The house, like its neighbor, dates from the mid-1920s. The street frontage of the two houses is of the same rather narrow width, though the Hixon house enjoys a much deeper lot. Professor Hixon, who became chairman of A.P.I.'s department of mechanical engineering, was an enthusiastic Rotarian and an amateur magician whose entertaining presentations were often mentioned in press reports. He was, as well, an accomplished photographer who produced an admired collection of nearly a hundred portraits of local African Americans. The collection passed to his daughter, but its whereabouts are no longer known.

Above, Hixon House, 115 Mitcham; below, Hardie House, 113 Mitcham.

Following the death of Hassie Terrell Hixon in 1931, Professor Hixon continued to live in the house. He and his second wife, the Opelika widow Mrs. Dorothy Greene Mitchell, remained there until his death in 1954.

The house now is owned by Auburn's St. Michael the Archangel Catholic Church. With additional construction behind the house, it is the center of student outreach for the church and obviously a stage for student humor, as passersby can see from the beckoning Pope in the upper left window in the accompanying photo.

A third surviving house on Mitcham Avenue was originally the Hardie House at 113 Mitcham Avenue. With the expansion of zoning for commercial use in this direction, it has been the location of several businesses. As a small residence, the house fits well within the bungalow category, notwithstanding that it shows few of the exterior Craftsman or Arts and Crafts details that typically embellish bungalows of the 1920s period of this one.

Over the years, the Hardie House has hosted a number of Auburn families with familiar names. C. J. Young once owned it and the adjacent McMillan House facing College Street. Young descendants Gilford "Buck" Young and "Sonny" Young lived in it.

On Moore's Mill Road

The Heard House, a Greek Revival wooden structure, was built in 1848 by John Eady, a member of the original settlement party that arrived in Auburn in 1836. The house, in a classic dogtrot style, featured a central hallway with two rooms on each side. The earliest section of the house is still supported on the original rock/stone pedestals. Supports for the roof are made of un-debarked timbers, still to be seen in the attic. In 1857 John Eady sold the house to T. L. Cobb, from whom John Frazier Heard purchased it in 1883, with a significant amount of adjoining land, when he moved his family into town from rural Lee County. In this house John Frazier and Fannie Zellers Heard raised their seven children. The home has remained in the care of Heard family members, including Heard daughter Annie Florence "Miss Annie" Heard, granddaughter Frances Williams Vowell, and the present owners, great-granddaughter Lynda Vowell Tremaine and her husband, Joel.

Below, Heard House in 1901; bottom, Heard-Tremaine House in 2016.

The house has been through several renovations. In 1901, John F. Heard added a dining room, the first indoor kitchen and bathroom, a bay window in the living room, columns in the hallway, and a wraparound front porch. Decorative mantels were made and installed over the four original fireplaces. Heard also put in decorative ceilings, comprised of individually placed wood slats, in the front bedroom and dining room. He also turned attic space into a bedroom.

A second major renovation project was completed in 1956. The renovation added two bathrooms, enclosed a side porch to make a family room, and remodeled the kitchen. In 2010 the existing bathrooms were updated, the wide-plank heart pine floors were refinished, and heart pine flooring was added to the family room and kitchen.

During the 2010 renovations the kitchen was completely rebuilt, including exposing a brick chimney and raising the ceiling to its original height of eleven and a half feet. A new marble-topped island was built from joists reclaimed from the renovation. A master bedroom suite and screened-in porch were added to the back of the house. Central heating and air conditioning were installed.

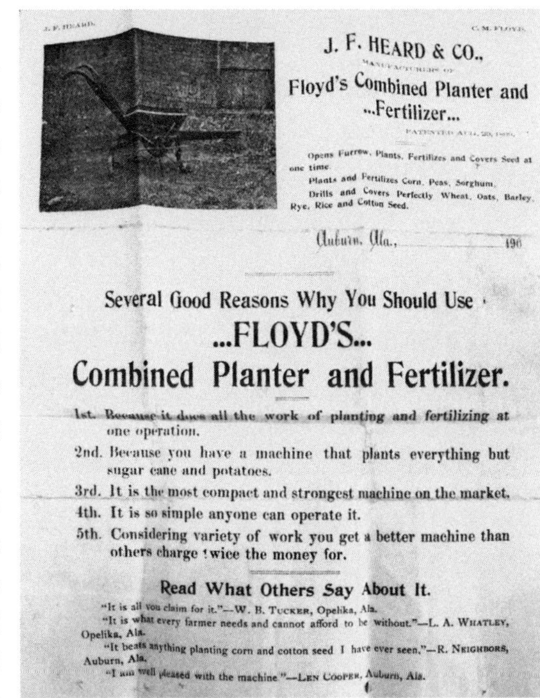

J. F. HEARD. C. M. FLOYD.

J. F. HEARD & CO.,

Floyd's Combined Planter and ...Fertilizer...

Opens Furrow, Plants, Fertilizes and Covers Seed at one time.

Plants and Fertilizes Corn, Peas, Sorghum.

Drills and Covers Perfectly Wheat, Oats, Barley, Rye, Rice and Cotton Seed.

Auburn, Ala., 190

Several Good Reasons Why You Should Use

...FLOYD'S...

Combined Planter and Fertilizer.

1st. Because it does all the work of planting and *fertilizing* at one operation.

2nd. Because you have a machine that plants everything but sugar cane and potatoes.

3rd. It is the most compact and strongest machine on the market.

4th. It is so simple anyone can operate it.

5th. Considering variety of work you get a better machine than others charge twice the money for.

Read What Others Say About It.

"It is all you claim for it."—W. B. TUCKER, Opelika, Ala.

"It is what every farmer needs and cannot afford to be without."—L. A. WHATLEY, Opelika, Ala.

"It beats anything planting corn and cotton seed I have ever seen."—R. NEIGHBORS, Auburn, Ala.

"I am well pleased with the machine."—LEN COOPER, Auburn, Ala.

Top, Swope House; above, flyer for Charles Floyd's planter-fertilizer.

John F. Heard was a builder. In addition to his own house featured here, for which he supplied some of the labor himself, he is credited with other buildings. The small house that stood next door to the family home on Moore's Mill Road was constructed under his direction for his daughter, Addie, at the time of her marriage to Arthur Swope. When Bobby Barksdale Dees purchased the house in 2003 from Heard descendants, it stood structurally sound with its original heart pine floorings and mantels and its original overlap oak board siding completely intact.

In addition to the John Heard Cotton Gin and Grist Mill northwest of downtown that appears on the earliest Auburn Sanborn map, the building in which his downtown business, J. F. Heard & Co., was conducted was also a Heard project. From that building, he and his son-in-law, Charles M. Floyd, supplied hardware to the community, featuring at one point the Floyd's Combined Planter and Fertilizer, for which his son-in-law held a patent. According to family legend, in 1889 Heard was responsible for the installation of the clock and bell in Samford Hall Tower. He built the supports for the bell and used a portable steam hoist from his cotton gin/grist mill to lift the 4,200-pound bell into place, where it continues to ring out.

The Heard family members have maintained their home through generations, paralleling their legacy of service to the town of Auburn. When Miss

Annie Heard was graduated from the Auburn Female Institute in 1895, she began her more than thirty-year teaching career. She was remembered as a "favorite fourth grade teacher" and as principal of the Auburn Primary School. Years later, her niece, Frances Williams Vowell, followed her as a "favorite fourth grade teacher." The legacy of service continued when Miss Annie's great niece, Lynda Vowell Tremaine, became a teacher in the Auburn City Schools and served as principal of Wright's Mill Road Elementary School. In 2019, Lynda Tremaine, as her husband Joel had before her, was serving as a member of the Auburn City Council.

South Gay Street

Sam Hurst, who revitalized the School of Architecture during his tenure as its dean, designed houses on two adjacent lots on South Gay Street. The first, planned for his own family, did not follow the traditional designs popular in Auburn, and a picture window in the bathroom at the back of the house was a particular cause for comment. The architect's wife at the time, Melinda, claimed that the picture window presented no problem and reportedly added that she would be happy to provide paper bags for guests to put over their heads when using the bathroom. A succeeding dean of the College of Architecture, Daniel Bennett, greatly admired the house and purchased it but wished to add a garage. Hurst, then at a new post in California, sent Bennett the plans of the house so that the new garage would fit with the original design of the structure.

Below, elevation drawing of Hurst House, 2030 S. Gay; bottom, Anderson House, 1104 S. Gay.

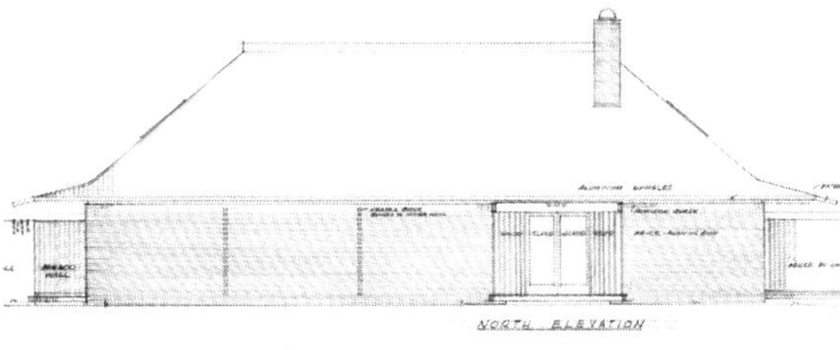

Although the house can no longer be usefully photographed from the street, as the present owners prefer a landscape that obscures that view, the original architectural drawings give a general impression of the overall features of the house. A source of amusement as construction on the building proceeded was the reported comment of one of the work crew that "what this place needs is an architect."

Sam Hurst also designed the house next door to the south for Dr. Robert Anderson, then vice president of A.P.I., and his wife, Margaret, the daughter of the long-serving dean of Home Economics, Marion Spidle. Dr. Anderson was thought to be a leading candidate for the presidency of Auburn University, but when the trustees chose Harry Philpott for the post, Anderson accepted a position at the University of Georgia similar to the one he had held at Auburn.

The Anderson House, like its neighbor next door, is a study in horizontality. Aside from the chimney stack protruding from the right side of the roof, no vertical elements are apparent, not even the line of small high windows under the street side eave. The low double-pitched roof line lends an oriental air to the design and emphasizes its firm attachment to the grade.

Brookwood Drive

Dr. John Winfield Scott, at the time dean of science and literature at A.P.I., designed and supervised the building of a large, elaborate house on the eve of the Second World War, with the intention, apparently, of occupying it himself. In the late 1930s Dr. Scott became extensively involved in his own personal building and property development. Auburn lore includes at least two different accounts for the fact that he never occupied this house, which small-town Auburn considered to be a mansion. One story is that because President Luther Duncan removed Scott from his post, financial considerations precluded his residing in his "mansion." The other explanation is that Mrs. Scott's heart condition prevented her using the upper floor, so that Dean (as he continued to be called) Scott built another house, with only one story, diagonally across the street on Brookwood Drive, where they lived until their deaths.

After several tenants occupied the structure pictured here, Emil Wright, a local banker and successful businessman, bought the building. It has remained in that family's possession ever since and is now occupied by the original purchaser's son and daughter-in-law, Dr. Emil Wright Jr. and his wife, Margaret, who raised their family here.

Scott-Wright House, 500 Brookwood Drive.

The house is noted for solid construction and large rooms, particularly two unusually large bedchambers, one upstairs and one down, both of which have anterooms, rather outsized for dressing rooms and of otherwise undetermined usage. The exterior appearance of the house most closely approximates the Tudor revival architectural style, with the steeply pitched roof, heavy chimneys, and half-timber effects. The metal windows, which have always been a problem to use and maintain, are fitted with an unexplained variety of arches. Scott set the house in a large acreage that includes extensive woodland that has remained undivided. A garage with two attached rooms matches the design of the house.

EAST MAGNOLIA AVENUE

The Baughman-Honour House was designed by and built for Ohio native William Dryden Baughman, who attended and later taught at A.P.I. It was constructed in 1929 by out-of-state contractor Fred Burt. The house is notable in this area for its striking French-Norman style, emphasized by a large turret in the front that spawned the local nickname, "The Castle." Its interior features French millwork, Gothic archways, and heart pine floors.

Sometime in the early 1940s, the house became the center of a local divorce scandal. Baughman, a teacher of engineering and building construction at A.P.I., began an affair with an out-of-town woman with whom he communicated through a private post office box. When this was discovered, the Baughmans divorced. Their son dropped the surname Baughman and had his name legally changed to William Dryden, his mother's surname. He was called thereafter simply Dryden. The second floor was not finished due to the Depression.

Honour-Baughman House, 420 E. Magnolia.

In 1949, Wilfred Honour, a faculty member in civil engineering and architectural construction, bought the house and surrounding property. The Honours left the house in the early 1960s and for years let it to a variety of tenants. One of those with an artistic sense of humor once fashioned a long Rapunzel-style braid and hung it from the high turret window.

In 1996, after the death of the Honours, Warren and Mary Ann Stiles bought the house and finished the second story, which included the Rapunzel tower. The house continues today as rental property owned by M. A. Stiles.

In a part of the town where many properties within walking distance of the campus were razed, the Baughman-Honour House demonstrated another approach. The house was saved and shielded the newer apartments, in a complementary style with small turrets, built behind it.

Below, Showalter House; bottom, the rear of the house about 1940 (from *The Runaway Train*).

East Samford Avenue

The house that Walter Burkhardt designed for Benjamin Showalter, director of extension teaching in the A.P.I. School of Education, is by far the most notable, authentic, and successful shingle-style house in Auburn. While "shingle style" refers to a house entirely covered with shingles, it also refers to a stylistic approach that rejects the "revivalist" inclination of many, even most, architectural styles that architects and builders had pursued for upscale houses before the Showalter House was built in 1931.

The Showalter House is skillfully adapted to the sloping site, even though the elevations are conventional. Beneath the living spaces was a garage floor, seen in a 1943 photo illustration from the successful children's book *The Runaway Train*. The Z-braced plank window shutters seen in this view are no longer used on the house.

From an aesthetic point of view, the building, once also the home of the Eugene and Alva Current-Garcia family, conveys modesty with a restrained entranceway and a homely, rural quality with its gray color. The current owners of the house use the space for an art studio/gallery.

Dayspring Natural Grocery, 223 Opelika Road

Of the numbers of classic Craftsman bungalows that once graced Auburn neighborhoods, few remain standing, and of those that do, few remain in their original form. For many years the Dayspring Natural Grocery on Opelika Road was the home of the Boris family, part of the small Greek community in Auburn. Mr. Boris was an employee of the treasured (now

Dayspring Grocery, 223 Opelika Road.

lamented) Auburn Grille, founded and run by the Gazes brothers. In the 1970s the building became the Dayspring Natural Grocery.

The footprint of the building is rectangular, the roof a simple gable type. The marks of Craftsman style are easily seen in the street view—brackets under the gable roof, exposed ends of rafters supporting the porch roof, and sets of double supports under that, themselves on masonry bases in a stepped design on both sides of the center stair. Underneath the porch, the front door with a large transom light above is flanked by double windows, each window composed of nine lights over one, a familiar Craftsman preference.

The appropriate and attractive current color scheme of the building—dark brown, cream, and white—could easily have been the original one.

Armstrong Street

The Moore-Tamblyn-Shaw House at 337 Armstrong Street was purchased in 1922 from Mary Samford, the adjoining property owner to the south, by William McDow Moore and his wife, Maria Giles Perrin Moore. The Moores had come to Auburn in 1911 to seek educational opportunities at Alabama Polytechnic Institute for their son, James, but James died in 1912 before that dream was realized. Their daughter Sarah Evelyn became an A.P.I. graduate in 1916, and their third daughter, Florida, married Jack Tamblyn in December of 1920. They were married in the Ingalls House on South Gay Street, and in 1924, their son, Billy, was born in the front bedroom of their Armstrong Street home. In 1942 the Moores sold the house to their daughter Florida Tamblyn, ". . . for the consideration of $1.00." Fourth generation Moore great-granddaughter Anne Tamblyn Shaw and husband Larry bought and restored the house in recent years, and it continues to anchor the extended Moore-Tamblyn family as a gathering place. Anne Shaw considers this one of the few homes in Auburn that remains under the ownership of the original family.

The Tamblyn House fits easily into the category of early twentieth-century Craftsman style even though it lacks some of the usual Craftsman features. It may be thought a local interpretation of Craftsman style and a thoroughly competent one, featuring the hipped roof, wide dormer, four-over-one double hung sash, and front door with upper divided lights. Built soon after World War I, the house was described in a 1922 insurance application as having ". . . three bedrooms and one bath, indoor plumbing, city water, electricity, gas space heaters, fireplaces in living room and bedrooms, clapboard siding, composite roof, and brick foundation pedestals." Originally there was a screened sleeping porch on its back southeast corner. Today the house has the original interior doors, hardware, windows, hinges for window screens, and even the original nail in the mantelpiece where Billy Tamblyn hung his Christmas stocking and the loose brick in the fireplace where he always imagined secret messages to be hidden. The only significant changes to the house include the enclosure of the screened sleeping porch, the addition of brick skirting around the entire structure, and, in the late 1950s, the replacing of wooden front porch support columns with poured concrete columns built by Jack Tamblyn, using forms he designed to replicate the original columns.

Tamblyn House, 337 Armstrong.

Historically speaking, the Tamblyn House is in the approximate location of Auburn founder Judge Harper's third and largest house, dubbed by a later tenant as "Cedre Villa" in recognition of the wealth of cedar trees on the property. Tamblyn family history, indeed, refers to the property's cedar trees as an economic resource that the family exploited in hard times, and a number of historic cedars remain on the property.

North Gay Street

The Wilmore House, built in 1901 for the John J. Wilmore family, was originally in a thriving residential neighborhood. It is said that when John Wilmore arrived in Auburn in 1888, he was dismayed by what he found but for lack of money to go further on the train and for fear of falling prey to a yellow fever epidemic in Montgomery, he was forced to stay in Auburn and fulfill his commitment to teach at the college. Over time he become a principal contributor to the college's emergence as a force in engineering education, eventually becoming dean of engineering and a mainstay of the

Top, Wilmore House, 413 N. Gay; above, the Wilmore House (ca. 1910).

A.P.I. administration. In 1897 or 1898, John Wilmore and Charles Cary acquired several properties at the Halliday estate sale, including the property on which this house was built and the much larger property containing the Halliday-Cary-Pick House, which adjoined the Wilmore parcel. From Drake Avenue to the north and the railroad to the south, the Wilmore House is the only remaining residential building on the west side of North Gay Street.

When Dean Wilmore died in 1943, the Cary family purchased this property from his estate. While General Lewis Andrew Pick, Cary's son-in-law, was serving in Burma during World War II, his wife, Alice, and her mother, Emma Cary, conducted a brisk real estate business. They purchased the Wilmore House, converting it into two apartments and renting them to tenants. Eventually the house was inherited by a family member, who recently sold it to a new owner, who has returned the building to its original single-family configuration, substantially updated the interior, and greatly improved the view of the house from the street. No records have been found to identify the designer and contractor for the Wilmore House. Considering that Wilmore was a trained engineer, one can only assume that he paid close attention to structural details as the building rose, but perhaps not so much to its aesthetic qualities. The design of the Wilmore House does not closely follow fashionable stylistic models of the time. In comparison, for example, to the Little House, just a block to the south across the railroad tracks, it is quite plain, notwithstanding the nicely proportioned first-floor bay window jutting toward the front. There is no explanation of the prominent glass-enclosed area, perhaps enclosing an original porch or perhaps a later addition altogether. Cross gables of the roof draw attention upwards and suggest that verticality was in the designer's mind, even though the building site afforded ample room to extend the design outward rather than upward. On the other hand, since nearby houses on the block were all single story—with the notable exception of the Drake-Samford House at the north end of the block—perhaps a building that would stand out among the neighbors would have been a desirable goal.

The absence of decorative exterior detail is puzzling and perhaps misleading. Was it simply removed as the house was renovated on occasion? A small circular window of stained glass on the south side of the house suggests that the original designer or occupant was not averse to embellishment, so perhaps some now removed evidence of decorative taste was once part of the design.

West Thach Avenue

E. L. (Edward Lee) Spencer was a major force in Auburn business and community life (see p. 99 concerning Lincoln Heights). His wife, Florence, and son, E. L. Spencer Jr., contributed significantly as well. The architectural culmination of the Spencer Sr.'s work in Auburn was a house on a large tract of land at first only adjacent to the town but now part of it.

Several Spencers, members of a North Carolina family, arrived in Auburn in 1920, but only E. L. Spencer Sr. remained permanently. He came with a UNC degree, decorated service in the First World War, and, like numbers of other North Carolinians, a shrewd intention to develop a lumber business,

The siting of the Spencer House.

which began modestly with a sawmill. By 1932 he had organized the E. L. Spencer Lumber Company only half a block from the competing Auburn Ice & Coal Company.

E. L. Spencer was an important supplier of building materials in Auburn; he leased tracts of timberland around Auburn and even farther away, and he also produced dimensioned lumber with his sawmill. Youngsters growing up in Auburn will remember their parents' dire warnings about playing in the huge sawdust pile that collected at the bottom of the Samford Avenue hill. The sawdust was so loosely compacted, it was alleged, children playing on it might be sucked into the pile and fatally suffocate!

Business success and community service led to an invitation to join the board of the

Top, the Spencer House, 1236 W. Thach; above, an interior view; right, the pine paneling was testimony to the Spencer family's lumber business.

Bank of Auburn in 1944. As Spencer business developed, the family lived at the corner of Samford and Payne Street, across from the new Lee County High School, in one of the trim bungalows that still stands in that place. The family cut an admirable swath of accomplishments across Auburn history. Florence Spencer, wife and mother, reached far from family responsibilities to extensive service with the Presbyterian Church, including service as its first female elder. Their son, Edward Lee Spencer Jr., following stellar records in high school, college, and military service, was a Fulbright scholar, after which he returned to Auburn to develop the family's lumber and building supply businesses, eventually becoming president of the Bank of Auburn in 1990.

It was perhaps to be expected that the family's contributions to Auburn and record of business success should be expressed in an impressive home: impressive in its location—looking over the town from a slight rise to its west; in its style—a modern version of a traditional plantation mansion; and in its materials—on the house's exterior, the carefully finished horizontal wooden weatherboarding makes a sharp contrast with the white columns of the giant portico, and a second-floor balcony over the entrance door is fitted with full surrounding side and transom lights below. The interior, in an altogether fitting acknowledgment of the source of the Spencer family success, is largely paneled in pine of varying shades, possibly its natural appearance years after milling and without obvious stain or clear finish. The design of the house was apparently E. L. Spencer Sr.'s own. According to family members, he acted also as supervising contractor. The principal builder was Bob McMillan of Opelika.

9

Close Quarters: Multi-Unit Dwellings

Auburn's reputation as "the loveliest village" was largely built on the picturesque college buildings of the campus and the churches and family homes of the surrounding town. The growth of student enrollment and staff and the subsequent growth of the town supporting that expansion introduced a variety of multi-unit residential building types in Auburn. The community had become accustomed to renting rooms in family homes to students, but the purpose-built rooming houses and early fraternity houses were prologue to a variety of multi-unit and multifamily residential buildings that represent if not a fundamental change in the character of the town at least a significant additional note to it.

The multi-unit residential buildings associated with the college are not the central focus here, but those had their origins in the twentieth century, with the earliest fraternity houses. This history is more fully set out in Ralph Draughon's account in *Lost Auburn*. Two of these early fraternity buildings survive, though neither is still used as a fraternity house. The 1901 Kappa Alpha fraternity built its chapter house on South Gay Street.

Below left, Kappa Alpha Fraternity House; right, the structure repurposed as Dr. B. F. Thomas's office.

There is some reason to think that it was designed by Frank Dudley, who designed the home of close friends Dr. and Mrs. Mell, enthusiastic patrons of the Kappa Alpha members. The fraternity building later became the office of Dr. B. F. Thomas and is still owned by members of the Thomas family intent on protecting this Auburn landmark. Now divided into several apartments, this rental property remains to testify to its rich Auburn history, both fraternal and medical.

In 1916, the Lambda Chi fraternity built on West Magnolia Avenue the chapter house that Nathaniel Curtis Sr. had designed for them. Today only parts of it can be glimpsed within and above the Toomer Place commercial additions surrounding it.

The first college foray into residential accommodations was the 1908 combined dining facility and dormitory, Smith Hall. The architect was chosen through a design competition and the contractor through a low-bid competition. The architect, William Warren of Montgomery and Birmingham, was an alumnus; the builder, J. A. Cullars, was an Auburn townsman. The building, facing Samford Hall across South College Street, has endured fires and restorations and many changes of purpose and tenants, but the merits of its design are still recognized by architects and public alike.

Top, Lambda Chi Alpha House as built; above, the house is now overshadowed by Toomer Place on W. Magnolia. Below, Smith Hall, 135 S. College.

The boarding house as a residential type is an essential part of Auburn history, but most such establishments began as ordinary single-family houses. Perhaps the largest and best known of these was Mrs. Terrell's. The house was originally a rather elaborate postbellum structure built by J. E. Gachet and inherited from him by his son, an Auburn dentist. Mrs. Terrell bought the house from the dentist when he

Top, Mrs.Terrell's Boarding House, Mitcham Avenue & North Gay Street; above, Cary Castle, 348–350 N. College.

left Auburn. Under her supervision, it evolved into a large establishment that housed and fed many an Auburn student.

In 1908, Dr. Charles A. Cary built the building known derisively as "Cary's Castle" on the property he owned next to his home on North College Street, the Halliday-Cary-Pick House (see p. 166). In 1892, when Dr. Cary arrived in Auburn to establish a school of veterinary medicine, there was limited student housing available. He was informed by the college that he was responsible for the housing of his students, so Dr. Cary's first thirteen "disciples" studied, ate, slept, and lived with the Cary family in their home at 360 North College Street. Each evening Dr. Cary and Mrs. Cary ate family-style with the students before sending them off to the third floor with a strict curfew. What an educational environment that must have been!

In 1908, with a growing number of students and surely some interesting adventures with the students living in his home, Dr. Cary decided to construct housing for his veterinary students at 348–350 N. College Street, next door to his own home. Dr. Cary's enthusiasm for the project was so great that he took a direct part in the building's construction during which he suffered a dangerous fall from the roof. A family account has it that Dr. Cary would not permit any attention to his injury except by his great friend and fellow veterinarian, Dr. McAdory.

Even with three stories, Cary's Castle sits comfortably among the one- and two-story homes on both sides of its block. It is, nonetheless, distinctive for its stuccoed walls and the design of its roof, variously termed jerkinhead, clipped-gable, hip-on-gable, or hipped-gable. The double curving wrought-iron stairs to the second floor are not part of the original design but were added in the 1960s.

The Castle may be considered one of Auburn's first private "dormitories." After Dr. Cary's death in 1936, his widow, Emma Heck Cary, rented to female students. According to local reports, she ran a tight ship with strict rules. Now, well over one hundred years later, this structure, located in Auburn's designated historic district, continues to function as rental property under the caring eyes of the Cary's great-grandson Charles Cary Pick.

Although we ordinarily attach some symbolic values to homes, utilitarian considerations may be uppermost in instances of multiple unit domestic housing. Apartment complexes such as Cary's Castle on North College Street, the Wright Apartments that until their demolition in 2016 faced the Presbyterian Church on Thach Avenue, the Moton Apartments on Martin Luther King Boulevard, or private dormitories such as Wittel Dormitory and Auburn Hall are all extant examples of utilitarian needs fulfilled.

As a rule, in the early years of the college most students and young professors boarded in private homes and in larger boarding houses. Local history is replete with stories of the bonds that developed between boarders and landlords. One good example would be Dr. George Petrie, who as a newly employed professor of history boarded in the home of Patrick and Annie Mell along with six additional student boarders. Dr. Mell was a professor of geology and botany and director of the weather service at the college. In later years Petrie wrote of Annie Mell: "She made us feel that it was our home and we were members of her family. She looked after us bodily and spiritually, fed the hungry, spurred the lazy, and comforted those in trouble. Everybody in town was her friend and her home was its center."

One extant example of a family home that took in boarders is the Lamar House at 311 North College, which is discussed at greater length and depicted in a photo in the previous chapter.

Hinds House

In August of 1913, V. Mitchell Drake began selling portions of the original James F. White property, which he had inherited. One of the first portions he sold, a lot on the corner of Ridge Grove and Main Street (Bragg and College), was to Warren Elmer Hinds for $500 to build a two-story Colonial Revival frame house. Dr. Hinds was head of the department of entomology at the college and was state entomologist at the Alabama Experiment Station on the A.P.I. campus. His wife, Edith, was active in the college community, and in 1913 she reportedly worked with President Thach's wife,

Above left, Hinds House in 1925; right, Hinds House as SAE Fraternity, N. College.

Nellie, as decorations chairman for Auburn's first homecoming celebration.

Professor Hinds and his wife moved to Baton Rouge, Louisiana, in 1924, where he became the head of the department of entomology at Louisiana State University and Louisiana's state entomologist. They sold their corner lot and frame house in Auburn for $10,000 to the Alabama Alpha Mu Fraternal Association, Sigma Alpha Epsilon. The fraternity added brick veneer to the house along with additional entertainment and living space. The SAEs remained at this location, except for a short time during World War II, until the construction of a new house in the late 1950s on "new" fraternity row on West Magnolia Avenue. When the majority of the student men were away in the service during the war, Auburn coeds lived in the house.

The North College Street Historic District describes the house as follows: "Circa 1914. Hinds House. Two-story Colonial Revival. Brick veneer exterior (added, 1925), originally frame gable, 12/12 slope with decorative dormers, asphalt shingles, two side-wall fireplaces. Arch front entry."

Other fraternities have subsequently owned the house, and at present, the Chi Phi Fraternity is still actively operating this property as a fraternity house—Auburn's oldest fraternity house. The SAEs were one of the first "neighbors" in the Bragg Avenue and College Street neighborhood, and they were one of the first to move on. Times changed—fraternities wanted more modern houses closer to the campus, and as the college opened up new property, fraternities began to move away from the center of the Auburn community on to college property. The SAEs departure was only the beginning of the changes that lay ahead for one of Auburn's oldest neighborhoods.

NEIGHBORHOOD RECOLLECTIONS

For almost thirty-five years the SAEs were part of the Bragg and College neighborhood and reportedly were good neighbors. One of the Lamar grandchildren from next door, Ceola Lamar Fancher, said she always remembered the fraternity boys being nice. She recalled, "They would come over to my grandmother Lamar's house and help with little repairs or chores, and she was likewise willing to help them with small tasks like sewing on a button. As a small child, when I came to visit 'Ma,' I remember them coming over and playing ball with us in the front yard."

Lifelong Auburn resident Ida Wright Folmar said, "When I was a college girl I remember the SAEs being great gentlemen. They had a wonderful housemother who truly felt like the boys were her sons. The housemother in those days cracked the whip and she was sure the boys minded their manners. She invited townspeople over for Sunday dinner and tried to make real gentlemen out of her boys."

Virginia Young Priest, Evans Young's daughter, grew up in the house on College Street directly across the street to the east of the fraternity house. She said, "The boys who lived there were always nice, but I have some funny stories about those days. Of course, there wasn't any air conditioning back then, so when the weather was warm their windows and ours were always open, and you could hear everything that was going on. The boys sat out on their front porch, and we could hear all they were saying, and they could see everything we were doing. We had a rule that we were always to make sure our blinds were closed. I remember I came home from a picnic late one afternoon and ran upstairs in a hurry to get ready for a date. When my date came to the front door, one of the fraternity boys hollered across the street and said, "Don't take her out. She hasn't had time to take a bath." Another one of the boys yelled out, "YES, SHE HAS!"

Dan Benson, who grew up on Bragg a few houses down from the SAEs, said, "As a kid I never went to any of their parties, but I loved it at homecoming when they would tear down their homecoming decorations. As soon as they piled all the wood from their float up on the trash I would go down there and bring it all back to my house. I love wood and still today I have a hard time passing a trash pile on the side of the road without stopping and seeing if there is any good wood in it."

Tom Sparrow, who grew up just two houses down from the fraternity, said, "I remember their initiations. There was a small balcony on the back of the house, and they would put the pledges below the balcony and drop eggs into their mouths. When it was time for initiation, we all hid our cats because they would make each pledge catch a certain number of cats. The cats that survived were let go after initiation, and that is probably why we always had so many stray cats on our street. The 'E Boys' were all pretty nice guys and having a fraternity as a neighbor was just part of growing up in Auburn."

Top, the building of Auburn Hall, 1937; above, Auburn Hall at 210 E. Thach; below, Wittel Dormitory, 205 S. Gay.

SAMUEL SYLVESTER WITTEL, BUILDER

When Samuel Wittel from Demopolis, Alabama, entered Auburn as a freshman in 1930, he found it extremely difficult to secure suitable student lodging. At the time, his father, Samuel Sylvester Wittel, operated a business in Demopolis that made handles, and he held the patent for a lathe that turned the handles. The senior Wittel saw a business opportunity in the need for student housing in Auburn and so in the early 1930s he and his wife, Estelle, moved to Auburn and began what would be a distinguished business career in property management and building construction. His first major project was construction of Wittel Dormitory for men (later known as Auburn Hall) at 210 E. Thach Avenue.

Sam and Estelle Wittel's granddaughters, Pat Tremaine and Barbara McIntyre, describe their grandfather as a builder and say he sketched a plan for what he wanted his buildings to be and then oversaw their construction. A local resident, John Curry, came to Auburn as a student in 1937 and lived in Wittel Dormitory. He tells many stories about how kind Mrs. Wittel was to all of the students. Curry got free rooming because each week his father shipped Mrs. Wittel two cases of eggs by train from down in Monroe County. Mr. Curry recounts that the eggs had to make two train transfers, but they always arrived in perfect condition—not a single cracked egg. The Wittels operated the men's dormitory until 1945, when the Auburn Alumni Association purchased the property and gave it to the college; it was renamed Auburn Hall.

At 205 South Gay Street, Sam Wittel designed and oversaw the construction of a second dormitory, also named Wittel Dormitory, which backed up to the original Wittel Dormitory site. This 24,000-square foot, four-story structure was designed to house the Wittel family, including the Wittel's son, Dave, and his family, and professional women, for whom there was limited housing in Auburn. The 1940 census shows twenty-two young professional women living in Wittel Dormitory (secretaries, stenographers, clerks, etc.). Enrollment rose dramatically after World War II, and Wittel Dormitory became the first private dormitory for female Auburn students. The structure features copper roof details, wood floors throughout, silver plate applied to the front entrance ceilings, private bathrooms, and Auburn's first elevator. In 2017, a new owner acquired the building and converted it into the boutique-style Collegiate Hotel.

Over the years, Sam Wittel built many other projects in the Auburn-Opelika area. He built and managed apartments, duplexes, and houses, and constructed the bowling alley on Opelika Road and the A&P grocery store in Opelika.

Moton Apartments

The Moton Apartments (700 Martin Luther King Drive) are one of the first public housing developments in Auburn, along with the East Park Apartments (Dean Road), which were constructed at the same time in 1952; the first tenants in the development moved in on September 2, 1952. These were segregated buildings—the Moton Apartments housed African Americans, and the East Park Apartments were for white people only. The Moton Apartments were named after Robert Russa Moton, a Hampton Institute-educated man who served as the second president of Tuskegee Institute from 1915–1935. Construction of Moton was funded with the assistance of a $250,000 construction loan from the federal government. The apartments were built to provide adequate housing for lower income citizens who previously had no other housing options. The Moton Apartments were closed in August 2006, at which time the City of Auburn and the Auburn Housing Authority began planning to develop the property.

Moton Apartments, 700 MLK, street view.

The original architectural style of the Moton Apartments mimicked that of the row house/barracks-style public housing that was constructed all over the United States in the early 1950s. The most well-known public housing project with similar architecture is the Altgeld/Murray housing in

AUBURN'S MOST UNUSUAL MULTI-FAMILY HOUSING

Bat House Uncovered

Almost every student at Auburn has heard about the mysterious bats that once lived in Samford Hall and the bat house that was built for them to relocate to and live in; however, not many have heard the actual story or seen the bat house. Well now there is evidence for all students to be able to experience and have true knowledge of these bat stories.

A fair amount of Brazilian Free-tailed bats once inhabited the attic and the bell tower of Samford Hall back in the early 1990s. Due to the fear that the bats were chewing the roof of Samford Hall and to the misconception of bats, action was needed to remove the bats from Samford. "The bats needed to be moved to another location but without being harmed," states Dr. Troy Best, Biological Sciences professor at Auburn.

Graduate students Mark Kiser and Mindy Mylum, with the assistance of the School of Forestry and Wildlife Sciences, worked on a bat house for relocation and roosting of the bats as their thesis project. A bat house was chosen to be built as a new home for the bats because Brazilian Free-tailed bats in the Southeast roost only in man-made structures. Auburn's bat house was researched and modeled after the University of Florida's bat house, which has become an outstanding success. "Auburn University Facilities built the bat house, which is a wooden house raised high on stilts, while Kiser and Mylum duplicated and monitored the surroundings and temperature of Samford Hall to match that of the bat house," says Best.

The bat house was being built not only to rid their existence at Samford Hall, but also as a "home" or a safe place for the bats to have to roost and relocate their colony. Auburn University and the School of Forestry and Wildlife Sciences made the correct decision by choosing to build the bat house as an alternate "home" for the bats instead of removing them without

worry of their safety. Bats, which may be the most misunderstood animal in the United States, actually rank among the most beneficial due to their enormous consumption of insects.

Bats suffer from a bad public image in much of the world; misconceptions and superstitions about them are numerous, states Best. Most bats are highly beneficial, intelligent, interesting, and possess fascinating abilities such as homing instinct and the ability to navigate in complete darkness by listening to echoes reflected back to them.

"Bats need to be appreciated by the public, but also people need to be aware of bats and knowledgeable of them. We want the Auburn community to be aware of the high bat population in this area and to not be afraid of them" Best states.

The bat house was not a success in terms of maintaining a permanent residence of the free-tailed bats from Samford Hall and throughout the community; however, it did remove the bats from Samford Hall, says Dr. Jim Armstrong, Auburn professor and Extension Wildlife Specialist. Armstrong was involved with the bat house project because of his bat education and experience through being a wildlife biologist. He feels that the hardest task of the project was removing and relocating the bats to the new structure.

"Bats are able to squeeze through a quarter-size hole without difficulty, so confirming that every hole or vent possible for a bat to enter is pend and blocked off is difficult work," Armstrong says.

Also, due to bats' homing instinct, the ability to return home after being displaced into unfamiliar territory, Armstrong knew that relocating the bats would be no easy task, but was definitely worth it.

The bats were removed from Samford Hall by placing a netting flap over the entrance ways and openings around the attic vents and between the walls and roof. This netting was tacked down at the top but not at the bottom so that it operated as a flap door when exiting. The bats would be able to leave through the flap, but not be able to enter back through because they are not able to lift it up to re-enter. Once all bats had been removed properly, the openings were sealed, says Best.

There are various factors and opinions on why the bat house was not a success by becoming a home and permanent roost for the free-tailed bats. Armstrong states that the area chosen for the bat house was heavily wooded and too thick for the bats to being forging.

"Free-tailed bats prefer open areas to being forging; not very many of these bats are found in woody areas. Because of these conditions, along with others, the bats did not stay at the constructed bat tower," says Armstrong.

Best also feels that the site of the bat house was a factor affecting the relocation of the bats and was not best suitable for free-tailed bats to being a colony. "Samford Hall is an open area; duplicating the structure, environment, and temperature of it into a bat house is very difficult. The duplications that were made from Samford to the bat house were excellent, but hard for the bats to adapt to and the area was not open enough for travel of the bats," Best states.

Although the bat house project was not successful in terms of maintaining a permanent colony . . .

(See full article at www.theloveliestvillage.org)

Chicago. The Moton Apartments were built on monolithic concrete slabs. These two-story structures were of concrete block interior construction with brick veneer exteriors, and the units were separated only by six- to eight-inch concrete slabs; providing no spacing between floors. Interior outside walls were painted concrete block with no insulation and no separation space for running electrical wiring or ductwork. The original roofs were well-worn pitched and asphalt-shingled with little to no overhang. The units did not have central air conditioning and heating.

The work to preserve some of Moton's past while encouraging redevelopment for a brighter future for residents and surrounding neighborhoods was a collaborative effort between the City of Auburn and the Auburn Housing Authority at the request of the Alabama Historical Commission. In August 2008, as part of the redevelopment planning process, interviews were conducted with previous Moton residents Verlinda White, Jessie Williams, and Idella Dowdell, who urged decreased density and provisions for developing a more suitable living environment with a greater sense of community.

The Moton redevelopment project was completed in 2011 with greatly decreased density (one-half the number of original apartment buildings), new landscaping, sidewalks, and adequate parking. The buildings were designed with new metal hip-roofs and matching hip-roof porches extending the length of the buildings.

Auburn's Earliest Student Dormitory?

The living accommodations that awaited prospective Auburn students did not seem promising in the early 1920s. In 1922, the *Montgomery Advertiser* reported:

> Auburn has no dormitory for boys and only a very small one for girls. A temporary frame building, constructed during the war, houses 165 boys while some live in tents. The town of Auburn is very small and accommodations for students in private homes is extremely limited . . .
>
> Dr. Spright Dowell spoke of the long neglect of the state legislature in providing adequate dormitory space for the 1,400 students many of whom are now

Auburn's earliest private dormitory, 1925.

> being compelled to stay in tents provided by the government on account of this neglect on the part of our state government.

And then, as reported by the *Columbus Daily Enquirer* on October 15, 1922:

> A fire of unknown origin completely destroyed the "Barracks" boys' dormitory, of the Alabama Polytechnic Institute at an early hour this morning [October 14]. The loss will exceed $30,000. The students rooming there, numbering about 250, saved but little of their belongings.

What's more natural, then, that some enterprising Auburnite would decide to build a private dormitory in town! This building on Glenn Avenue is sometimes said to be the first private student dormitory in Auburn (though Cary Castle predates it, see p. 208). It was built in the 1920s and sits perpendicular to the street on land that was once part of the extensive holdings of Mary Cox; the dormitory may even have been her own project. The building was later purchased by the Alabama Commission for Human Rights and used for their offices for many years. It is now unoccupied, allegedly for sale, and likely to be demolished in order to develop more fully the substantial undeveloped property around it.

Duplexes at, below, 442–444 N. Gay Street, 1978, and bottom, Miller Avenue.

Duplexes

As an Auburn building type, the duplex deserves an in-depth study of its own. But the present survey can only document what these duplexes look like and where they are, not often who designed or built them and why. It is the case that most, perhaps all, were rental units, although occasionally an owner lived in half and rented the other half. Auburn duplexes appeared in several styles and configurations. The architectural term "duplex" has acquired a great flexibility, but here it is confined to the form in which a single residential structure is divided into two apartments with a separate entrance for each.

The rationale for building in this way seems most readily accounted for in economic terms, though some "politico-aesthetic" considerations (that is, regard for zoning ordinances) may be involved as well. Duplexes are more economical to build because at least one wall serves both apartments and because some utilities may be provided from single entry points rather than two. To conform to the character of a residential neighborhood, the footprint of a duplex is ordinarily about the same size as the footprint of a single-family house.

During the 1920s and 1930s, duplexes were built in many Auburn neighborhoods in the rather plain style that Depression-era homebuilding necessitated. On North Gay Street, the Auburn Ice and Coal Company built the duplex among the row of rental properties it constructed on lots available on the east side of the street. It became an early home for the Gritz and Coppedge families soon after they came to Auburn.

Another duplex in about the same style, although with the amenity of broader porches at both entrances, was built on Miller Avenue. For many years, the western half of the building was the home of Isbell Goff, longtime secretary of the Auburn Presbyterian Church.

Although similar in style but somewhat more elaborate for its larger size was the duplex on East Glenn Avenue. Two such duplexes were built side by side in this location. One of these was the home for many years of Elizabeth "Tootsie" Wilder and was moved to another location no longer remembered. Thus far, the mania for raze-and-redevelop in this part of Auburn has not taken the remaining Glenn Avenue.

Below, Wilder Duplex, 318 E. Glenn; bottom, 130 Bragg Avenue Duplex.

Plain-style was not always the character of the Auburn duplex. To an extent, "stylishness" correlates with size; the more stylish duplexes are usually larger than plainer ones. Consider the duplex at 130 Bragg Avenue, now the office of East Alabama Electric, Inc., an assembly of roof line, windows, entrances, materials, and site attractive enough to compete with any single-family house of the same size built at the same time. The building still exists, though it now

Duplexes at: top left, Samford Avenue; top right, 344 Thach; above left, 217–219 Casey, and above right, 533–535 Wright's Mill Road.

houses a commercial enterprise, like all the development that surrounds it.

Although more conventional in style, the duplex on the corner of Samford Avenue and Armstrong Street is quite as attractive as the one on Bragg, and fortunately, it is still a residence, apparently now converted from duplex to single-family home. Some longtime Auburn residents have no memory of this building as a duplex, notwithstanding that its appearance argues that it was built to be one.

An idiosyncratic feature of a number of small Auburn duplexes is the pair of arched rooflets protecting their front doors. Three of these buildings are still standing, perhaps more "charming" than "stylish" and certainly not "beautiful." Typically, they stand close to the sidewalk or street. The same rooflet feature is also found at the front door of the Bottoms House, which suggests it may have been a stock item with builders supply dealers.

301 E. Glenn.

Without the arched rooflets but also in a cottage style is the duplex with twin porticoes among several older buildings on the north side of East Glenn Avenue, now enclosed behind a solid wall adjacent to the sidewalk. The duplex is part of a group of residences all behind the wall, developed as "Shady Glenn" by contractor/developer Jim May.

Duplexes designed to fit into streetscapes without

Top left, 254–256 Payne Street; top right, 300–304 Payne Street; above left, 543–545 Wright's Mill Road; above right, 451–453 Wright's Mill Road.

standing out among their neighbors are invariably built of brick on previously unimproved lots. Two on Payne Street are good examples. The first pictured is said by an owner to have been the first duplex built in Auburn, although its style would not suggest that it is. The other, far more modest duplex fits comfortably on the same side of Payne Street.

On the other hand, duplexes that replace homes in older neighborhoods that suffer redevelopment are more likely to be designed to signal passersby: "Look at me!"

Two-story duplexes appear to have offered fewer possibilities for the imaginative styling their one-story relatives received. One of the earlier examples was built on South Gay Street in a vaguely classical revival mode. At first glance the building might be taken for a standard single-family home. The giveaway—two small windows above the front door, the location of a bathroom for each of the two units in the building.

A house first built as a duplex on Wright's Mill Road, now apparently converted to a single-family home, is distinctive in its simplicity, a welcome contrast to other two-story duplexes.

Despite the efforts of their designers, many of these two-story duplexes appear as rather ordinary and undistinguished domestic accommodations in Auburn neighborhoods. However, some effort for stylishness was made in these neighboring duplex buildings on the corner of Samford Avenue and

Top left, 328–330 E. Magnolia; top right, 339–341 S. Gay;
center left, 219–221 E. Samford; center right, 358–360 Armstrong;
above left, 354–356 Payne; above right, 360 Payne.

Armstrong Street. They were built for Dr. Luther Duncan in the early 1930s. It is clear that they were built to the same plan, varied by the location of entrances and the shape of the small central opening on the street face.

On both the Armstrong and Samford duplexes, the eight-over-eight window sash and the central projection under an accented gable in the facade relieves the otherwise utilitarian feeling of the buildings. On the Samford Avenue twin, centering the front door in the projection and placing it under a split pediment gives the building a more sophisticated appearance that the Armstrong Street duplex lacks. The brickwork on both buildings includes randomly placed off-color units that fortunately are barely noticeable from the street.

Two buildings on Payne Street typify the more recent insertions of duplexes into mostly single-family neighborhoods. The duplex pictured opposite on the lower left stands just as built, while the building on the lower right has been modified from its original duplex configuration into four apartments.

Top, 350 East Magnolia; above, Duplex Court.

The final duplex pictured that stands on the unimaginatively named "Duplex Court" appears to be the only actual duplex in that place. The building itself is unimaginative, strictly utilitarian, built of standard concrete block adorned only by a coat of white paint and a half-hearted portico at the front door.

10

Surviving by Relocation

An article of faith among preservationists is that where possible, buildings should be kept on their original sites. The reasons that buildings sometimes cannot remain on their original sites are many and, from the preservationist point of view, usually suspect. The alternative to removing a building by destroying it is to move it to another location. Auburn has a long history of promoting survival and preservation in this way. So far as reliable records are concerned, that history begins with the relocation of the chapel or assembly hall (see p. 20 text and photo) of the Auburn Masonic Female College from its North Gay Street location to the campus of the Agricultural and Mechanical College of Alabama, where it became Langdon Hall.

The often-told story of this move is available in at least two versions. In one, the building was placed on logs and rolled the block and a half from its original North Gay Street location to the campus, which then consisted of Old Main and, a little later, the utility and shop buildings. The story is altogether quite possible, for the original building would have been raised on heavy wooden plates that would have easily withstood the rigorous journey to the new site. And certainly students and town laborers could have provided sufficient manpower to do the job.

Facing page, from top: early view of Langdon Hall, 152 S. College; Langdon Hall today; the Armstrong House on Armstrong Street; Armstrong House at its present location at Gold Hill.

The alternate story is that the chapel was disassembled on its original site and reassembled on the campus. This account comes complete with the name of the person who produced drawings used in the reassembly process. He was William D. Wood (see p. 20 text and photo), a student who, according to newspaper accounts, was awarded a prize for his drawings of the chapel at his graduation from the college. What makes this account especially plausible is that it would have been far easier to reassemble the building upon the high brick basement that its new site required than to transfer it smoothly and intact from rollers.

Substantial alterations over the years—removal of the tower and elements of its decorative Gothic treatment, encasing the structure in a brick veneer, adding a portico, and changing the style to a more classical mode—have produced the attractive assembly hall that today is one of the featured buildings of the original campus.

Whichever story is true, the process of relocating the chapel was a primitive one compared with the elaborate preparations, machinery, and rearrangement of roads and utilities that contemporary relocation of buildings requires. Nonetheless, cost and inconvenience are often enough outweighed by other factors that compel relocation of buildings, reasons that are variously historical, aesthetic, sentimental, economic, or some combination of these.

The antebellum Armstrong-Ensminger House had presided over Armstrong Street, overlooking the edge of Pine Hill Cemetery, since the 1850s. The builder, of whom we have no record, gave the single-story house a then fashionable Greek style, with a wide and deep front porch behind square columns under a hipped roof. The columns were a standard local treatment; antebellum columns in the round were rarely used, perhaps in recognition of the skills of available local builders. An outbuilding in a complementary style was later placed close by the main house, apparently having been variously used as office, cook house, servants' quarters, and student rental units.

The patriarch of the Armstrong family, former Confederate Captain Henry Clay Armstrong, acquired the house after the Civil War. Armstrong distinguished himself after the war in a variety of public positions on the local (as trustee of Alabama Polytechnic Institute and Tuskegee Institute), state (as superintendent of education), and national (as

U.S. Consul General in Rio de Janerio) levels. After Henry Clay Armstrong died in 1900, other family members remained in the house. The Ensminger family, which succeeded the Armstrongs as proprietors of the house in the 1940s, judged that the picturesque qualities of the building on the original site had been unacceptably degraded by multi-unit and smaller residential properties to both sides.

Above, the Armstrong Annex at Gold Hill in ruins. Below, the White-Harris House when on Warrior Court; bottom left, the Harris staircase after the move; bottom right, the staircase restored.

Consequently, they moved the main house and the smaller companion building to open sites near Gold Hill. The main house, with an unobtrusive addition to the rear, now occupies a site in view of State Road 147. The original office annex building was relocated to a different site not visible from the main house. It was, for a time, a charming rental unit but now stands abandoned and in ruin.

The largest and most impressive of the known antebellum Greek Revival houses that once stood in Auburn and have been relocated from their original sites, and the one most elaborately restored, is conventionally known as the White-Harris House. Built in the mid-1850s by James F. White, its original location was on Warrior Court, a short side street off Bragg Avenue. It had so many owners that it was amusingly known as "the seven-name house" or the "White-Drake-Echols-Newton-Hubbard-Overstreet-Harris House."

In time, the neighborhood around it had become so crowded with commercial development that a few years ago the house was moved by the John T. Harris family to their property in Cusseta to be used as a family guest house. John T. and Eleanor Harris were married in the house when it was owned by the Newtons. Their six sons, in honor of their parents, moved and renovated the building. It is two stories, in typical Greek Revival style, with a small balcony that was extended the full width of the house when the building was renovated. Its crowning glory is a mahogany staircase as grand as the one lost in the Drake-Samford House. Preservation purists deplore moving historic structures from their original sites, but this house was saved and returned to its former splendor by relocation to Cusseta. It is now known simply as the Newton House after decades of a jumble of owners and renters. Mary Eleanora Reese, in an early history of Auburn, wrote that George W. Shelton and Sam Williams built the house, as well as other antebellum houses and the antebellum Methodist church.

Above, the Harris House (now the Newton House) at its present location in Cusseta. Below, the Neva Winston House on S. Gay; bottom, the house after its move to Kiesel Park.

One of Auburn's premier antebellum homes stood comfortably and notably on South Gay Street from the 1850s until the mid-1990s, known casually as "Neva Winston's house" and more formally as the Nunn-Winston House, named for the only two families that owned it on its original site. Samuel Nunn, an early Auburn settler and once trustee of the East Alabama Male College, had left the house to his daughter, who sold it to Thomas Harris Winston, from whom it was ultimately inherited by the unmarried Neva Winston.

The house, in typical Greek Revival style, was saved from threatened destruction by motel interests that acquired the property. Through efforts of the Auburn Heritage Association, the building was moved to Kiesel Park and restored there by the city. In the restoration project, the original square columns were replaced with round ones. The Neva Winston House is now available to the public as a meeting and entertainment venue.

For reasons that seem to defy logic, the United States Postal Service abandoned their handsome in-town New Deal-era post office in order to build

Top and above, the Steadham-Stewart House at 316 Opelika Road, and after its move to N. College Street.

another on Opelika Road—inconvenient, sweltering below its glass roof, understaffed, and so crowded oftentimes during the day that lines for service extend well into the entrance lobby. In the course of this mistake, the long row of distinguished—in some cases antebellum—houses that once lined the south side of this entrance street into Auburn was obliterated. One of the few survivors of this residential neighborhood is the Steadham-Stewart House, which had once been owned by General H. P. Harrison. It was rescued by the efforts of the Danny Blessing family, who moved it to Highway 147, the northward extension of College Street.

The original portion of the house, seen here, had a standard plan for 1850s Greek Revival cottage-style homes in this area. Subsequently, a leftward addition, said to have been built by one of owner Dr. Steadham's patients in lieu of paying the doctor's fee in cash, was added for rental income. To the extreme left was a gazebo-like extension, not visible in these photographs.

Glenn Cottage, not originally within the town limits, stood on a prime development property west of Auburn along the road to Loachapoka. As the structure was about to be razed, George Konstant, who was at the time restoring an antebellum house nearby on Chadwick Lane, noticed the old Glenn Cottage sitting up on a hill in the center of a site being cleared for development. When he inquired about the house, he was told it was his for the moving.

The Konstants had purchased property on Chadwick Lane in 2003, then consisting of one large house, two smaller houses, and a barn. Their family

Below left and right, Glenn Cottage on the Loachapoka Road, and as part of Konstant House on Chadwick Lane.

Glenn Cottage was split and its chimneys removed before being moved.

lived in one of the smaller houses while they were restoring the big house. Glenn Cottage was added as a wing on their main house and is now part of the larger structure, called Water Oak Manor. Although it is unrecognizable as the Glenn Cottage in the photograph on the facing page, which shows the wing that it became to the right, the historic fabric of the structure, at least, has been saved. Water Oak Manor is the Konstants' family home and is also used as an entertainment venue.

The cottage relocation was done by I. L. Davis House Movers. On the day of the move the Konstants let their children stay home from school and had relatives and friends come in to witness the big event. When the structure had been readied for the "pull," Mr. Davis reportedly told Mr. Konstant, "Don't you go too slow and hold me up." From start to finish, the pull took no more than *ten minutes*, and the Glenn Cottage was once again safe.

Top, the Boykin-Drake-Guthery House on N. College; above, the house now at Noble Hall.

Boykin-Drake-Guthery House

Another house from the antebellum era, now known as the Boykin-Guthery House, has survived two moves. The house was built around 1851 by Wallace Drake on North College Street in the area now designated a historic district. The owners moved it in the early 1920s to Bragg Avenue, selling the original site to A. L. Thomas for a new house in a then fashionable "Spanish" style, designed by his friend and former Auburn faculty colleague, N. C. Curtis. To avoid its destruction on Bragg Avenue, Ann Pearson, the mistress of Noble Hall, moved the Boykin-Drake-Guthery House to the grounds of Noble Hall on Shelton Mill Road in 2008. At its new home, two alterations are noticeable—a lengthened flight of steps and a higher foundation under the principal front approach, necessary to account for the steeper grade, and a dormer to facilitate the use of the attic space. This move was also engineered by I. L. Davis House Movers.

Zellers-Pace House

The Zellers-Pace House was home to Peter and Angeline Zellers, who migrated to the Auburn area from Troup County, Georgia, just prior to the Civil War. Eventually, two Pace brothers married two Zellers sisters and ownership of the house went to William Henry "Harry" Pace and his wife Annie Lou Zellers. The Harry Paces raised their nine children in this house before building a new "Sears-Roebuck" house on the southwest corner of South College Street and Donahue Drive in 1922 (now demolished). Mr. Pace, a 1911 A.P.I. graduate, was a farmer, dairyman, and one of the earliest county agents for Lee County.

For some years, various Pace family members lived in the house, and eventually it was divided into two apartments and used as rental property. One family member who lived in the house until she was four years old remembers that "it had a dog trot down the middle, and once you left the front porch you were almost immediately out the back door. The living

quarters were two rooms on each side of the hallway, and I remember the original kitchen was in a small building out back with a porch that connected the two buildings. There was a deep well just outside the kitchen where water was drawn each day in the earlier years."

The house with surrounding land was sold for development of a Walmart complex in the early 1980s. At the time of sale, the house sat on a rise or slight hill, which was cut away for the shopping development. The house by then was in such poor condition that the family would have given it away to anyone willing to have it moved. Mrs. Louise Turner to the rescue! Mrs. Turner saw possibilities in this old house and engaged I. L. Davis House Movers to move it to its present location off North College Street in the Farmville area.

From top, Zellers-Pace House before its move in the 1980s; as restored today near Farmville; an older photo of its curious front entrance.

On its original site, the Pace house was configured just as shown in this modern photograph, although without the south wing added after the move. The house, on Alabama Highway 147 (2270 North College Street), is now owned by Scott and Kristie Morrell. An earlier photograph reveals the elaborate front entrance to the house, any analysis of which is problematic in the extreme. The doorway with surrounding transom and sidelights appears to have been insinuated into an open dogtrot hallway. Curiously, the pilasters stop shy of where they ought to if intended to frame an opening. The arrangement suggests some expediency, as if the area immediately above the doorway had to be cut away in order to accommodate the transom, and that preexisting pilasters were left unaltered. The two cut lines extending to the ceiling have no obvious explanation.

With thanks to Robert Gamble, a further analysis of the history of this house is summarized here:

Assuming the two interior chimneys replaced earlier end chimneys, one could hypothesize that a frame, end-chimney dog trot had undergone an extreme makeover in the prosperous 1850s, with the result pictured here. Certainly, that's possible. An original gabled roof could have been replaced with a hip, another pair of rooms with intervening hall built across the back, and interior chimneys inserted between the two resulting pairs of rooms on each side. Far more than most folks realize, antebellum Alabamians remodeled—sometimes massively—rather than starting from scratch. As to the Auburn house: it is still difficult to account for the strange pilasters to either side of a rather nice doorway!

Dillard-Lane House

The Lane House is so called after its most notable resident, General James H. Lane, although the house stood at the corner of Thach and College Street for thirty years before he resided there. The frame house was built in 1853 to be the home of the Dillard family. In the 1880s the appearance of the house was substantially altered as shown here in the earliest available photograph. A later resident was Emory Glenn, the college treasurer. General Lane, who had served as an aide to Stonewall Jackson, became professor of civil engineering at the college after the war ended. He purchased the house in 1884. His daughter, Kate Meade Lane, was the last family resident.

Below, the Dillard-Lane House after it was altered in the 1880s; bottom, the house in Cary Woods.

One of Auburn's grande dames, Mollie Hollifield Jones, purchased the house in 1960 to be the home of the Woman's Club. The club moved the building from the southwest corner of Thach Avenue and College Street to its present location in 1962, engaging architect Frank Orr to advise it on preservation of the house on its new site in the Cary Woods section of Auburn. Through close analysis, Orr was able to determine a great deal about the original lines of the building. With his guidance the appearance and plan of the house was restored as close to its original appearance as he could determine.

BURTON HOUSE

Top, Burton's Four Story Cottage, E. Magnolia; above, Burton House now at 10 Roden Court in Opelika.

Robert W. Burton was as much an institution in Auburn as the bookstore he moved from Opelika and reopened on South College Street in 1878. Although the move was reportedly at the invitation of the faculty of the A&M College, another version is that he moved to Auburn because of his displeasure that Opelika had begun to allow liquor sales. His local reputation rested not only on this successful business but also on his talents as an author of humorous accounts of local color and descriptions of usually rural places and travel. In Auburn he and his wife built a handsome residence on East Magnolia Avenue, still remembered as the "four story cottage," so called in his own account because he paid for it by selling four stories to the Philadelphia magazine *Golden Days for Boys and Girls*. The house had, in fact, only a single story. The Burtons raised their son and two daughters there. Miss Lucile, as the unmarried older daughter was usually called, became a mainstay of the Auburn Presbyterian Church, serving as its treasurer for many years and, as leader of the local Women's Christian Temperance Union, an enthusiastic advocate to younger Auburnites for alcoholic abstinence. According to their accounts, at meetings of the WCTU in the "four story house," where she lived on after the deaths of her parents, bottles of various (allegedly human) organs, steeped in alcohol, were displayed to demonstrate the disastrous effects of that poison on the human body.

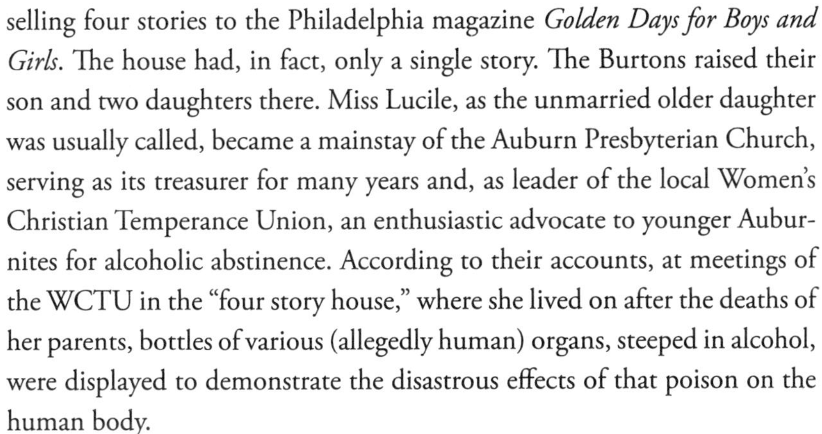

Mr. Burton's bookstore survived him by many years and was finally absorbed into Johnston & Malone Bookstore. The "four story cottage" on Magnolia Avenue enjoyed a different sort of survival. The Burton House was donated by Evans Realty Company to the Alabama Council on Human Relations. It was dismantled and moved to Opelika, where it now is part of the Darden Center complex. Over the years it has had several different uses, including being a Head Start center.

Wilder Duplex, 226 Glenn.

Wilder Duplex

Elizabeth Glenn Smith Wilder was a native Auburnite, a member of important Auburn families, and a force in Auburn in her own right. She had been secretary to the dean of engineering at A.P.I. and once served as a house mother and honorary member of Pi Beta Phi sorority. Mrs. Wilder, known as "Dee" or "Tootsie" to her friends in Auburn, lived at 226 Glenn Avenue, directly east of the corner of Glenn and Gay Street, where the Kappa Sigma fraternity house was once located. Her home was a duplex. Once the corner fraternity house was removed, Auburn's implacable urge for development threatened Mrs. Wilder's home. The duplex, however, was not razed but instead taken to a new home in north Auburn, the exact location of which is no longer remembered.

Trammell House

The Trammell House was built in the 1890s by the Cullars Brothers Construction Company and bears all the hallmarks of those late nineteenth- and early twentieth-century Auburn builders. J. V. Trammell, who worked with the Alabama Department of Agriculture, bought the house in the late 1930s. The last member of the Trammell family to live in the house was Frances Trammell, who moved out in 1982 when the property was sold to a developer.

The house was moved south of Auburn to the Sand Hill Road area in anticipation of its restoration. The work of moving the building was handled by the I. L. Davis Company, the proficient house moving company responsible for many projects of this type in eastern Alabama and adjoining areas of western Georgia.

As is common when buildings are moved, a small group of onlookers, many of them members of the family that had lived in the house for more than forty years, gathered to watch the process begin. Among them were John and Mary Trammell Freeman from

Below, Trammell House, 305 S. Gay; bottom, the house en route to Sand Hill Road.

Montgomery and Alton and Betty Little, parents of Lucy Little, who was largely responsible for rescuing the house from demolition by the purchaser of the property.

Top, Presbyterian Manse on Thach Avenue; above, the manse now on Turk Road.

Presbyterian Manse

Auburn Presbyterians built their minister's house, the Presbyterian Manse, in a more-or-less Dutch colonial style. It stood on Thach Avenue to the west of the 1917 church, where it became the home of the long-serving Reverend Samuel Burney Hay. Dr. Hay left the Auburn ministry to become president of Tuscaloosa's Stillman College. He was succeeded in the Auburn pulpit and in the manse by a distinguished church scholar, the Reverend John Haddon Leith, who launched a rebuilding program for the church. The old 1917 Akron Plan church was replaced in 1954 by a new Burkhardt-designed building in classical style because, it was claimed, the older building was unstable and uneconomical to stabilize. Many, both members and non-members, were dismayed by the decision and dubious about the rationale. The manse, too, was removed to allow further extension of church development westward from the new sanctuary. Fortunately, this small part of the old Presbyterian campus was relocated to a county site rather than demolished. It became the home of longtime church custodian Willis Turk, for whom the Lee County road on which it is now located was named.

Graves Cottage

For more than forty years, the cottage on West Samford Avenue at the corner of Auburn University's Patterson Greenhouse Complex served as the state headquarters for the Garden Clubs of Alabama. The cottage was originally one of the several athletics cottages that once occupied the rim of the Graves Center Amphitheater. Through the years, various campus constraints and organizational changes reduced the day to day use of the cottage for the

Garden Clubs. As a result, they donated the building to the Auburn University Department of Horticulture. At the same time, the Alabama Nursery and Landscape Association (ALNA) needed a temporary location to serve as a headquarters. For many years the ALNLA was located on the corner of Samford Avenue and South College. When relocation from that site was imminent, an agreement was reached for the ALNLA to upgrade and then occupy the Garden Club cottage in exchange for scholarship support for horticulture undergraduates. Presently, the surviving Graves Cottage is once again threatened. The university's plans to redevelop a large number of horticulture program venues have been shelved as of this writing.

Top, the Graves Cottages sat above the Amphitheater; above, the surviving cottage (far right in the top photo) on Samford Avenue. Below, house at Frazier's Park.

Frazier's Park

Even though it stretches the category of "preservation by relocation," Frazier's Park was a noteworthy part of Auburn's built environment that is today still expressed in the modest house located where the park once operated. The house was built of the remnants of the clubhouse that anchored the park. Though the authors of this book could not locate any photographs of the park, it is still vivid in the memories of those who used it.

Frazier's Park consisted of several acres owned and developed by William "Whack" Frazier in the

1920s and '30s. As remembered by the Vickerstaff family and recorded in *Lest We Forget*, "This place provided all types of entertainment for this area. Big-time bands and entertainers like Cab Calloway, Nat 'King' Cole, and Ella Fitzgerald all appeared here. Frazier Park also provided a ball park, picnic area, lake area with paddle boats, food, and other entertainment." (While the park was an African American institution, visiting entertainers with national reputations also attracted a white audience that was segregated in a roped off area.)

Frazier Park was also remembered as a place for Sunday school and 4-H Club outings. The Palm Garden dance pavilion, topped by a large umbrella-like canvas top, facing Bragg Avenue proved a popular Saturday night attraction for the African American community. A group of local self-taught musicians, it is believed, furnished the music. The park, however, was the scene of violence in 1940. According to the records of the Auburn City Council, Dr. B. F. Thomas presented his bill to the council for his services attending to a prisoner who was beaten up at Frazier's Park. The demise of the park itself followed shortly thereafter during a Fourth of July celebration—a popular annual occasion at Frazier's Park—when owner Whack Frazier was killed on the premises. Frazier's Park as a business did not survive the death of its owner. The property ultimately was auctioned at the courthouse due to non-payment of property taxes. The successful bidder, Andrew Gentry, left the property to his son, from whom the Conners firm of developers acquired it.

Below, architect's drawing for Boy Scout Lodge; bottom, the "hut" after removal to Azalea Avenue.

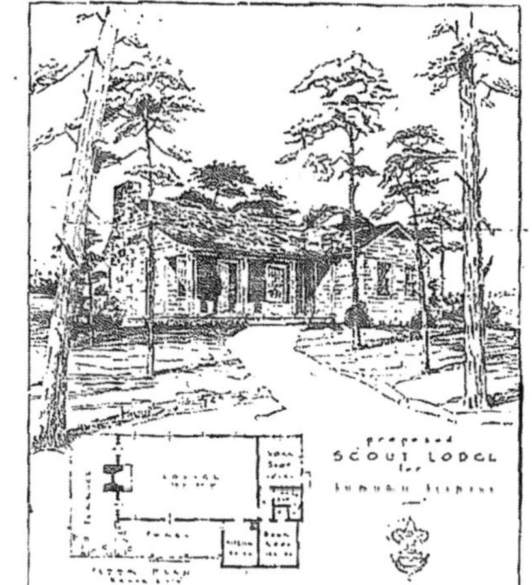

BOY SCOUT HUT

A drawing by the architect Milton Hill of the proposed Scout Lodge that appeared in the *Lee County Bulletin* bears scant resemblance to the building that, after being moved, now stands on Azalea Avenue. College employees constructed the Boy Scout Hut, as it was usually called, to Hill's plans on college property not far from the President's Home. The principal feature of the building was a large meeting space, with a stone fireplace, entered from the front porch. Several smaller

auxiliary spaces adjoining the large hall were sometimes living quarters for the scoutmaster, often a college student. As relocated, the smallish yellow frame building has little of the charm of the lodge in its original setting. The appearance from outside suggests that only part of the original was moved, as there is no integral front porch, no chimney, and no projecting wing on the right side.

From top, W. A. Cullars House on S. College; as moved to Chimney Acres; as the Whittlesey (Cullars) House at Chimney Acres today.

Cullars House

The home of William A. Cullars, a project of the three Cullars brothers, stood south of town on US Route 29, now a busy part of South College Street. After the death of Cullars in 1937, the property was sold to Alabama Polytechnic Institute, which established its swine research project there, providing a popular name for the former family home—"the pig house." A portion of the house on its original site is shown in a photograph of family members on and beside the front porch.

As the home site gave way to commercial development, the house was moved to Chimney Acres, a development of houses in period style, and ultimately became the home of the R. D. Horne family, who completed the renovation.

The general configuration of the main block was retained, although the pedimented portico replaces the original full-width porch at the front of the house. The entrance with side and transom lights is evidence that, as builders, the Cullarses introduced sophisticated design elements even in a simple rural homestead like this one. (A blurry photograph of the house on its original site may be seen on p. 82.) The original high-ceilinged single floor has been modified to provide a second floor under the steeply pitched hipped roof for additional bedroom space.

Robinson House

Longtime professor of mathematics Alexander Jude Robinson built his house in what seemed at the time a distant location on Magnolia Avenue at the western edge of the town. That ultimately proved not far enough for the group of largish faculty homes originally built there. First fraternity houses and then student apartment buildings invaded this neighborhood so that family residences were leveled in the face of the onslaught—except for the Jude Robinson house.

The building seemed attractive enough and moveable enough to appeal to a new owner, who had it transported—as seen in the accompanying photographs. Later it was purchased by a new owner, Walter Giddens, who gave it an entirely different appearance, more appropriate to a rural setting, changing the siding to unfinished lumber and adding a full-width front porch and stone for the chimney. In the course of some renovations, it was discovered that some of the materials originally used had been supplied by a Tuskegee building supply company, Conner Brothers Construction, which later grew into a large construction business in Auburn.

Top, Robinson House being moved; above, after renovation.

Prather House

As commercial interests intruded more and more on areas that once were rural, especially through the eastern outskirts of town where once the Prather farm and Prather's Lake were located, residential developments grew over the land and around the lake, and commercial projects swallowed most of the spaces along the highway between Auburn and Opelika.

Not all of the buildings that had been cherished on the changing landscape were lost, however, for moving a building like the Prather House proved both desirable and possible. It was relocated to Chimney Acres along with other houses moved there because owners thought them too valuable to be lost to demolition.

Above, Prather House as relocated to Chimney Acres; inset, detail of the Prather House entrance.

A MOVING EXPERIENCE: AN INTERVIEW BY EMILY SPARROW

A myriad of special individuals has contributed to the structuring of Auburn's built landscape. Of all we encountered, no group of artisans proved more memorable than the Ira Lee Davis Jr. family, who refer to themselves simply as "house movers." The highly specialized skills of the Davises have been exceptionally significant in protecting many architectural treasures of Auburn's past. For more than fifty years, the Davis family has worked to relocate structures to new and safer locations, out of reach, at least for a time, of the wrecking ball of "progress."

I. L. Davis & Wife Pat: Master Relocation Specialists

I. L. Davis Jr., always referred to as "Junior," came with his wife, Pat, and their family to the west Georgia-east Alabama area in 1961 and joined Junior's father, I. L. Davis Sr., always referred to as "Senior," in the family business. Senior, originally from Oklahoma, had relocation work experience as far back as the late 1920s New Mexico oil boom, where he worked driving the skid shacks in the oil fields. In 1951, Senior followed promising job opportunities and moved his family to South Carolina and later Augusta, Georgia, to work on a major relocation effort, the Savannah River Plant Project, which was being built for the production of plutonium and tritium used in production of the H-bomb. In this project, more than six thousand people and everything else along with them, including at least six thousand graves, had to be relocated before plant construction could commence.

Eventually all that remained of the original towns were the paved streets, curbs, and sidewalks. In an interview Junior recalled, "We even moved the outhouses." As he spoke of his family's willingness to take risks and work hard from daylight to dark, and of their determination to complete projects, there was a deep expression of family pride.

Corps of Engineers and Alabama Power Company projects, including the development of lakes like Eufaula, West Point, and Weiss, among others, provided the work opportunities that brought the Davises to the Chattahoochee Valley area. Junior explained, "Back then there was lots of work, and we didn't have lots of heavy equipment to make our 'catches' and 'pulls.' We used twenty-four by twenty-four-foot wooden beams that were seventy feet long, and we used hand jacks, but now we use steel beams and have a complete hydraulic system. We now have five trucks, fifty to sixty sets of beams, and we have our son, Allen, who is the best mover of all. He's been moving houses thirty years."

The Davises explained that because of the heavier weight of a brick house you "catch them off" differently. They have even moved a house built on a slab, but the Davises explained that it was not very practical. In describing the moving process, they talked as if it were a simple matter and minimized the difficulties, saying, "We just slide steel beams underneath whatever we're moving, jack or 'catch' the whole thing off the foundation, support it with cribs [wooden support frames], roll sets of small wheeled dollies under the structure, and we're ready to pull. Once we get where we're going, we just sit the house or building down on its new foundation and move all the supports away."

The speed with which a pull is completed depends on many factors including weight, obstructions along the way, and the roadways which must be traveled, but Junior said he could move some houses as fast as forty to forty-five miles per hour. When the Davises moved the antebellum J. W .W. Drake house from Bragg Avenue to Shelton Mill Road, it only took a half hour, and reportedly a wine bottle that was sitting on a mantel at the beginning of the move was still sitting upright in the same spot when the house arrived at its new location.

Pat Davis takes care of what she calls the hard part of the moving process—the paperwork—and she said, "The biggest thing nowadays about moving houses isn't about moving houses—it's about getting the permits." She makes the permit applications, which have to come from utility companies, fire departments, police and/or sheriffs, and city administrators (city business licenses), and she gets the police escorts and deals with insurance (travelers are the people who write special insurance for movers).

Pat told us they had a man working with them who did all the paperwork, but he died, and the work all fell to her. She said, "When I drive by the cemetery where he's buried, I almost want to go in there, dig him up, and give him a boot in the backsides for leaving me with the work." Besides explaining changing rules and regulations, she also says costs have increased greatly and it is more and more difficult to find people who want to work. Pat added, "Who wants to take on a hard job that has dangers when you can sit on the porch and make money?"

The Davises estimate moving costs based primarily on distance, square footage, and potential obstructions along the necessary route. In Montgomery, they moved the very large Italianate Ware-Farley-Hood House for the Landmarks Foundation from near the Alabama Capitol to Old Alabama Town—a \$100,000 job. The Davis family's business card proudly displays a photograph of that Montgomery move.

Auburn endures in part because of the talents and skills, family pride, and strong work ethic possessed by the I. L. Davis family. We feel honored to have become acquainted with them and to know them as master relocation specialists.

11

Bits and Pieces: Monuments, Memorials, and Remnants

Even as we applaud those who have undertaken to move buildings rather than see them destroyed, our sadness at the loss of others is mitigated a little by another kind of preservation. The loss of Auburn's buildings—buildings that constituted a record of the town's history and held much of the memory of what it was—is by any account regrettable. Still, sometimes the remains of those buildings are preserved and cherished, to become a different part of the built environment or to persist as mementos. Here is a collection of the remains of an older Auburn, of the bits and pieces that cameras can now record.

The most striking instance of the reuse of building parts—and to many the most gratifying—is the entrance portico to the home of Auburn University's ROTC program, the Nichols Center. The monumental portico once served in a more conventional way as an entrance to Broun Hall, an expanded version of one of the school's earliest engineering buildings. In 1910 additions were designed by Nathaniel C. Curtis (see p. 23) and built by the Birmingham Building and Improvement Company. The columns, entablature, and pediment were composed of limestone and terra-cotta and are faithful copies of authentic Greek style. Broun Hall was razed in 1984. The classical portico was dismantled and stored by the T. M. Burgin Demolition Co. of Birmingham. The architects for the Nichols Center were Barganier Davis Sims Architects Associated of Montgomery; the contractor for the project was Construction

Below, Broun Hall with 1910 additions (destroyed); bottom, Nichols Center with Broun Hall Portico.

One, Inc., of Columbus, Ohio, and Montgomery.

The urge to modernize or replace Auburn buildings has rarely produced such striking results as those at the Nichols Center. Even so cherished an institution as Toomer's Drug Store endured a regrettable modernization that produced a bland, virtually blank appearance on the main corner of town in place of the thoroughly "un-modern" charm of the original (which today would probably be considered chic). Some months ago, nevertheless, America's online yard sale, eBay, offered what were claimed to be the original doors to Toomer's Drug Store. The photographs lead one to believe that the claim was accurate. Where these bits and pieces are now is not known; one hopes that an Auburnite somewhere has given them a new and useful home.

Toomer's Drugstore original doors.

Another Auburn landmark, Burton's "Four Story Cottage," was preserved by relocation to Opelika. The attractive cast-iron fence, however, was saved by former Auburn mayor Jan Dempsey, part of which she installed on her property at the corner of Ross Street and Magnolia Avenue. For twenty-five years, the fence enclosed the yard in front of Betsy's on Ross, a doll and toy shop. It continues today, standing guard as time and traffic fly by.

Auburn's city authorities decided that the next residential block on South Gay Street did not need the charming Victorian home that Opelika contractor Thomas Plant had built for his daughter, Mrs. Wilhelmina "Bill" Ingalls. Although J. A. Cullars was not the builder, it is likely that he produced the bulk of these elements in his workshop, which was less than a block from the Ingalls house. Some years later, when several of the house's decorative elements needed to be replaced, the originals were reproduced by J. A. Cullars's nephew, Alfa Cullars, with the original patterns on the original machines, then still located in the Cullars shop on Samford Avenue. A collection of these remains was gathered

Burton House Fence.

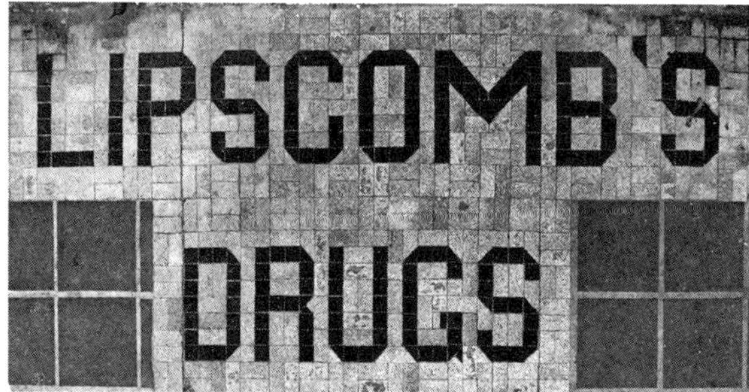

Above, clockwise from top left: Heard & Swope cast iron entrance, N. College; Lipscomb's Drugs entrance; Cullars Store cast iron entrance plate; Wright and Co., ceramic tile entrance, N. College.

by William Dean and stored in the basement of the Cullars House at 427 South College Street, now the offices of William Dean Realty, until an opportunity arises to reuse them.

Early commercial advertising efforts were sometimes devoted to unobtrusive (and sometimes less expensive) building identifiers—thresholds at store entrances. Although these are fast disappearing, a few remain or have fortunately been recorded shortly before being destroyed.

The demise of the Tiger Theater as a principal source of entertainment for Auburn students and residents was perhaps the first episode in the transformation of the downtown from a collection of small homegrown village businesses into a mall of franchise fast food and glitzy gift shops, among which only a few old-timers remain. When the theater went dark, some effort was devoted to adapting the building for other uses, but eventually it was so transformed by the Gap clothing store chain that only the emblematic tiger head remained, repositioned on the facade, to remind Auburn of what once was there.

As a "pleasure palace," it did not reach for the glamour of big city theaters, but in its heyday going to the movies was always a treat, served up for many years by stalwarts such as the manager, Gus Coats, and the unflappable Mrs. Sparrow taking tickets.

Aside from the numerous markers placed in later years by local historical associations, many others have appeared over the years to commemorate events, groups, or buildings that marked Auburn as a special place well worth remembering.

Above, Tiger Theater facade emblem, N. College; left, Tiger Theater; below left, Auburn Founders Monument, S. College and Magnolia; the marker reads as below:

AUBURN—ALABAMA
SETTLED BY JUDGE J. J. HARPER AND OTHERS
FROM HARRIS COUNTY, GEORGIA, IN 1836.
THIS REGION WAS OPENED TO SETTLEMENT
IN 1836–37 BY THE REMOVAL OF THE
CREEK INDIANS TO LANDS WEST
OF THE MISSISSIPPI RIVER.
ERECTED BY
THE ALABAMA OFFICERS CLUB
DAUGHTERS OF THE AMERICAN REVOLUTION
MARCH 16, 1936

Confederate markers and memorials

Right: Auburn Female College plaque beside Auburn Bank, North Gay Street. The wording is: *On these grounds, the site of the Auburn Female College, on March 4th 1861, simultaneously with the raising over the Capitol at Montgomery, Ala., of the first Confederate flag, a similar flag was raised by Betty Dowdell.* Below left: Stone commemorating mobilization of Rebel regiments, on the front lawn of Sunny Slope, S. College Street, and inset at bottom, the plaque from the stone. Center right: Auburn Guards plaque, beside railroad station, Mitcham Avenue.

Church cornerstones

(Counterclockwise from bottom right) St. Luke C.M.E. Church, inserted into bell monument in front of the church, Donahue Drive; Sacred Heart Catholic Church, inserted into the wall of St. Michael's Catholic Church (now Methodist Assembly Hall); Hamill Memorial Sunday School building, inserted into the garden wall at Auburn United Methodist Church, E. Magnolia and S. Gay.

War memorial

To Auburn men killed in the First World War, Thach Avenue, south of Samford Hall.

Plaques from University Buildings

These items are now located in Auburn University Special Collections storage. 1) In Memoriam from Alumni Association 1861–1865 to the Students Who Fought under the Stars and Bars of the Confederacy; 2) Seal of the Wirt Literary Society; 3) Julia A. Hamiter, August 17, 1839–April 13, 1857, Daughter of Joel Hamiter, Barbour County, Alabama, Who Munificently Endowed the Chair of Natural Science of the East Alabama Male College as a Monument to Her Memory; 4) Charles Coleman Thach, LL.D., presented to the College by the Class of 1921, bronze bas-relief by William Spratling; 5) Bronze bust on granite pedestal memorializing Alabama Governor Thomas Goode Jones. This 1955 bust by Margaret Whetstone is apparently a copy of the 1943 original by Herbert Adams placed in the Hall of the Alabama House of Representatives. Why it was created and where it was originally displayed is not recorded; 6) "In this hall then located upon another site, in the great political debates immediately preceding the Civil War spoke David Clopton, Thomas J. Judge, and Wm L Yancey of Alabama, Seaborn Jones, Benjamin H. Hill, Albert Toombs, and Alexander H. Stephens of Georgia, and William Brownlow of Tennessee"; 7) Bronze bust by Martin Deutsch memorializing Alabama Governor Bibb Graves was the centerpiece of a semi-circular brick seating arrangement in the Graves Center.

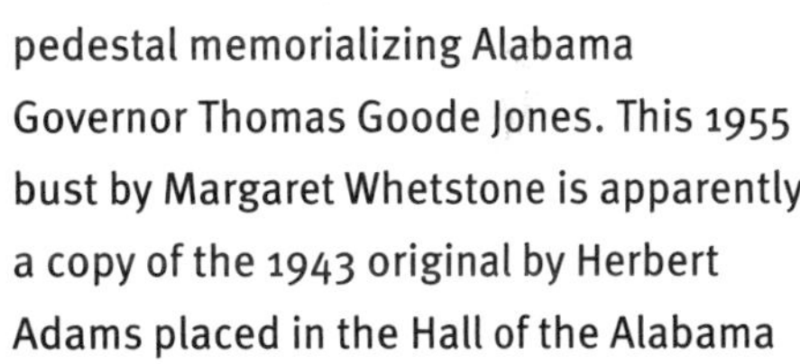

Dr. Cecil Yarbrough Relics at Pebble Hill

Two relics associated with Dr. Cecil Yarbrough's years living at Pebble Hill are little remembered and little noticed in Auburn's landscape. Dr. Yarbrough built a four-unit apartment building (1) to the north of his residence on Debardeleben Street, naming the complex "Mary Jane Apartments" for his granddaughter, Mary Jane Ennis. When the building was removed, this (2) reminder was left in the ground to mark the place where the Mary Jane Apartments once stood. A second remnant of Dr. Yarbrough's tenure at Pebble Hill is at the spring that lies quite hidden far behind the main house, now in the overgrown back yard of a house on Ryan Street. Around this spring Confederate troops once camped. Dr. Yarbrough improved it with a (3) concrete surround, inscribing (4) his name at one side and the date, 1921.

4

The Dynamo

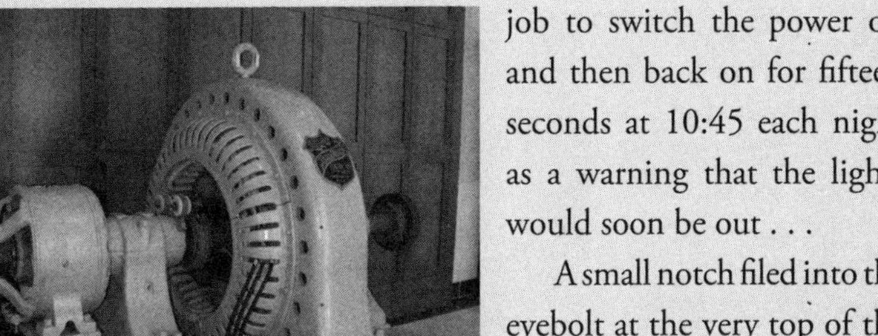

It is hard to believe that an important part of Auburn's history has been quietly rusting away behind Broun Hall, unnoticed for almost twenty-two years. To the average student, it looks like a broken piece of junk left over from a building renovation or an unsuccessful experiment. Even faculty that walk by may have no idea of its storied history—of the innovation, the heritage, and even the tragedy that surrounds this ugly hunk of metal, wires, coils, and bolts.

In Dr. Jim Lowry's Broun Hall office, when our conversation turned to the five horsepower Weston dynamoelectric generator that was parked in the grass next to the electrical engineering faculty parking lot, it was hard for me to imagine that this cumbersome and rusted old thing was once the sole source of electricity to Auburn University and the city of Auburn—and an unusual bit of history.

The generator was first installed inside the basement of Langdon Hall in 1886. Though not very powerful by modern standards, the 240 volts it generated with steam and coal was enough to light up the town from Ag Hill to the end of College Street.

To save money and energy, the generator was turned off promptly at eleven o'clock as residents and students headed off to bed. The generator's operator was typically a student, and it was his job to switch the power off and then back on for fifteen seconds at 10:45 each night as a warning that the lights would soon be out . . .

A small notch filed into the eyebolt at the very top of the iron frame is a reminder of the power and danger that once surged through this now dilapidated machine. In the early 1900s, a man was electrocuted by the Langdon Hall generator. At that time, it was traditional to mark a dynamo with a notch each time someone was killed by its electrical current. Fortunately, Auburn's generator only has one such notch. One hundred years later it still serves as a small but meaningful reminder of the potential danger of electricity.

In 1923, after thirty-seven years of service to the Auburn community, the generator was retired. It was moved from Langdon to the electrical labs where it served as a teaching tool for countless engineering students. It came to its present parking lot resting place in 1985, when the lab building was torn down to make way for the construction of Broun Hall . . .

Dr. Lowry says he would like to see the old dynamo restored and moved to a prominent location on campus to commemorate its important place in the Auburn community. Until then it sleeps quietly in a bed of weeds . . . as busy students hurry by to their next class, their next tomorrow.

— Laura Steele

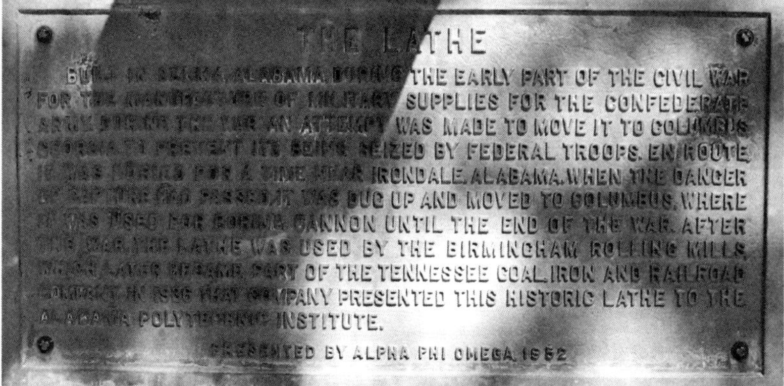

Other Auburn Curios

Top left: Pan, garden statue, concrete with marble chips (original metal pipes missing); first installed in Auburn University President's Home flower garden; present location 270 Hillcrest Drive, Auburn. Top right: Commercial sign from Pruet's Shoe Shop, painted wood. Original location: east side of first block of South College Street; present location unknown. Center right: The Lathe. Cast iron on brick base. Placed on north side of Samford Hall in 1938. Bottom right: The Lathe's plaque was donated by Alpha Phi Omega service fraternity in 1952.

Index

D

T